CREATING CULTURE CHANGE

STRATEGIES FOR SUCCESS

PHILIP ATKINSON

Rushmere Wynne
England

*To Ann, Sarah
and Jonathan*

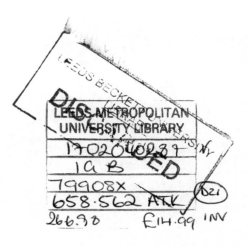

CREATING
CULTURE
CHANGE

STRATEGIES FOR SUCCESS

PHILIP ATKINSON

Rushmere Wynne
England

First published by IFS Ltd 1990
This edition January 1997
© Philip Atkinson

British Library Cataloguing in Publication Data. A catalogue record for this book is available from the British Library.

ISBN 0 948035 43 9

Designed and typeset by:
MacWing

Published by:
Rushmere Wynne Limited,
4-5 Harmill, Grovebury Road,
Leighton Buzzard, Bedfordshire LU7 8FF
Tel: 01525 853726
Fax: 01525 852037

Printed by:
Redwood Books Limited
Kennet House, Kennet Way
Trowbridge, Wiltshire BA14 8RN

Acknowledgements

There are so many people who have contributed towards my understanding and the practice of implementation of culture change that it is difficult to single out just a few. However, I would like to thank the following as well as all those people who have attended my seminars and workshops over many years. It was through an exchange of views that I was able to gain a greater understanding of the dynamics that can shape our businesses for success. Thank you.

Philip Atkinson

Jim Schroedinger, Colin Rutherford, George Turner, Steve McGoldrick, Andy Methven, John Ewart, Keith Greenough, Nora Kellock, Jan Soderholm, Tom Gross, Pierre van Esch, Malcolm Hill, Vance McQueen, David Shepherd, Stuart Smith, Morris Foster, John Ryan, David Buchanan, Alan Sinclair, Robbie Taylor, Malcolm Hill, David Deeble, John Lynch, Brian Coolahan, Neil Roden, Nick Schofield, Vince Hoban, Garth Heron, Richard Tinkler, Peter Taylor, David Aussie, Ian Miller, Brian Murray, Hugh Newman, Judith Dunker, Iain Smith, Paul Quay, Alan Hughes, Adam McLachlan, Dennis Reay, Peter Johnston.

Contents

Introduction: You Can Shape Your Culture, Now

Culture change is *the* critical 'business issue' for organisations as we enter the next century. Imagine what your business could become if you knew you couldn't fail in implementing a strong and healthy culture! Now, just take a minute to imagine your business as a successful, vibrant, competitive entity run by staff with strong Leadership skills who have mastered and routinely practise their change management capabilities. It is a common occurrence for staff to work cross-functionally to prevent problems arising. Continuous improvement is 'business as usual' for customer service.

This positive image can become a reality for all organisations if the Senior Managers who run them understand that change and improvement do not exist by accident but by design. They need to take ownership of the cultural issue. Planning for a new positive culture begins with confronting the core issues facing many businesses.

HOW CAN WE SHAPE, ENGINEER AND CREATE A SUCCESSFUL HIGH PERFORMANCE-DRIVEN BUSINESS CULTURE?

Passion and planning are the key elements of the drive to achieve this new culture. It starts by examining those things which have hampered the implementation of Total Quality in recent years. Looking back and understanding the reasons for failure is critical in helping us focus on an error-free implementation plan for culture change.

In all honesty, over the past ten years, Total Quality (TQ) was seen as a panacea for all organisational problems, and perhaps it may have been if the behavioural and cultural components had been driven intensively into the business – but often the methodology or techniques of TQ were only partially understood and realised. There were many perceived variants of TQ, many not addressing the behavioural issues at all! Generally speaking, very few initiatives with the TQM (Total Quality Management) label were really that – many were simply dressed-up training programmes designed around some form of a quality system or quality accreditation. Those programmes established partial success in discrete areas and these were mostly driven by participation, often referred to as quality circles. Very few initiatives actually designed and installed a positive 'culture' for the business, but those that did were enormously successful.

Figures for successful implementation of TQ vary, but it is not unusual to find a 90% failure rate. There were many reasons for failure, but the most important issue which those that failed had never addressed was shaping the culture of the business by becoming customer-facing. There were some partial successes with companies achieving accreditation to certain quality standards, resulting in the infrastructure of the business being technically improved, but the means of delivering error-free service often remained the same. In some cases, acquiring standards led to more bureaucracy and actually slowed down the delivery of customer service.

Only by addressing the culture, the living breathing fabric of a business, and shaping a strong and committed staff working cross-functionally, will TQ work. This means committing to creating a highly energised staff through continuous development and leading by example. Core to this process is another major issue needing to be confronted for the next century: Leadership.

Make no mistake – without Leadership there is no change. Companies which fail to meet the Leadership challenge of their particular business will fail to grow a healthy and vibrant business culture, and TQ will be no more than a fad that was never implemented. Every organisation faces the challenge of equipping those who manage with the skills to master and initiate corporate change.

Failing to grow Leaders confronts every organisation. Most, however, do little to provide their business with a healthy core group of change-masters. It goes without saying that companies with a highly trained managerial group, an elite core of change-makers, will succeed while those who rely solely on the technical skills and experience of their managers will achieve their goals only in the short term.

This book is about Vision, Leadership and Change, for without these core components of a culture will not prosper. What has been instrumental in motivating me to completely revise my book *Creating Culture Change* has been the disappointing lack of healthy success in implementing TQ in Europe and the US. What appeared great in theory has failed to be implemented in practice. This book highlights the key components of a successful drive, together with strategies for implementation.

The chapter outline of the text focuses strongly on the behavioural components of change. Those who have used the original text as a vehicle to help their organisations improve will have found that success lay in addressing 'Corporate Culture' first. That remains my key message.

The book is divided into four key sections and need not be read sequentially.

SECTION I: THE STRATEGIC ISSUES.

CHAPTER 1: Pursuing Excellence: Vision examines the importance of understanding the behavioural dynamics behind TQ. It addresses the issue that many so-called TQ drives have been little more than problem-solving Workshops or training programmes with the TQ 'badge'. Understand that real culture change requires a curiosity about how other successful organisations function and how 'Modelling' can be used as a tool to rapidly improve performance.

CHAPTER 2: The Building Blocks of a TQ Culture. Seasoned practitioners may wish to skip through the first part of this chapter because it outlines the contribution of leading figures in the field of Quality. The remaining larger portion of the chapter deals with critical issues of a successful TQ Drive.

CHAPTER 3: The Economics of Culture Change are reviewed here with a strong emphasis placed on measuring and reducing the unnecessary high cost associated with Rework. Rework in the Service sector is explored and suggestions put forward for measuring and mapping these apparently intangible costs.

SECTION 2: MANAGING TRANSITIONS: THE KEY ISSUES FOR CHANGE

CHAPTER 4: Cultural and Behavioural Change examines the conflict between partial sub-system or partial change through the application of systems to the detriment of using the behavioural approach. Clear views are expressed using the new 9 S's framework for examining both Hard and Soft S's. Resistance to change is explored with powerful suggestions for combating the negative attitude.

CHAPTER 5: Shaping a Total Quality Culture builds on Chapter 4 and outlines the key components of an effective culture at the same time as describing diagnostics tools. Core components of effective cultures are outlined. The stages we go through are covered by the Transition Curve. Chapters 4 and 5 are essential to understanding the basics of Corporate Culture.

CHAPTER 6: Leadership for Beyond the Next Century focuses upon the importance of Leadership and suggests that this is not a 'magical' process which is acquired by virtue of holding a management job title. The core components of effective Leadership behaviour are outlined.

CHAPTER 7: Pitfalls to the Implementation of Culture Change focuses upon the sensitive role of the key actors in the process of change. The relative relationship between external consultant and internal facilitator is examined and the chapter then focuses upon the role of the TQ manager in a more traditional production environment exploring the ideas of commitment and effectiveness.

SECTION 3: CORE COMPONENTS OF SUCCESSFUL IMPLEMENTATION

CHAPTER 8: Meeting Customer Requirements promotes the balanced view that before we concentrate upon developing resources to delighting the external customer we need to focus all our energies on getting people within the business to row in the same direction. The view that requirements are not met and lead to rework is founded upon 'behavioural' factors that people prefer ambiguity, adopt tunnel vision and display a win-lose mentality when working with others.

CHAPTER 9: Right First Time is an attitude best reflected in performance measures. It is argued that the starting place for setting new performance measures is in service functions. We should start with setting 'behavioural' standards first and then cascade the concept down towards manufacturing.

CHAPTER 10: Taking Preventative Action strongly projects the view that a firefighting culture formed upon functional silos will only be destroyed when sufficient energy is diverted to preventing problems arising. Prevention and planning are discussed as well as the two key components of problem-solving; the logical and creative approaches are explained and the climate and process of solving problems are described as being critical in the process.

CHAPTER 11: Teamworking and Participation is critical if we want staff to truly adopt cross-functional working as 'business as usual'. This requires more than participation and involvement. It requires people being prepared to work with individuals from radically different backgrounds and perspectives. Forming a flexible team only happens after extensive development of people and this can be facilitated through the development of the style of managers through team-building, profiling or psychometrics as part of a development programme.

CHAPTER 12: Development, Learning and Training is the second most important element of a TQ drive, after Leadership. Equipping staff with the skills, attitudes and knowledge is the focus of this chapter. Core training issues are discussed which relate to the design, the quality of training, objectives and outcomes, changing attitudes and developing group working.

SECTION 4: IMPLEMENTATION AND CONTINUOUS IMPROVEMENT

CHAPTER 13: Readiness for Change concentrates upon the strategic and the tactical issues for implementation. Cultural Surveys and Management Audits are critical to understand the organisation's current 'status'. Tactical issues are also discussed, including such issues as the mix of internal and external change-agents, the focus for training and the continuing drive to embed TQ in the culture of the business.

CHAPTER 14: Implementation and Review is essential when assessing initial efforts to change a culture. Review will enable any requirement to change direction of the drive. It also highlights key issues which need to be addressed. It is important to measure how well values are communicated, Leadership practised and then focus upon the tactical areas of how well the concepts are being applied on a tactical level.

CHAPTER 15: How Do We Create a World Class Total Quality Culture? No book written on culture could fail to make reference to those who had gone before and managed Quality successfully. We explore some aspects of what makes Quality a 'Total' concept in Japan, and how it can be made to work here.

The book has been written with the purpose of becoming a practical handbook which can help you understand and shape the dynamics of culture change. I trust that anyone interested in the process of change will find this of value, so the text is not addressed to one particular group of people. However, it soon will become apparent that the message in the text is directed towards the senior officers or Managers of companies who are charged to take ownership of this complex process.

The book has been substantially revised and includes material previously unpublished. I hope it challenges the reader to think in different ways and to understand that when planning change for others, change first has to start with 'self'.

Phil Atkinson
Transformations (UK) Ltd.
11 Alva St., Edinburgh EH2 4PH
Tel 0131-346-1276/0131-226-4519, Fax 0131-346-1618.
Web Site http://www.lookhere.co.uk/transform/
e-mail: phil@transform.win-uk.net.

CHAPTER I
Pursuing Excellence: Vision

SHAPE YOUR CULTURE

'What are the leading companies doing to shape their culture?' This question was asked by the CEO of a company shortly after acquiring a Division of a UK Finance House. The issue was debated when the top team of the newly acquired company first met to discuss strategy for the future. Immediately, the top team was focused upon change and improvement. The conversation soon concentrated upon 'Corporate Culture' and it was clear that they needed a quick understanding of 'how' a new culture could replace the existing outmoded, bureaucratic, slow-to-respond and negative culture of the newly acquired business.

They made short work of their post-acquisition integration strategy, setting themselves 90 days to turn the culture and the business around. Within a calendar year, the old business was to be totally revitalised and functioning at a pace, speed and delivering service quality better than ever considered before. It worked for the simple reason that the top team had a strong Vision of what the company could be. They rejected the self-limiting beliefs of the previous owners, set objectives, formed a firm optimistic attitude and communicated and implemented best practice throughout the network. This company is GE, one of the world's leading businesses which understands the power of culture and uses all leverage at its disposal to design its corporate culture the way it wants it. It looks for positive ways to make things work and relentlessly drive home the culture issue.

Financial Services Business

Old Culture	New Culture
Short-term Volume-driven	Strategic – Value added
Slow and unresponsive	Time-based competition
Autocratic style	Leadership through people
Departmental in outlook	Cross-functional
Hierarchical	Flat organisation
Status-driven	Achievement-orientated
Control	Trust and challenging
Directed	Empowered staff

DESIGN YOUR CULTURE

Imagine being able to shape and design a 'Corporate Culture' the way an architect designs a house. What would you do first? How would you set empowering Values which would inspire others to perform within set standards? How many Values would you work on and how would these relate to the goals of the business? How would you ensure the Values are energising, positive and customer-focused? How much effort would you put into agreeing the performance standards you would want your most senior managers to achieve? How would you ensure that the Values which you believe are important to the business are consistently practised daily? How would you ensure that Values were translated into behaviour – especially that practised by managers? What methods and measures would cause this to happen? These are all questions which I work through with Senior Staff when discussing the importance of implementing effective change and, more importantly, they are questions which are often never considered, far less answered, by too many Senior Staff within organisations today.

It's fairly obvious that here I am talking about the importance of culture, the fabric of the business which is driven by staff and is a critical issue for many companies today. Understand now that Corporate Culture is central to inhibiting or enhancing the performance of a business. A poor culture does nothing for staff. A strong focused culture can inspire staff to achieve their unlimited potential which will have a significant impact upon corporate performance. This is a double win for staff and for the company. Understand that every business has a culture – sometimes it is operating along powerful defined principles and driven by the top team, but often a culture exists by default, changing by accident and usually influenced by the arrival and departure of key players in the corporation. We estimate only 5% of large businesses have a definable culture which has been shaped consistently by the top team. If in doubt, consider your own organisation and the degree of consistency in displaying the desired culture to staff and to customers. If 75% of the top team members are in harmony and visible in living the values that would be excellent – if less than 50%, there will be confusion in people's minds about behaviour which is to be encouraged and that which is not.

THE DICTATOR IN THE BANK: A NEGATIVE CULTURE

A senior executive within a large Bank had a reputation for creating a climate of fear. On occasion, he would visit his Direct Reports and deliver their mail for signing. His approach was novel and demeaning. He would knock on his chosen victim's door and throw the mail for signature (which had been carefully placed in a large blotter by a secretary) across the room snarling 'sign and deliver back to me'. This and other negative behaviours were very strong in shaping the culture of this Executive's function and were sure to create fear in even the strongest member of staff. Needless to say, the results of a cultural survey indicated that this area was ripe for improvement. Thankfully, the executive was moved to a small team where his less than human style was not so damaging, before being moved out.

Culture is the most important aspect of a business. A positive vibrant culture will ensure that staff expend their energy in the interests of the business because the culture will reflect the accepted way of managing or leading. More negative cultures will create a climate where staff are driven to do things because they fear the consequences of 'not doing so'. Some companies have interesting cultures where nothing in particular is valued or communicated – people just do a job. You can imagine that the results are less than awe-inspiring.

Now consider your response if placed as a person in a weak and negative culture. Over-control and a failure to positively motivate to achieve certain outcomes will impact upon your job satisfaction and, ultimately, your self-esteem. A strong positive culture will create the opposite view where a positive approach to work will include a certain degree of challenge or stretch for staff.

Stretch is a good thing for staff because, when managed professionally, it can enhance the skill base and boost self-esteem. And we all know that being stretched beyond our comfort zones can immediately build up our self-confidence. This is central to empowering staff to improve their experience and their self-confidence. An analogy to illustrate the point is important. Those readers who have children will have committed to take action to help develop their self-esteem and confidence at every opportunity. It is a pity when the same people who practise this skill successfully with their children fail to do so with the people they manage at work – thus failing to tap the potential of their most important creative resource.

Forward-thinking companies recognise that they employ more than the arms and legs of their staff: they commit to their aspirations, their visions and their dreams. How much more sensible it is to utilise the talents and dreams of the people while they are working for you. I wonder how often the most creative element of a person is lost to a company and actualised when he is 'away from work'.

WANTING TO CREATE THE RIGHT CULTURE

Knowing *why* a company is pursuing TQ or Culture Change is not as important as *how* to implement it. Even now the 'old traditionalists' debate whether or not a TQ Culture is desirable. Senior Staff in some companies are still debating whether they can afford to pursue TQ or Culture Change. They may be interested to know that they can't afford not to if they value their positioning in their market. This can also be reflected by some Senior Staff in large Governmental agencies or quangos in the public sector. The reason I say this now is that some in the public sector have a mindset which states that only organisations with huge resources can effectively change and develop a performance-driven flat culture. Some of my most effective clients at causing change have been those in this sector and achieved a great deal even though funds and budgets are limited. I argue the case that in these situations all we have to work with is the most important resource in the business – the people. By working closely and listening to people, significant change can be caused to happen. What I am really saying is that it doesn't matter in which sector of the economy you operate, it is the quality of the people who lead and manage that matters. *Before we have quality management we need quality of management!*

MODELLING EXCELLENCE

The critical question asked by Senior Managers should be 'How do they do that?' when discussing how best practice is displayed in customer-focused and high performance companies. Personally, I ask 'How can I help you speedily achieve your culture change targets?' based upon a detailed 'Modelling' exercise.

Modelling* is a tool of organisational change which has not been prominent in helping companies focus their direction. Benchmarking is the poor relation to Modelling, because it tends only to focus tangibly upon those processes which are easily definable and observable. Modelling is a process examining the complexity of business performance by

* Modelling. Transformations UK Ltd 1996 ©

observing and copying the style of the key players and the culture of a business. It can be a very comprehensive exercise including the use and application of problem-solving tools, techniques and methodologies to Human Relations strategies for improvement. Some Modelling is evident in the EFQM's (European Forum for Quality Management's) model for business improvement – but this neglects the behavioural processes inherent within most businesses. Modelling, if conducted rigorously, can identify those factors which caused success to happen and help transfer these speedily into the 'host organisation'.

Modelling goes beyond Benchmarking to examine and detail the success of corporate performance by examining which 'Values' and 'Behaviours' are most likely to accelerate the performance for businesses.

Modelling is a complex process because central to it is understanding the decision-making models of the top team of leading companies, including the personalities and their strategies of influence which make things happen. Many have worked with leading figures in the business world to model the way they manage – featured in the book *Control Your Destiny or Someone Else Will*. Examples of these models include leading CEO Jack Welch of GE (General Electric) fame, and Bill Gates of Microsoft, writer of *The Road Ahead*, and John Harvey Jones, writer of a trilogy on best practice for managers in the UK. Other biographies make some use of Modelling, but do not capture the detail of observing specific behaviours and critical incidents in the life of a business. There are many instances of business biographies from the original Victor Kiam of "I liked it so much I bought the company" fame, through Townsend's *Up the Organisation*, to the 90s equivalent of General Schwartzkopf's success in leading the Desert Storm campaign.

Modelling can be used within any business to examine how key 'Change Makers' have reacted successfully to critical incidents which have taken place within the company. We use it extensively as part of a 5 Day Leadership programme to highlight and differentiate between effective and ineffective behaviours in a Leadership role. If required, only the leading companies in innovation and change then tailor the behaviours into their appraisal scheme which is unlike any other in terms of effectiveness. Here the appraisal is focused upon how well the Values of the business are reflected in the behaviour of the core Managers who control key resources in the company. This powerful tool increases its effectiveness when used in 360 degree assessment exercise when direct reports, internal customers as colleagues (external customers can also be involved in this exercise) and the Boss objectively complete an assessment based upon 'how am I doing?'. Managers receiving feedback from this exercise can then focus their energies on those areas where there is a discrepancy in their behaviour which is sent and that which is received by others. This stimulating exercise is central to moving managers speedily towards a positive leadership role, and away from the traditional function of 'control and administration'.

Modelling has long been considered as a powerful tool for Sports people who wanted to emulate their 'role models'. What has been learnt by 'trial and error' over a lifetime by a renowned athlete can be learned in months by aspiring pupils. By modelling athletes, swimmers, tennis players and others, it is possible to accelerate learning so that performance which took years to improve for athletes can be improved learnt and achieved in months. The detailed process of Modelling can be applied in any setting and used to the advantage of organisations. What is critical for this to take place is moving toward understanding that other innovative techniques for creating culture change can be incredibly powerful and contribute to the bottom line very quickly. Without getting into detail, this approach to organisational change is unique in providing a speedy route to implementing best practice in terms of behaviour. And since all behaviour is focused upon achieving results, those responsible for Change Management could invest some time in learning about this important process.

EXAMINING THE BEHAVIOUR OF OTHERS TO IMPROVE PERFORMANCE

When perceived over the past 20 years, change has been rapid, and we can see the collapse of companies who failed to manage change by assuming that the past world of business would roughly equate to the future. Looking back, we can learn a great deal from some of the manufacturing giants who first drove the improvement for Quality. In those days, Senior Staff talked of how they could assure Quality for their customers or how they would reduce unnecessary Rework costs. I remember in those early days there was little talk or understanding of the word 'Culture' when discussing how to implement TQ in an engineering or a plastics business. And as the Quality Revolution emerged in the 70s and 80s we heard the phrases Total Quality or Total Quality Management. To those of us first engaged in the Quality revolution TQ was a term which related to significant organisational change focusing upon the beliefs and values of a business and founded upon Organisation Development (OD). OD was the movement which centred upon using the applied behavioural sciences to help organisations change, because even then it was understood that Values Systems and Behaviours were critical in causing massive shifts in corporate effectiveness when applied in a tangible and practical manner.

In those early days, our interpretation of TQ was strategic and concerned with changing the fabric of the business for the better. It was a rigorous approach to meaningful change. Change was geared heavily towards measured improvements. It was never a quick fix based upon the use of shallow principles and programmes which bore little credibility in bringing about significant change – but in reality many were just that!

In so many ways Total Quality, with a heavy emphasis on Corporate Culture, has helped companies come a long way in improving bottom line performance. Those who went along the route of a 'watered down' version of TQ achieved little and with it the reputation of TQ as a change process took a tumble.

TQ still means significant and lasting change through investing in prevention and creating a strong business culture. In the eyes of too many TQ is seen as a process which is no more than a quick fix.

CULTURE CHANGE = TOTAL QUALITY

For me Total Quality and Culture Change are synonymous if TQ is described along the lines I have discussed, as will be highlighted in Chapter 2 on the Building Blocks of Culture.

So what is Total Quality? My understanding is that it is the synthesis of the hard and soft sciences for corporate improvement. The tangible science of Quality Assurance and its tools and techniques are skilfully assimilated under the larger and more powerful umbrella of the Applied Behavioural Sciences to promote a change in the business culture. Changing the climate, the very fabric of an organisation, is critical to improving performance. Only by utilising the skills from hard and soft sciences is it possible to create the changes required for businesses today. Focusing just upon the 'left brain', rational problem-solving processes will never pay dividends to any business without the right attitudes, behaviours, passion, belief and spirit associated with 'right brain' creative thinking. Likewise, a commitment to the teamworking spirit will do little for improvement in a company without sound, sensible tools and methodologies for deliverables. Bringing together these two approaches to change is what Total Quality is really about and much of the best practice in TQ is founded upon those who have already achieved a great deal.

MODELLING AND THE JAPANESE EXPERIENCE — *Recommendation*

It comes, therefore, as no surprise that after discussing Modelling best practice, we make reference to the Japanese experience. I would find it impossible to write about TQ and Culture Change without reference to the Japanese and their huge successes of the past 30 years. Understanding the steps to their success fed my curiosity in looking at the process of Modelling.

We can learn any of the methodologies or 'how tos' from those who implemented error-free quality first and captured World markets in the process. It is natural that reference will be made briefly to the TQ revolution in Japanese companies, then a more open description of TQ and Culture Change will be presented in Chapter 2.

The most important issue is that those in the service sector in our economies need to understand that a great deal can be learned from the advances in Manufacturing in this and other countries. Because effective Quality Management was first witnessed as working in Manufacturing Industry and especially in Japan it is wise to invest some time in examining their successes. And when doing so we should move beyond any national stereotyping in terms of 'the Japanese are compliant and will do as they are bidden'. This is no more than a simplified generalisation, is negative and does not explain why we in the US and Europe choose not to drive change as effectively. For instance, the national characteristics of the Japanese, the Germans or any other race do not necessarily make a big difference in how well they instigate change. What is important is rigour of analysis and a passion for 100% implementation and review. So the comments on 'ease of implementation' being nationally based are nonsense. In honesty, if managers want a process to work they can always find a way, no matter in which national, commercial or industrial culture they reside.

My interest in learning from others and Modelling was stimulated by a ten-day trip to Japan with the purpose of visiting companies who were implementing or had implemented a huge change in culture. I was keen to learn those things which were least apparent about the way they approached change or continuous improvement – Kaizen. I was also interested in how the other 20 people on the self-financed trip would respond and how they would reframe the Japanese experience.

One day in particular which stands out was our visit to one of the 30 Toyota plants in Japan. During that trip we had the opportunity to exchange views and debate key issues. On such occasions some discussions did get out of hand.

The statement below is the result of a heated discussion with a group of Toyota Managers who had been kind enough to take us through one of their most innovative production plants. We had just completed a two-hour tour of the Toyota plant in Toyoda City. We had been sitting with the Senior Management Team and asking questions about TQ. At first our hosts were bemused. To them, TQ was no more than business as usual!

Of our party of twenty, most asked questions trying to identify the critical issues to work on to emulate the Japanese approach to Quality. One or two asked embarrassingly naive questions implying that the Japanese approach to excellence could be quickly imported into European and American businesses – that is, once we have the secret! The question which created a most interesting response is printed beneath their question below.

"How long will it be until we in the West catch up and overtake you?"

The Manager who had conducted the tour spoke in clear English and his response was simple and to the point.

"We estimate it would take you 20 years to be where we are now, and by that time we will have progressed further. We have moved from a Quality philosophy of measuring defects on an acceptable quality level basis. We are now working on reducing our defect rate to below 5 to 6 parts per billion. Our last product recall was 1969 when we first started introducing what you know as Total Quality Management."

On reflection, the response from the Toyota General Manager was extremely kind. He could have made a few points about the way we do business in the West, but he didn't.

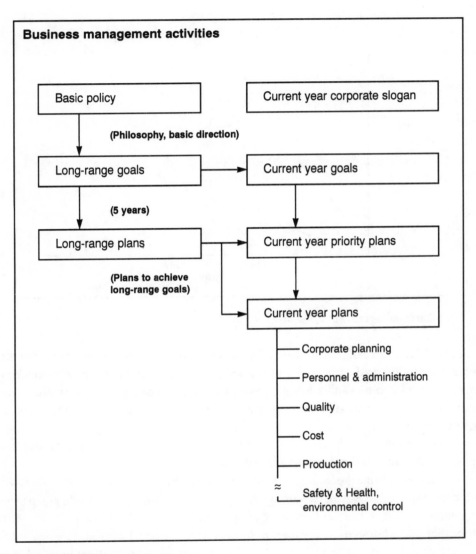

Fig. 1 Basic TQC activities at Toyota

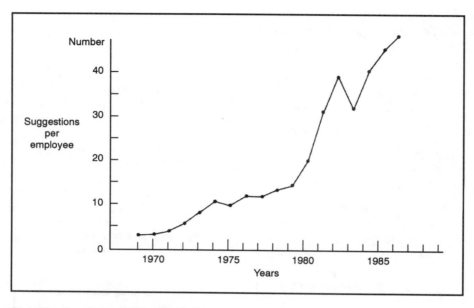

Fig. 2 Employee suggestions at Toyota

We left that meeting hall in silence. We had been exposed to depressing statistics. Each day the twelve hundred employees at this plant, including service and non-manufacturing personnel, produced two and a half thousand cars. Over two cars per person per day! The European equivalent was eight cars per employee per year! All employees participated in Quality Circles.

Staggeringly, the average number of ideas processed per year in Toyota was one hundred and eighty per employee, of which 98% were implemented.

Can you imagine the feelings of inadequacy as our party of twenty left the plant? We had been exposed to so much during that past week, visiting two leading Japanese companies (service sector and manufacturing) every day. We had absorbed so much information and witnessed Quality Improvement at close quarters. How could we remember the most important points and how would we, as a group of representatives from industry and commerce in Europe, start to to initiate change in order to improve our competitive edge?

A GLOBAL VIEW ON THE IMPORTANCE OF TOTAL QUALITY

In reality, we must move quickly to implement rather than argue about change. Over the past thirty years we have lost so many of our markets because of a failure to commit to Quality. That is the truth. We could improve our delivery, but we do not. Is it any wonder the West is suffering from the biggest trade deficit in history! How many industries do we have to lose before we take note and take action? Failing to create a competitive culture through TQ will lose our competitiveness in World markets.

For example, the Western automotive industry has been decimated in recent years. Most of the US-owned automotive companies have established joint ventures with the Japanese. One out of every four cars sold in the US is Japanese. Nine out of the top ten banks in the world are Japanese. It is almost impossible to buy a non-Japanese hi-fi component, camera, TV set, VCR or other household electrical appliances. The Japanese are now exporting white goods – Western producers always believed this would never happen, because no one ships fresh air – it costs so much! JVC has entered the film industry in the US, one of the last bastions of American business. The examples of Eastern success are too numerous (and too depressing) to pursue and yet we could provide just as good service and products if we were committed to implementing TQ.

WHAT ARE WE DOING ABOUT IT?

Where are we going and is there any hope of a revival of Western dominance? Perhaps we could learn from the East and implement some of their ideas and practices gradually.

Senior Executives have been learning from others – whether they do anything is open to debate. Study Tours organised by various bodies have been flying executives to Pacific Basin countries for the past ten years. The success of Japan, Korea, Indonesia, Taiwan and Singapore have been witnessed at first hand. But did those Executives learn and transfer best practice back into their companies?

Many Management Teams had hoped that after their Senior Staff were exposed to TQ in the East, TQ might be promoted and put into practice in their own company. Some organisations have benefited. Others have not. Many have hoped that 'exposure' by itself might help to rekindle the flame of Quality.

Of the hundreds of executives and managers from Europe and the US going out every year to Japan, Korea, Hong Kong etc. to see the way they do business, most return armed with case studies, brochures on TQ practice and briefcases full of information. This is the 'resource' which can form the foundation and which is applicable and transferable to Western Industry. But what happens to this body of knowledge? The answer is pessimistic. Some of us think a large proportion is lost forever. We believe only 5% take note and really create change.

We would suggest that the percentage of managers reading the material, analysing and presenting it to their management team, and maintaining the momentum and enthusiasm for change, is low. The reason for this is the 'Western quick fix mentality'. We do not seem to take TQ or Culture Change very seriously.

Summary

This chapter has highlighted the key point that in order to promote Total Quality, the culture of the business has to be right. We have also highlighted that Culture Change is a complex business which cannot be imported straight from the shelf. In too many instances, TQ was confused with other quick fix change initiatives which have been founded on methodologies, problem-solving skills or particular techniques or accreditation standards. TQ is really the coming together of organisational and technical change to change the fabric, the culture, of a business. Too many TQ initiatives are inaptly named or 'badged' because the depth of analysis they were based on is shallow and does not address stimulating a fresh and vibrant business culture.

So what progress can be made? I think it important that we focus upon Modelling as a discrete process for engendering and implementing change. We also need to understand that change is a behavioural not a technical process. And, most important of all, we need to understand 'how others have created change' first in order to work through our strategy for successful implementation. Chapter 2 deals with the core components of TQ and addresses some of the reasons we have been less than successful in implementation.

Bullet Points

- Find out what the leading companies in your industry, and in the World, are doing to create a performance-driven culture.

- What key words would best typify the negative and the positive elements of the culture in your business?

- If you design your own culture – what words would you use – how would the culture look and what would people feel about it?

- What Values would drive your culture and how would these translate into behaviour?

- What opportunity for stretch is there within your business and how often is it practised?

- Modelling is the most dynamic process of change and yet very few practise it!

- Learn from the experience of others.

- Understand that if even you work in the service sector you have much to learn from Manufacturing and vice versa.

- Others have succeeded or failed using similar processes when perhaps your sector was unaware of these – so learn from them.

- Learn from other cultures, not just your own.

- Total Quality = Culture Change.

- Total Quality and Culture Change is an issue for every company wanting to operate well beyond the 21st Century.

- Differentiate real Culture Change from the shallow projects which were inaptly named as full-blown quality initiatives.

- Understand that change comes about through the Applied Behavioural Sciences, not using 'quick fix' or 'flavour of the month' techniques.

CHAPTER 2

The Building Blocks of a TQ Culture

The main sections of this chapter concentrate upon defining Total Quality and drawing upon some of the approaches which fall within the Culture Change umbrella. But first we quickly examine the contribution of some of those who helped shape Quality over the years. Whole books have been written around the contributions of just some of the names and subjects mentioned below, so please go to the relevant texts if an in-depth understanding is required of their work.

MAJOR CONTRIBUTORS*

The major figures in the world of Quality include Dr. Deming, Juran, Crosby and Conway. Deming and Juran visited Japan after the Second World War in order to help them rebuild their industry. They helped the Japanese improve their quality through the use of Statistical Process Control (SPC). In effect, the techniques of the West were married with the philosophy of Management from the East.

Since that time, many companies in the West have been pursuing a variant of Total Quality Management and have committed to quality helping set up the EFQM in 1988.

COMPARISON OF COMPANIES IN THE EAST AND IN THE WEST IN TERMS OF QUALITY

If we look at a comparison of quality products from the 1950s to today, we see a big difference in the commitment to quality in the West and in Japan. We can note that quality improvement has increased much faster in Japan from year to year than in Europe and the US.

* A detailed booklist is provided in Appendix 2

Dr. Juran recognised and published this many years ago, but companies in the West took little interest. Thirty years ago, the Japanese were noted for poor quality products and this was evident in the cheap toys and textiles they exported. Today the Japanese and other Pacific Basin countries have greatly improved their quality and have overtaken us in most international markets.

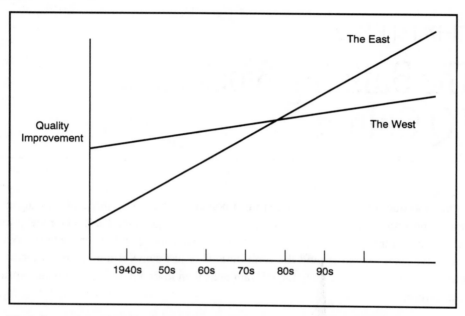

Fig. 3 Comparison of Quality improvement of companies in the East and the West

Much of Japanese TQ expertise is a direct result of the Korean and Vietnamese Wars. The US invested heavily in Japan to ensure that equipment and technology could be repaired quickly and sent back to the battle lines. The experience of working with Quality Systems gained during these two major conflicts has had significant influence on the Japanese approach to Quality.

With this experience they have retested and learned new ways to improve the Quality of their products and services. They have now captured many European markets and this goes far beyond the manufacturing arena. Japan has now sited its major banks in key European and US cities and the finance houses are well established to compete with their counterparts. Some suggest that the Japanese tend to target a market and go for it. The interesting thing is they don't keep this a secret from us Westerners.

Over a decade ago it was acknowledged that Japanese companies had targeted the pharmaceutical industry and the financial services sector. As far as the pharmaceutical industry is concerned, the Japanese are huge users of 'prescribed drugs' and feel that there is an opportunity to move into a new manufacturing area which will have huge payoffs to a relatively new industry. They have made significant movement in financial services at the same time, as any walk down any major European city will testify by the presence of their banks and other institutions. In the City, the presence is obvious as new Japanese financial services businesses have locked into the financial infrastructure of the UK economy. This is also prevalent in other European countries.

A commitment now by companies to changing the culture of their business to TQ is perhaps the only guaranteed way for protecting and improving their market in the long term. In the past twenty years consider the loss of market share in industries like the automotive, motorcycle, electrical household components including TV, audio equipment, video, watches, shipbuilding, electronics, camera, photocopier markets, etc. Providers of these items were aware of the competition and their zeal for quality, but did little. They refused to take Quality seriously as a competitive issue.

Twenty years ago, the Japanese had little part to play in world banking and finance. Today nine out of ten of the top banks in the world are Japanese.

The increase in the demand and provision of financial services in recent years has been a sufficient incentive for the Japanese to move into Europe. Their banking sector can easily service new initiatives in this area. Many of the providers of pharmaceutical services including Johnson & Johnson, Dow Merrill, etc. have developed TQ Drives to improve their performance and compete with the Japanese – but what of the financial services sector?

The tradition of banking and insurance has not moved sufficiently forward to understand the concept of Culture Change. Only the most knowledgeable and enlightened CEOs of companies in the banking and finance sector have taken note and developed programmes for changing their cultures.

It is impossible to discuss TQ and culture change without referring to the tremendous progress made by the Japanese in TQ. And consider the progress they have made by siting new manufacturing units in Europe and the UK and the success they have achieved over the past ten years. This success has come about by changing and improving the culture towards 'empowerment' and away from 'management control'. Control has been replaced by trust and this is critical in any successful TQ drive. We note that flat structures must be driven by empowered managers who can operate in an environment of ambiguity and thirst for continuous improvement. Being Japanese by itself is not important. But what is important is the culture they create to enable and cause improvement to happen through the desires, the skills, creativity and personal drive of the most important resource of all – people. Quite simply, the Japanese have no special advantage over us, they simply examine the process of doing a job and try to improve upon it. More importantly, they listen to their people and implement their suggestions for improvement. To quote Mr. Ohno, one-time chairman of Toyota.

"QUALITY is both about thinking why something is done, and why it is done that way; then thinking differently to improve it."

SOLVE THE PROBLEMS BY BUILDING A STRONG CULTURE FOUNDED ON TQ, RATHER THAN THROWING MONEY AT THEM

Rather than changing the business culture to exploit the ideas and improvements of our people, a typical Western response to Japanese competition in Western markets is: "We will invest and drive them back into the Pacific". The US felt they had to respond to the influx of Japanese cars in 1978 and suggested that the automotive industry should invest a great deal of money in new technology, robotics, etc. This initiative was orientated to improve Quality, protect market share and give the American product a competitive advantage. The US car industry believed that throwing money at a problem would solve it. In particular, a major automotive manufacturer said that they would invest $40 billion in the next ten years and send the Japanese back in to the Pacific. They were wrong. They invested over $68 billion in that decade and still lost market share. However, their share price rose in 1988 when they sold off spare capacity and admitted that they were trying to hold on to a realistic percentage of the market. Their position has improved radically since they have committed to a total change of culture.

Quality is about attitude. Spending money does not promote Quality, although it may provide the tools. Throwing money at problems does not make them go away. Investing in technology is not a route to TQ. You may invest in the right technology but still implement it poorly. Total Quality is something which is engineered through effective human relations and goes beyond the quick fix of problem-solving techniques.

Japan now manufactures one out of every four cars in the world and targeted, created and achieved a manufacturing platform in Europe. Now Nissan have well deserved dominance in the North East of England as Toyota have set up an equally effective operation in Derby. There is a hardly a week goes by when we do not hear of yet another Japanese or Korean business locating in the UK. The news is good for employment but what about the impact upon home industries?

YOU WON'T DO IT!

Some years ago a British Department of Trade and Industry delegation visited Japan. The group was composed of Senior Managers from companies, Civil Servants, Trade Unionists, Academics, Consultants, etc. During a cocktail party on the last evening of the tour an English manager asked a Japanese economist why they had opened up their factories and talked frankly with the group about Total Quality issues. Did they not realise that the group would go their respective ways, implement the approach in their companies and come back and compete successfully against Japan?

The Japanese economist replied: "It will take you 7-10 years to catch up with us and by that time we will be even further ahead – but we don't mind sharing our secrets with you, because we are confident you won't do it!"

For the reader, this is all pretty depressing in a book orientated towards promoting TQ in Europe and the US. But writing platitudes and confirming prejudices does not and will not create the needed change in commerce and industry today.

Honest, plain speaking is required. In many areas we produce mediocre services and products. To make matters worse, there are too many in industry and commerce who think that change is not necessary – thinking we can return to the early 1970s, before things started to get tough! It is not going to happen. Senior officers in companies have to be able to learn to become responsive, to anticipate and plan for change. They have to be able to turn their companies around and anticipate the competition becoming better in every way. They have to lead by example.

HAVING THE ANSWER – BUT DOING NOTHING

What is of key concern is that when we have the means of resolving problems, we studiously ignore them – often because we have to learn to change personally first. We have a great deal of difficulty achieving this. Or sometimes, because of a 'quick fix' mentality, we will ignore needed changes, or say it won't work. Why? Often because it means we have to lead the change and that pushes us out of our comfort zones.

XENOPHOBIA – IT IS NOT THE JAPANESE, IT IS THE WAY THEY PREVENT PROBLEMS OCCURRING

It is easy when writing on TQ to compare Western with Eastern practice in organisations. This book is no different – but we must be aware that the Japanese are not our only competitors. They are quoted frequently because the comparison with the performance of Western companies is extreme. They seem to have developed in their companies a climate where TQ is the guiding influence. This, understandably, has resulted in diminished market share for Western nations.

Some European managers claim that the Japanese and their Pacific neighbours compete unfairly and this has led to a decline in Western dominance in markets. They further claim that TQ is a natural product of their culture and that 'they' will always have a natural advantage over the rest of the world. This is nonsense. Many of the ideas which the Japanese and their neighbours employ are not new to Western eyes. The techniques and approaches to Quality were the product of Western minds, such as Deming and Juran, and were exported to Japan just after the Second World War. The Japanese took a long-term view, incorporated the ideas into their manufacturing base and constantly sought innovation. The Japanese put far more emphasis on implementation plans and reviewing changes. In the US and Europe often the loop of culture change is frequently not closed, and the reason is that Senior Management often do not understand the concept of 'Culture' and its relationship to cross-functional working and improved performance.

CASE STUDY: Japanese Companies Seeking Innovation

In 1950 Toyota developed Statistical Quality Control, nothing new to Western industry. In 1951 they introduced their first Suggestion Scheme. Total Quality Control was introduced in 1961. Nineteen-sixty-two saw the advent of Quality Circles and in 1963 this became a company-wide programme. In 1965, Toyota improved quality to such a standard that it received the coveted Deming Prize. The company went on to further success in 1966 when it introduced a company-wide Quality assurance system (there are still many companies in Europe who do not have such a system). In 1970 it received the first 'Japan Quality Control' prize. Nineteen-seventy-nine saw the development of a programme to improve managerial ability. Nineteen-eighty-three saw the beginning of the 'Improving Office Campaign' and in 1985 this was extended to a 'More Spontaneous Office Activities' programme. Since then, the company has been working on general 'Quality Improvement'.

Companies like Nippon Denso ran a similar change in culture starting with Quality Control in 1956, receiving the Deming Prize in 1961, introducing Quality Circles in 1964, deployed resources to promote the "100% Reliable Products and Service" drive and in 1983 the campaign which was to herald Nippon Denso as producing the world's No. 1 products and the world's best Corporate System – reflected in its approach "Nippon Denso of the World, TQC by everybody".

It is difficult to denigrate such efforts with excuses. They, the Japanese, the Koreans etc. simply took the body of knowledge relating to Quality as it existed and put it into practice. This is hardly unfair competition. Perhaps we have a great deal to learn about how we easily discard sound sensible approaches to effective management.

REJECT STEREOTYPED BELIEFS

The sooner we in the West move away from the old stereotypes about unfair competition, dumping cheaper unit price items on European and American soil, cheaper wage costs etc., the sooner we can start our drive to be the best in the world. It is not yet too late. For companies to establish Superior service delivery and manufacturing excellence, the race to catch up must start now. It is no good in 2005 complaining about the advantage our competitors have over us – without putting some of their ideas into practice now. All that stops us is simply 'Managerial Mindsets'.

IS TQ CULTURALLY BIASED TOWARDS THE EASTERN CULTURE?

If their practice was 'culturally biased' we would expect that Eastern companies based in Europe and the UK would have not developed as well as they have done. We are constantly surprised to find that the particularly 'Japanese approach' to the management of Quality has worked in Japanese companies such as Nissan, Hitachi, JVC, National Panasonic etc. in the UK with British workers. There is nothing magical about their culture – they just apply the principles. Companies such as Jaguar, British Airways, Mars, Corning Glass, Dow Chemical, CMG (Computer Management Group), Cable & Wireless, General Electric and many others have succeeded not just by looking and admiring the Japanese but by applying ideas on improving the Quality of what they do.

So in order to understand the concept of TQ and separate it from any national culture, it is important to examine the philosophy which underpins the approach. And before we go any further it is important to understand that there are no differences between the service and manufacturing industries. All organisations provide services which customers consume. Ensuring that all staff understand that they provide a service to either an external or internal customer is critical in implementing Culture Change.

WHAT IS TOTAL QUALITY?

It is a strategic approach to producing the best service we can – through constant innovation. It is a recognition of the importance of concentrating on the services you provide as a business. TQ is a refocusing upon service to the customer being tantamount to success and improvement as a business. If you don't like pleasing the customer with right first time business, get out and do something else!

Over the past ten years there has been a constant intellectual battle between Quality being a manufacturing rather than a 'customer service' issue. This is complete nonsense. Many manufacturing companies can produce zero defect products, but the company's 'Quality' in a metaphysical sense is very poor. There is still so much to let companies down which goes far beyond the product they make. The quest for Service Excellence is very much the issue for most companies to achieve in the next few years. Quality is a corporate issue. It affects every company and ultimately will determine the success or failure of any business.

Quality Assurance in many manufacturing businesses may appear right, but there are other functions and departments in the organisation which can let the business down. This is a reversal of traditional thought about QA but not about TQ. For instance, the right product delivered at the wrong time can have catastrophic impact upon both buyer and seller. In a research report conducted twelve years ago it was found that 95% of companies deliver their product late. This late delivery can have just as much impact upon future buying decisions as increasing the price of the product by 5%, and yet too many businesses still only deal with

TQ as relating to the more tangible sides of the business. TQ is first and foremost a 'Service Excellence' issue!

Other service-related issues which can cause problems come from functions who don't even touch the product. For instance, Accounts and Invoicing can create problems. Delivering the right product, but invoicing incorrectly, can delay payment back to the supplier for as much as three months or longer, but many people in 'support services' don't seem to realise the impact of their behaviour and their less-than-quality standards.

Salesmen promising the earth in 'back-up' can leave the customer disappointed, cold and indifferent to further trading with his company when the cold hand of bureaucracy – staff who never meet the customer but are expert at 'Service Prevention' – fails to provide the customer with the level of service he requires. Sometimes it is important to remind 'support functions' that without a 'Sale' there is no business. So respect the Salesmen and support their efforts. There is no need to generate a war between functions just because a salesperson promises X and support functions have to change their plans to provide to 'customer requirements'. It is critical to understand that all staff should be 'customer-facing' and 'support services' should provide to those who liaise directly with the customer.

The conflict between 'customer-facing ' staff and those who provide support services should be resolved. Overall, whether staff actually meet the customer or not, my belief is that the following phrase should be at the foremost of the minds of all staff in every function:

"Quality starts with me and is my responsibility."

TQ DIRECTED TOWARDS MAINTAINING THE COMPETITIVE EDGE AND SECURITY OF THE BUSINESS

Without doubt, the drive towards TQ comes about for a number of reasons, but generally there are push and pull factors in operation.

Many senior officers of organisations pursue TQ because they fear the future. They know the environment is constantly changing and that they are constantly being reviewed by their customers. Some customers such as Ford, Jaguar, Marks and Spencer, IBM and many Japanese companies refuse to do business with vendors unless they can prove that the quality of service and product they provide meets their exacting standards. Witness the number of companies recognising that BS 5750 is only the foundation for full accreditation as a vendor by Ford. The only way they can do this is by being rated on a sliding scale of the Ford Q101 System which requires a real drive for detail.

Senior Staff in organisations understand that to continue to do business with customers will require dedication to get things right, first time, every time. Some company officers decide to pursue TQ as an act of faith. They know it is the right thing to do. Dow Chemical, a major American chemical company, pursued TQ in a year of record profits.

Nothing was wrong with its performance. The product range was excellent Quality. But the over-riding motive behind the initiative was 'while the sun is shining let's get out and fix the roof'. Years later the company is glad it did – because the Japanese focused upon its very successful and thriving pharmaceutical markets.

Paul Quay, a Senior Manager with whom I worked and who was responsible for the European TQ Drive within this company, was flying out to Switzerland and started up a conversation with a fellow passenger. He discussed TQ with this new acquaintance – and then said that although there was no threat in the ABS Plastics market (another successful part of the business), the officers of the company thought it would be a good idea to promote TQ in this area. The passenger produced his business card and handed it to Paul. He was the Plant Manager of a chemical plant producing ABS Plastics and when Paul turned the card over he found that the reverse of the card was in Japanese – as was the origin of the company.

This prompted an investigation into companies in the West and East producing plastics. The data generated reinforced the belief that the company had to improve quality in order to maintain its edge. We established that 50% of the ABS companies in the East had been set up in that year – and of that total, 50% were exporting plastics to Europe.

What might have been known in one area of Dow, a small section in marketing, was not common knowledge throughout the structure. Acknowledging that continual improvement is the only factor that keeps you ahead of the competition must be communicated to everybody. The resulting TQ Drive helped people share the perception that their company had to be 'vigilant' and constantly needing to appraise its competitive position in order to grow and succeed.

AN ORGANISATION-WIDE COMMITMENT TO QUALITY

TQ is an organisational-wide commitment to getting things right. But our experience helping companies suggests that the initiative can come solely from the production people. At a TQ presentation for a multi-national engineering company, it was noticeable that the Marketing, Sales and Financial Directors were absent. The Sales Director said he was busy with buyers from Italy. The Financial Director stated that he had to see the Company Secretary and the Marketing Director that he had an appointment with a Public Relations agency. The TQ message had not been well 'sold' previously. Some were not listening, evidenced by the non-attendees still believing that Quality was not a priority and had nothing to do with them. Quality starts with 'support functions'.

RECOGNITION THAT TQ PROBLEMS ORIGINATE IN AREAS OTHER THAN MANUFACTURING

Many problems do arise in units which service manufacturing units. The following examples illustrate the 'cause' of Quality problems in areas other than production. For instance, the enthusiasm and zealous appeal to customer service displayed by the Salesman to the customer who will agree to any modification with the customers, not understanding or caring about the chaos created on the shopfloor. Likewise, the Designer who feels that he knows best and does not need to talk with the operative making the component he designs about the use of particular techniques in manufacture. Another example is the Purchasing Manager who fails to appraise suppliers because he doesn't have time, which leads to significant problems with material management. Another example is with Accounting when a Manager who experiences cash flow problems from customers and consequently withholds payment to Suppliers changing the 30- to a 60-day payment period – then wonders why components are not delivered on time, etc. These are all classic examples of problems which arise in non-manufacturing areas. They are not treated as Quality problems although TQ is a support function issue first and foremost.

The impact of these decisions in service units can have a horrifying effect on Quality on the shopfloor. That is why we talk of *Total* Quality.

FOUNDED UPON QC, INSPECTION AND SPC

Total Quality Management is founded upon these areas of Quality Management. It is always desirable for a company to have developed some level of Quality Control, QA System and SPC prior to TQ – but it is not essential. Now this might sound strange – but it"s not. TQ is concerned with turning a company around in terms of improving overall performance by focusing upon Quality. TQ is an umbrella term for *continuous improvement starts at the top*. If these and other initiatives have been going for some time, TQ is a guiding influence which can bring them all together in one Drive.

TAILORING TQ DRIVES TO THE ORGANISATION

TQ Drives are often not designed and tailored to the needs and maturity of the company. TQ drives are frequently designed around the capability and experience of consultants. Few consultants in the TQ area are behavioural scientists by training or through experience. Too many are technical or engineering focused and have picked up aspects of the applied behavioural sciences on programmes. When trying to change a culture, ensure you work with someone who understands and drives change much deeper rather than at a surface level. Change starts with behaviour and radiates out through the organisation. TQ is not a system which can be taken from the shelf. It is a serious and deep study and application of changing the very fabric of the organisation – in honesty it is about changing Managerial Mindsets.

For instance, British Telecom engaged upon a major TQ Drive some time ago and as well as focusing upon systems, also focused upon people through its innovative Customer Care programme. It is committed to long-term change and has a grand vision of where it will be in the the next five years. The endeavours are now becoming part of its culture and recognisable signs of success are strongly evident. But, because of the sheer size of the company, the full impact of the Drive may take up to 15-20 years to realise after starting 10 years ago. This does not mean that TQ has been unsuccessful, but that the initiative has to follow certain stages before the real benefits accrue.

TAILORED DRIVES FOR CULTURE CHANGE

For instance, we have worked with three different chemical companies, all American owned. But the TQ initiative in all three companies has been radically different. Although the three companies did produce similar products, their cultural base, the Quality methods they employed and their 'management style' were all different. Consequently, what worked for one company wouldn't work for others.

Organisations employ differing technology, have different histories and backgrounds, serve different markets, with different products, employ people from different cultures – so the drive to improve Quality has to be managed differently.

DRIVEN BY TOP MANAGEMENT

A major theme which runs through this book is commitment. If senior officers in organisations fail to drive TQ it will fail. Getting the Drive started is not where the responsibility for change finishes. Long-term 'Ownership' is the role that Senior Management take on. They have to lead others by example. They will have to demonstrate new ways of working and, through actions, reject the old ways.

DEPENDENT UPON THE ACTIONS OF EVERYONE

The great danger of talking about Senior Management commitment is that others within the structure assume that all the effort must come from the top. Wherever people fit within the hierarchy they have a part to play. Quality initiatives need to be generated and driven by everyone within the company. Of course, we can't expect this to start from day one of the TQ Drive, but over time everybody should have a responsibility.

A NEVER-ENDING PROCESS

Total Quality is a process which goes on forever. There will never be a time when Quality and Service Excellence is 100% right. There will always be new ways of providing and improving Service Excellence. Again, in the past there has often been too much emphasis placed on that tangible product, the manufacturing or distribution side of a business, and I can understand why this is so! Historically, we can see the greatest changes and performance improvements in terms of concrete and tangible examples, often in manufacturing areas. It is because these areas have been most able to 'demonstrate' improvements that those in support functions have thought the same principles were not applicable to their functions.

To support the view that too much emphasis is placed on manufacturing and the soft 'intangible' side of the business remains defocused, Deming, Juran and other Quality gurus claim that 80% of Quality Costs originate in areas other than those where the product is touched by people.

So TQ is far more than a Quality Assurance system! The quest for quality is not over when a company receives its accreditation to a Quality standard, although some companies feel that their drive is over as soon the certificate goes up on the wall in the Reception area. It begins with the recognition that people – the staff – the most important resource, are critical in driving the process of continuous improvement.

TQ IS BASED UPON RIGHT FIRST TIME AND PREVENTION

TQ is a preventative strategy replacing rework, firefighting and crisis management with planning, co-ordination and control. This means Company Officers, orientating themselves to generating the long-term resolution of the really important problems which impact upon the organisation. In order to do this, we have to spend less time putting things right after they have gone wrong.

TQ AND RELATED QUALITY IMPROVEMENT INITIATIVES

TQ is the umbrella under which a great number of Quality initiatives can be managed, including SPC, Taguchi Methodology and Just in Time. It is not the purpose of this book to detail the growth of these approaches to Company-Wide Improvement, although they are briefly explained towards the end of this chapter with further reading suggested in the Appendix 2.

These techniques are no alternative to Culture Change. In fact, it is impossible to meaningfully establish these practices without a TQ culture. Let's explore some of the initiatives which underpin TQ and look at developments in recent years. I will highlight the techniques and methodologies which have appealed to and support the wider concept of

Culture Change. Application of these approaches alone will not engender the changes most organisations require.

QUALITY CIRCLES

For too long many managers have confused the growth of Quality Circles with TQ. Quality Circles are groups of people, often structured as normal work groups, who meet on a voluntary basis together with their direct supervisor to discuss 'improvements'. They may discuss productivity improvement, suggest new and better ways of doing things. The important point to note is that they are voluntary in nature. They meet because they want to. They can be based in manufacturing or service areas – although most have been established in production-type environments.

Quality Circle members will have had some training in problem-solving. They will work on a project and present their proposals for change to management. Basically it is a 'bottom up' change strategy. Commitment is given from the top of the organisation and managers throughout the structure should help facilitate change. There have been many successful QC activities, but equally, a great number of initiatives have failed. They fail for all sorts of reasons, the most obvious being lack of visible support from senior management, blockages to implementation of improvements by line management, and lack of momentum and direction.

Quality Circles helps to create the environment for change but often fails. TQ as a structured approach does not rely on volunteers – it is a structured company-wide strategy for change driven from the top.

CUSTOMER SERVICE

Many service companies use this approach to improve the Quality of service to their customers. It can be a great boon and often works. The most notable examples in recent years have been the British Airways campaign and the radical turnaround of SAS with the leadership of Jan Carlson, who created the 'moments of truth' concept. This term refers to the time each customer can take to make up his mind about a company. Often this can be as short as a 15-second interaction. Carlson highlighted that there are literally millions of opportunities each day when staff can demonstrate excellent customer service. By focusing upon the millions of positive 'moments of truth' created each day by staff, Carlson turned the airline business around. He saw to it that his staff, at all levels, were trained to be totally customer-orientated.

Well-designed customer care programmes can work remarkably well. However, there can be two problems to consider in providing customer service training. There is little point investing a great deal of time on external PR activities focused upon influencing the customer when there is little emphasis on improving the provision of service excellence to the internal customer. Often there is a major confusion and too much emphasis is placed upon 'smile training', just greeting the customers and adopting the 'have a nice day' approach, when there is little substance or improvement offered to customer service. There can be too much gloss and a few 'quick fix' slogans stated on counting the 'Customer as King' and 'Exceeding Customer Expectations' when what really is required are genuine attempts to improve customer responsiveness.

Effective Customer Service is based upon changing the attitudes of 'boundary personnel', the people who come into contact with the customer. Telling the customer how great the company is by using advertising does not work and is very patronising. What most companies don't understand is that 'all customers are intelligent' and they see way beyond the 'pop psychology' which is used to promote the right customer-focused image within the marketplace.

To illustrate this point, some time ago a company spent a great deal on a TV campaign focusing upon its apparent speedy response and concern with exceeding customer requirements – hoping to influence other potential prospects to become committed to the company as subscribers of an 'insurance' policy. Eight thousand disgruntled viewers wrote to complain to the company and stated that their experience did not match that expressed in the TV advertisements. The senior officers of the company reassessed their strategy and wisely decided to improve their customer service through action not advertising.

The second problem with some Customer Service strategies is that, by their very nature, they tend to focus only upon processes which take place between the customer and the organisation – thinking that only this interface is critical. This interface is very important, but if the company has developed excellent relationships with the customer – without substantially improving the service provided between internal customers and suppliers – the overall quality provided to the customer will remain poor. Here 'Service Excellence' provided to the customer is portrayed as being high, but in reality it is not. Behind the customer exchange there may remain confusion, animosity and conflict between functional silos in the organisation, but at least the customer may be shielded from it in the short term.

Total Quality Service or Total Customer Care can be incredibly powerful. Emphasis should always be on the internal dynamics of the organisation, recognising that meeting the requirements of the internal customer is as important as meeting the needs of the external customer. British Airways saw the good sense of adopting both approaches – using Total Quality Management inside the company and Customer Care with its passengers.

QUALITY CONTROL AND ASSURANCE

Traditionally these functions are concerned with checking for errors during and after the process of manufacture. Controlling, at its most basic, can take place at Final Assembly. Here everything is checked to see if it works. If it does not, it is rejected and either reworked or scrapped. If there is a major problem with a product, or the company is becoming more Quality conscious – knowing that too many errors are being shipped to the customer – it can develop a Quality Control System. A QC System is very useful and helps identify where errors arise, but does not create a change in the culture of the business and does not cause 'Service Excellence'.

The big problem with traditional QC activities is that there is a heavy requirement to depend on the activities of Inspectors. When companies experience a Quality problem there is a natural inclination to inspect, inspect, inspect! This creates an increase in errors spotted, but does not prevent their arising in the first place. And this is just as evident in the Service sector where supervisors and managers devote 50-75% of their time checking and controlling errors rather than building a culture to prevent them.

The problem with this rigid QA approach is that there is a focus upon people trying to inspect Quality into the product. Quality can only be designed and manufactured in at every stage – not inspected in after the event. TQ, by its very nature, rests on changing behaviour and providing the right preventative mentality. TQ is not inspection-orientated and focused upon rows and rows of managers checking and controlling what everybody else does. QA is an essential component of TQ, but only a small part of the wider jigsaw of Culture Change. QA and the many preventative strategies employed will however prosper and grow quickly and will work well if built upon a healthy TQ Culture

From Quality Control we have the growth of Quality Assurance Systems. These are designed in order to verify that all attempts are made to reduce non-conformance from the product specification. QA Systems enable us to check for progress, identify and isolate where a product is in the 'production process'. Quality Assurance is founded upon the Inspection approach – but is strongly preventative in nature and many practitioners have adopted a very proactive view to 'foolproofing' processes – but often QA is still understood as an 'inspection' activity. Although the majority of people in a QA section in a business may be inspectors, the QA Manager should be spending an increasing part of his time developing sophisticated systems to ensure there is not a breakdown in Quality processes in the company.

In summary, TQ is partly founded and reliant upon Quality Assurance techniques. TQ does not contradict QA but goes far beyond it. TQ relates to all functions in all areas. It is a behavioural intervention requiring attitude change – although it is founded upon measurement and control.

STATISTICAL PROCESS CONTROL

SPC, as it is known, is widely accepted in industry as a method of regulating conformance to requirements for a product – in other words it gives you the tools and techniques to measure the performance of an operation. From measurement you will be able to assess whether things are running smoothly or whether there are requirements for adjustments to fit within certain control parameters.

Simple charting is an extremely useful technique of SPC. Operators may test every twentieth item or randomly, and record it on a chart. Recording and measuring allows comparisons to be made. Most products will have specifications and it is to these that the measurements relate. Measurements that fall outside agreed tolerances indicate a potential problem – it could be as simple as a machine requiring to be reset or inferior material being used. Whatever the cause, SPC allows us to measure conformance to specifications. It provides the data upon which we create Corrective Action.

TQ requires SPC. It is a valuable tool and must be taken seriously. Too often it is not. Two instances, although perhaps extreme, will illustrate the point. The stories are based upon a discussion with operators on the use of SPC.

One chap at a CNC machine fails to plot any data on the graph in front of him. In discussion I ask him why he failed to do so. His honest reply, "Today is Tuesday, the man from. . . (the customer) doesn't come until Friday. The charts will be marked up then." It is clear that charts in this case are used for impression management purposes and to fox the customer. They have little intrinsic value to the organisation – although creating a sham for the customer and meeting apparent 'customer requirements' on the surface and only in the short term. Worse still, the example set from the managers who control the system is indirectly communicating that "SPC and Quality isn't important".

The second case involved an operator's refusing to complete the charts. When he was asked why, he said: "They are a waste of time. I have been filling charts in for the last three months. There are plenty of times when there have been problems which have led to reworking the product and these are recorded accurately. But what is the use – nobody takes any corrective action – so why should I waste my time filling in the forms?"

SPC is an extremely powerful technique **if used properly.** We know many companies who use the technique to best advantage, but there are too many who abuse it and use it for the wrong reason to benefit from its use.

SPC works marvellously – even in service areas. To be successful it requires total commitment and someone who can explain the use of statistics simply.

TAGUCHI METHODOLOGY

Dr. Genichi Taguchi is famous for his methods for improving Quality Engineering at low cost. This approach to problem-solving helps quantify the loss due to lack of quality of a performance characteristic and directly relating it to its deviation from the target performance. Taguchi methodology demonstrates the efficient use of analytical and experimental techniques to identify the real cause of a problem. Taguchi Methodology concentrates upon design of products, reducing variation of performance characteristics and parameter design.

Most companies in Japan and, increasingly, the US are using this methodology in system, parameter and tolerance design. The American Supplier Institute is foremost in promoting Taguchi. This approach and tool of TQ is not widely understood in the UK and Europe. The rigorous application of Taguchi Methods, although not a subject of this book, is gathering ground in industry. It is suggested that it should become a vital interest to European engineering and manufacturing managers. Taguchi methods are very unlikely to be applied successfully in a culture which is not heavily committed to TQ.

JUST IN TIME

Just in Time principles are concerned with improving productive efficiency and reducing waste. Most perceive this to be a means of strictly regulating the flow of materials into the company – which is restricted in outlook. JIT is used as a technique for minimising storage of excessive inventory through planning and meeting the exact requirements of the customer. JIT also requires the use of fairly analytical techniques for correcting problems in the manufacturing process.

Preventative Maintenance, Foolproofing, Set Up Time Reduction are some of the outputs of this approach. It is impossible to create JIT **without** the TQ Culture. It is possible to reduce inventory in the short term – but if there has been a failure to remove the problems underpinning excessive inventory, the problems will be intensified.

BARRIERS TO TQ IN RECENT YEARS

Clearly there are many initiatives which fall under the TQ umbrella – but require the TQ Culture to make things happen. It is for this reason that many innovative programmes fail. Management perceive a technique as being useful and apply it in an environment and culture which is hostile and where it cannot grow and prosper except in the short term. It is therefore impossible to try to inculcate a sub-culture of improvement within a business which does not possess a culture of continuous improvement.

REPUTATION FOR THE SHORT-TERM FIX

Too many companies fail to give TQ a chance and think it will give quick payoffs. It can if given the right drive and impetus. It is very important to understand that TQ *will* work in the short term but only with long-term commitment and a very detailed plan with review and feedback sessions to close the culture change loop. Overall, the belief has been sold by too many consultants with a technical background and who lack a strategic and behavioural perspective that TQ will produce results in the short term (See Chapter 3 on the Economics of Quality). They are right that TQ will work but not with the box of tricks composed of systems.

Overall, there is an expectation that the cost of reworking processes and wasteful practice will drop considerably in the short term. This will only happen when there is a major investment in preventative-type activities, and, in the long term, only if the senior officers of the business commit to sustaining a planned and sequential approach to continuous improvement.

If TQ or a related activity, ie. JIT, MRP or Quality Circles, does not live up to the short-term expectations of Senior Staff – new projects are not given an opportunity. Just as projects are starting to gather ground, senior officers introduce a new management 'fad'.

NEGATIVE ATTITUDE: WE HAVE SEEN IT ALL BEFORE

The frequency with which we are told by workshop participants that TQ is no more than Briefing Groups, Quality Circles, Participative Management, MBO, is incredible. We are also reminded that many of these approaches failed in companies in the past – so why should TQ work now? The matter to deal with here is addressing the Managerial Mindset which needs a stiff change in direction. Managers who control functions are either in favour of or against Quality improvement. If they are opposed to the view that the organisation has the capability to improve customer service and growth for the company in the future, my advice is to encourage them to pursue their career with one of your competitors who equally shares their lack of challenge, growth and improvement!

TEN REASONS TO MAKE IT FAIL

Attitude and resistance to change are major problems in Commerce and Industry today. Good ideas for Quality improvement can be rejected by the group who are intent on making ideas fail. Sometimes they portray the NIH approach, 'Not Invented Here'. "It's okay for the production people where all the problems arise – but no good for the service side."

DIGGING UP THE PAST AND MAKING IT REALITY

Too many people in organisations live in the past. They remember the problems created between units and functions and the personalities involved. They generate stereotyped images of people, and Win-Lose attitudes towards work are created at every opportunity. There is a chance that the past will relive itself. We should spend more of our energy thinking and planning for the future – rather than reliving old battles.

NATIONAL DRIVES FOR QUALITY AND ACCREDITATION

The national approach to Quality improvement in the past 15 years has tended very strongly, especially at the outset with the National Quality Campaign, to be totally 'Systems' focused. The subliminal message was that BS 5750 (ISO 9000) would deliver the competitive edge for the modern business. This is far from the truth, with many companies winning the said accreditation and still failing to win new markets. In too many instances it has been used as a PR tool for potential new customers or companies have been pushed into it by powerful purchasers who fail to understand the dynamics of Quality improvement.

> *However, please note that success in achieving ISO 9000 has often created a failure to promote TQ in the same companies.*

In the early National Quality campaign there was so much emphasis given to BS 5750 that many Chief Executives and senior officers became confused, believing that the secret of TQ lay in application of systems. Unfortunately, it was perceived that the Quality Manager within the company now had responsibility for Company-wide Quality Improvement. No doubt the first attempts at Quality improvement were 100% driven in Manufacturing areas.

The publicity and videos incorporated in the initial DTI packages reinforced this belief and were all geared to the promotion of systems – implying that this was what Quality was all about.

There is still a great deal of confusion today and this even extends to TQ conferences. At many venues at which I have presented papers on Culture Change there have been many instances of other speakers talking on 'systems and ISO 9000' – although their sessions were described as 'Implementing Total Quality and Culture Change'.

The latest initiatives have been 'broader' and are starting to focus upon the key 'Cultural' issues. The British Quality Association (BQA) and the Institute of Quality Assurance (IQA) are now providing an excellent service for their members and advancing the body of knowledge (QA), but still a great deal has to be done. There has been little to promote the broader idea of TQ.

Overall, there is a shared belief that Company-wide Quality is the responsibility of the Quality Assurance Manager. The longer this is evident, the longer it will take TQ to get off the ground. Although many of the early issues in Quality Improvement have been reworked and improved, the fundamental belief that Quality is a behavioural and cultural issue has still to be understood.

SUMMARY

TQ is about Culture Change and should never be confused with sub-system change. This chapter has highlighted the importance of learning from others. It has attempted to portray the image that Quality Improvement can be learned through the Modelling process described in Chapter 1. Models to draw from are either manufacturing in industry type or Japanese in terms of speed of implementation. TQ has been defined and some of the methodologies have been explained as well as reasons for failure being highlighted. TQ is not an exact science and what works for one company may not work for another. Developing an individualised approach and using a comprehensive view of Quality is the way to ensure that implementation is successful.

Bullet Points

- Don't underestimate the time and effort required to achieve the real benefits of TQ. It is a gradual process and is built upon a commitment to constant innovation.

- It is time that we in the West were honest about our losses in market-share. Fifteen to twenty years ago people could predict the loss of market-share in motorcycles, cars, TVs, shipping because of inattention to the Quality of product and service. We did nothing about it.

- If by 2005, companies have failed to become committed to TQ, there is serious doubt that they will have any market-share at all.

- Deming and Juran exported Quality Assurance and the related tools to Japan with ease. Why is it so difficult to import these back into our own culture? The simple answer is based upon Managerial Mindset.

- My great fear still is that we can be exposed to the secrets of TQ, have the answer to improving performance, but find ten reasons why we should not do it!

- Don't get wrapped up in moaning about unfair competition. Reject stereotyped beliefs about Japanese culture. TQ can work here. It is only culturally biased in favour of those who want to prevent and improve the way they do things.

- TQ is orientated towards maintaining the competitive edge of the business. It is not a short-term programme, a cost-cutting exercise or a new productivity prescription.

- Total Quality impacts upon everybody, everywhere in the organisation. It is as much the responsibility of the Financial Accountant, Purchasing Manager, Designer, Salesman, Personnel Specialist as of the QA specialist.

- Understand and reinforce the belief that 80% of Quality problems originate in areas other than manufacturing.

- TQ is the umbrella which covers all improvement activities including: SPC, Quality Circles, Customer Care, Just In Time, Taguchi Methods etc.

- TQ Drives must be tailored to the special needs of the organisation. What works in one culture will not work in another even if both companies are in the same industry.

- TQ must be driven and owned by Senior Management, Ownership must reside 100% at the top.

- TQ is a never-ending process. It does not end when a certificate is nailed to a Reception wall – the ISO 9000 series are important, but building a strong fabric to your business driven by strongly committed managers is critical.

- TQ is attitudinal change – it is about changing managerial values and leading by example. It is about changing Managerial Mindset.

- There are many barriers to TQ – the principle one being management orientated towards the latest quick fix.

- Success for organisations will come from persistently imposing the belief that Quality of service is what will keep them in business in the long term.

COMPETITION IN THE PLASTICS INDUSTRY FOR THE 1990s. WHO WILL SURVIVE?

Competitors in The West

Arco	Hoechst
Montedison	Enichem
Union Carbide	Monsato
Dow Chemicals	ICI
Shell Chemicals	BP
Borg Warner	BASF
Bayer	Du Pont
Rohm & Haas	General Electric

Competitors in the East

Mitsui	Mitsubishi
Toyasoda	Nanya
Cheing Mei	Samsung
PT Polychem	Hannam
Lucky Gold Star	Ext Resin
Asahi	Idemitsu
Grand Pacific	Taita

CHAPTER 3

The Economics of Culture Change

Billions of pounds and dollars each year are wasted by organisations fixing things after they have gone wrong. These costs never show up on the Profit and Loss Accounts or the Balance Sheets but they are a wasted resource. Most organisations fail to measure how much they have to invest 'putting things right' and when they do become aware of the horrendous cost, they start to take action. Many TQ or Culture Change drives have been initiated to reduce these costs and build a culture of prevention and planning, to replace the old 'rework culture'. This chapter focuses upon the invisible cost or economics of Rework. After working with many Service and Manufacturing businesses to build a strong Right First Time Culture, it has always been possible to reduce unnecessary waste. The following three cases illustrate the size of this apparent invisible problem.

100 WAYS TO OPEN AN ACCOUNT

Working some time ago with a large financial services business, I was amazed to find that there appeared to be as many ways of opening an account as there were Branches in the Commercial network. Although a procedure had been designed which detailed the process for opening new accounts, this was often disregarded by many in the Branch Network. There were many reasons for non-adherence to the procedure. Some staff felt the process was too bureaucratic, other Branches had evolved their own way of 'doing business' and others thought that their way for opening accounts was improving 'customer service'. Whatever the motives of these people, it created major problems for account-handling at Head Office. Often this led to significant degrees of 'reworking' certain internal processes which further added to confusion as well as wasting people's time. The institution decided to run a Pilot

Project to estimate how much it was costing their company. With a wage bill of £100 million a year many of those involved in the exercise understood that this could amount to at least £30 million.

In other words 30% of the time of all staff employed in the organisation was being wasted doing things right second or third time. Tremendous effort and scarce resources were devoted to doing things again – which could have been done right first time. Believe me, this is only the tip of the iceberg.

We believe that in the Service Sector true waste or misused resource can amount to anywhere between 40% and 50% of labour cost.

INSURANCE SALES CREATING REWORK

Consider a large insurance company. This organisation has a direct Sales Force interacting with customers as well as acting as agents with Independent Financial Advisors. The Sales Staff are keen to sell the products and do this quite well. However in this example the Sales Consultants meet with new prospects and agree and sign a deal. In this case, many Sales Consultants would 'close the sale' but neglect to complete all the paperwork. Attention to detail in completing the paperwork is critical because it sets up a legal agreement between the Customer and the Company. If the detail is wrong or inaccurate, the company can commit itself to huge costs being paid to the customer.

Also, incomplete information is fed into a central administration processing unit requiring staff to contact the new customers by phone and later by letter to glean all the necessary details to ensure that the legal agreement will be set up. We calculated that as much of 30% of a member of staff's time in central processing could be wasted completing this exercise – an exercise which was in the domain of the Sales Consultant. I was concerned, not just with this unnecessary cost, but also that this builds up a very negative perception in the customer's mind about the efficiency of the company – when continually required to go over old ground with those who administer the system.

PATIENT RECORDS DUPLICATED NINE TIMES

Likewise, I remember working within a hospital and, during one particular project, we established that patient records were duplicated an amazing nine times! We understood the reason for this. It was necessary to have duplicated records when a patient was being treated by several departments within the hospital. It soon transpired from cross-checking that the Patient Records were not consistent. There were fundamental errors between one department and another regarding the very important issue of the patient's pharmaceutical history. Clearly this could create major problems if a Doctor or other staff member made decisions about a patient based upon inaccurate information. The economics of this error would be very high if the error became the subject for legal action against the hospital authority.

WHO PAYS FOR THESE ERRORS IN SERVICE DELIVERY?

The customer pays and funds the 'right second or third time' mentality which many organisations allow to drive their business. When something goes wrong and the company 'reworks' the process, the customer pays and this could easily amount to 40% extra on the cost of the consumption of a service of product. This is a wholly unnecessary but real cost which never shows up on the profit and loss account or the balance sheet. It can, and does, cost the average Service business at least 40% of its wages bill. Some suggest that it can amount to a great deal more, especially within the Public Sector.

A REVIEW OF THE COSTS OF QUALITY

In 1978, the UK Government estimated that £10,000 million or 10% of the UK's GNP was wasted on Quality. The National Economics Development Office stated in 1985 that between 10% and 20% of a company's sales revenue can be attributed to quality-related costs.

The costs of getting things wrong are very high and tend never to be measured. We estimate that quality can cost a manufacturing company anywhere between 5% and 25% of sales turnover, a service company anywhere between 10% and 40% turnover and, for some of the more inefficient and large public sector organisations, the costs will be very high indeed.

The high costs experienced by service providers are often associated with the 'internal cost' of putting things right after they have gone wrong. This never shows up in any form of costing for the simple reason that costs associated with putting right what is wrong are often not measured – not even by companies who are pursuing Quality Improvement.

Senior staff in organisations are frequently unaware of how much it costs them to 'get things wrong'. Most Financial Directors will have little idea of how much providing 'Non-quality costs them each year. The 'Cost of Quality' (COQ) never shows up on a balance sheet, profit and loss account or operating statement. In many cases, managers have never been asked to measure the price of 'Non-quality' and would not know where to start.

The term 'Cost of Quality' is really a misnomer – it is more accurately described as the cost of Non-quality, a measurement which indicates how much it costs per year to provide Quality in everything the company does – whether service- or product-related. There are other terms which refer to the same measurement and they include the Cost of Non-conformance and the Price of Quality. The different terms relate to the same concept. For the sake of brevity, we will refer to Cost of Quality as COQ.

UNBELIEVABLE FIGURES: COQ

When the high figures of COQ are first quoted, they appear unbelievable. People wonder how their company actually makes a profit. The proof of such figures has to be explained with examples. But they are real and tangible! It is possible to monitor COQ in all activities – service and manufacturing alike. Companies like IBM, Corning Glass, Jaguar and British Telecom originally experienced COQ as high as 40% of turnover. Many senior officers openly admit this when the first steps in a TQ drive are taken. Most companies without a rigorous approach to Quality may well be operating in excess of this figure. If you doubt this, one or two days' data collection can produce horrifying results. Even now, when the Quality Revolution seems to be pretty well advancing in many businesses, I come across a number of organisations who, having never heard of this concept or having heard and understood the concept, have taken no action to improve performance. Most important of all, it must be remembered that COQ is the symptom of a cultural problem within the business and this usually resides between, rather than within, functions.

Costing Quality is an extremely important activity and, when doing so, companies need to understand it is an issue of developing the right Mindset, rather than just measuring in a mechanical and logical manner. Research into COQ has driven many companies to promote TQ in order to reduce unnecessary cost in the long term. This is easily achievable and possible.

However, it can be a healthy sign if companies pursue the TQ route for its own sake – believing that the current devotion to Quality is poor, and wanting to change things for the better. Organisations portraying this 'act of faith' will gain more benefits than those who perceive TQ as no more than a long-term cost-reduction exercise. However, having said this, it is important for companies to have a yardstick to assess progress and to disclose wasteful activities. COQ measurement helps here.

Costing quality is an exercise which organisations have to pursue if they wish to improve their competitive edge. Assessing the cost of quality creates the thrust needed. We are surprised at how many companies have openly proclaimed that the cost of quality is 40%. We feel that in the Service Sector, where costs of quality appear to be 'non-measurable' and intangible, the cost of quality far exceeds the figures quoted. But to get a better idea of the costs associated with non-conformance, we need to ask what is the cost of quality, and how can it be measured?

MEASURING EVERYTHING AND UNDERSTANDING NOTHING

When we are asked to assess costs, one of the greatest problems we experience is that we tend only to isolate those things which can be measured from those which are intangible or non-quantifiable. The first mistake is to measure only tangible items, eg. direct labour for rework, scrap wastage, materials. Many organisations make this mistake and come to the conclusion that the cost of rework is low. Would that this were true.

If this formula is used as a measure, it will not reflect the true costs. While working on a quality assignment with a US multi-national telecommunications company we were surprised to find that the COQ was calculated using this simple tangible method. The costs of manufacturing rework were low, 3-5% of manufacturing costs – but the rework in the service area was not calculated. We know this was extremely high because installation teams often had to return to customers in Eastern and Northern Europe, South America, Canada and the USSR to fix or recalibrate the product. The costs incurred, including salary, bonus payments, accommodation, air travel and entertainment, were never included in the 'cost' for that project. Although a team of five men could be away from the plant for ten days, working with a customer with a defective component, the costs incurred were not transferred to a particular product or project. Therefore, the COQ was inaccurate. No one seemed to mind too much until a customer asked for 10% off his invoice. When queried, the customer said he refused to pay the 'rework' costs of the company. The company spokesman denied that he was being charged for rework activities. The customer agreed that this might be true at the surface level, but someone was indirectly funding all this unnecessary rework, and it was probably him!

FIRST ASSESS THE COQ IN SERVICE AREAS

The major costs associated with getting things wrong rest in the support or service area of a business. Deming states that 85% of quality problems are created by people who never touch the product. It is common practice for companies to start collecting data which relates to manufacturing first and, in too many cases, managers responsible for Service Departments are less than willing to share such information. They claim that it is difficult to measure 'waste' and 'non-quality' in a service area. This is nonsense. All company functions and departments have goals and objectives and these should be able to be translated into responsibilities handled through various grades and levels of management. Tasks are allocated to managers to reflect the goals and objectives, and resources are distributed to ensure that work is completed on time. If service people say their effort and output is intangible, it is time to revise department goals. This is referred to in Chapter 12 when we discuss Departmental Purpose Analysis.

Over the years we have amassed a great deal of evidence from some companies that many of the problems are created 'unintentionally' through those in the service area.

SALES STAFF UNWITTINGLY GENERATING REWORK

Consider an organisation producing a standard technological product for the telecommunications industry.

I have a very high regard for those in Sales on that very difficult interface with the customer. However, in the example presented, Sales staff are functioning in an independent manner – not assessing the consequences of their actions on those who have to deliver the product and service to the customer.

Those running this company were very keen to promote the growth and market-share of their product over competitors. Salesmen spend a great deal of time with interested customers and are keen to agree to their special requirements. Sales staff, in this example, agree to modifications to their standardised product. This should work out fine for the customer – but they should be aware that modifications and changes to otherwise standardised equipment should remain within acceptable levels. The changes to the original standardised product if they become excessive will create countless and time-consuming rework for others in manufacturing to produce. In this example, Salesmen would agree to any spew to get the sale, which created real problems for all the other areas of the organisation.

If this practice gets out of perspective, soon the managers recognise that customers are keen to have 'specials' manufactured. The company starts to get a great name for becoming 'customer rather than product led' (there is nothing wrong with this as long as the company can produce the product economically).

If this practice continued of specials being made, more and more sales would emerge. As new sales poured into the company this in turn created problems further down the line. For instance, it generated a need for extensive further research and development for designers and draughtsmen, it created problems for inventory control who have to order non-standard components, it created problems for the shopfloor who have to develop different approaches to production and assembly. In one case, this degenerated into the company's moving from 'selling what it made to making what it sold'.

Although orders flooded into the company, the back-up service for the salesmen was not as good as it needed to be. Salesmen needed Engineers to agree to the feasibility of technical detail or modifications. In many cases, Sales staff, because of their ignorance of the complexity of 'modifications', omitted to define customers' requirements in sufficiently specific terms to develop accurate design drawings from which to manufacture. Part numbers of components were guessed and ordered. Materials Management problems arose and the company wondered why its stock of inventory was so high. New materials and components were being bought in while existing standard items, no longer required, sat dormant in the materials control section. The impact this had on the rest of the company was predictable. Its competitive edge was harmed almost permanently.

Management had failed to recognise that their market was changing and had failed to change the way they did business and delivered to the customer. The few agreed modifications to customer requirements had turned the large-batch production line into a jobbing shop. Because the change had been gradual, no one had noticed. Many senior managers had failed to grasp the fact that a company's back-up system must be 'spot on' if the Sales staff are promoting 'customised' products to customers. We strongly supported a customer-driven rather than a product-led strategy for this company to pursue – but they must have the right culture to support this approach, right the way through the company. The quoted company failed to understand that companies can still go out of business with *full order books* – if they fail to promote the internal dynamics to support the external push for customised sales.

HOW DO WE ASSESS THE COST OF QUALITY?

COQ is composed of three key elements. The largest proportion contributing to the COQ is the Cost of Errors. In other words, the action that has to be taken to do a job over. We often refer to this as Rework. This cost is very high. Traditionally, we measure only the tangible aspects of the manufacturing process: materials, scrap, and direct labour – but neglect to measure other costs. What about measuring the cost of indirect labour? Some examples have already been highlighted but many people in service functions fail to recognise that this cost is very high. A typical example includes the costs associated with Sales staff visiting clients to put right what was wrong. For instance, a Sales Manager responsible for Northern Europe calculated that each week he spends two days away (40% of his available time) discussing Quality problems with clients. Not all the problems were associated with poor quality manufacture: 50% of the time he spent apologising for late delivery, inaccurate invoicing, poor after-sales service, etc. What concerned him most was that he wasted so much time. He calculated it was costing the company a fortune, although it would never show up on a balance sheet.

The cost of his two days each week was at least 40% of his direct salary in addition to expenses including travelling, accommodation, etc., and the 'opportunity cost', which couldn't be calculated, of what he could have done in the two days if he had not needed to get involved in rework. The Sales Manager was busy and the customer was satisfied at the end of the day, but he had not added any real value to what he did – selling the product. He spent an inordinate amount of time fixing the mistakes which others had created for him. He 'reworked' the errors of others.

In another company we heard that the Finance Section had just employed two well qualified members of staff. We were surprised to find what they were to spend their time doing. The Purchase Order System in the company was too complicated. Line Managers were confused and often incorrectly quoted the codes of purchase orders, especially when dealing with suppliers. Consequently, suppliers were invoicing the company with inaccurate

Purchase Order numbers. Payment was delayed and it created a large number of problems with 'internal control'. The two new staff were employed – not to develop a new system or make the old one work, but to rework all Purchase Orders to check and ensure that resources were deducted from the correct departmental budget.

How many people in companies spend all their time reworking the errors of others? Does it not make sense to prevent problems arising and get them right first time? Some companies have whole departments engaged solely in rework.

CUSTOMER SERVICE DEPARTMENTS AND REWORK

Some companies boast that they have the largest Customer Service Departments in the industry. They may also claim that they provide a warranty which is second to none. This is not something of which to be proud. It means that the company is committed to 'getting it right second time'. The cost can be tremendous. At the start of working with one company, a colleague visited the Customer Service Unit to find that the size of the unit had grown and an increased staff were now sited in a new office complex. As he walked around the new office area – he wondered what impact this unit had on the COQ for the company. No one seemed to think about doing things right first time to prevent errors arising.

Order re-entry, retyping, unnecessary travel and use of the telephone, conflict and fighting between departments are just some examples of waste which contribute to the COQ. These are all assessed as leading to the cost of 'doing things again'. To get into further detail there can be two types of rework which relate to internal or external failure. If the product fails in the field the costs can be attributed towards external failure. If failure is in-house, it is internal failure! It is interesting to examine ratios between different companies in the same industry. These two areas can be further subdivided into necessary and unnecessary rework.

Necessary rework would be associated with redrafting a document or redesign. It is unlikely and, some would argue, undesirable to hinge on getting creative pieces of work absolutely right first time. But there comes a point when rework becomes unnecessary. It is to these areas that we would turn first to reduce waste. The interesting point about rework is that very few of us create rework for ourselves. Our supervisors and managers would comment and our inefficiency would stand out. Rework is usually created for others – probably the person who is next in line. It is created for you by those who feed you information, decisions, materials and resources. And you in turn can be a major source of rework for those in the company who depend on you. If you don't do your job right first time – someone has to fix it.

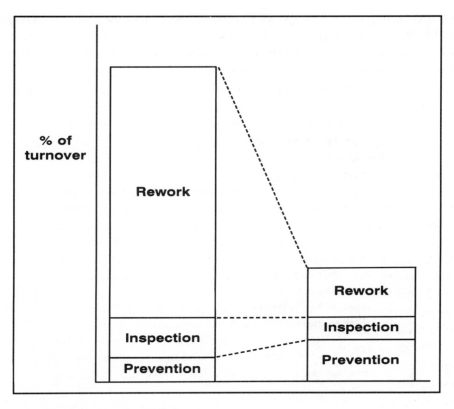

Fig. 4 Quality costs before and after TQM

THE COST OF INSPECTION OR APPRAISAL

The secondary element of the COQ is Inspection costs. Typical examples include the costs associated with maintaining quality control, the cost of calibration of tooling, the cost associated with policing a system, etc. The cost of inspection is high, particularly in administrative areas. People spend a great deal of time checking. Some of this inspection is necessary and some is unnecessary. It is the latter element that we want to eliminate.

Inspection activities are pursued by companies who have major problems with product and service quality. If things are not right – inspect, inspect, inspect. Inspection does not build Quality into the product – so is wasteful. Is it so unusual that many large companies have very strong Quality Control and Assurance sections? One thing we must remember – no amount of Inspection will increase Quality. Prevention is the key.

Working with an Investment Administration Department in an Insurance company I soon became aware that many of the staff 'checked' their output at least nine times before passing the information to the Accounts Department. One would have thought that this thorough checking would have spotted all possible errors. But when I talked with Accounts about the service Investment Administration provided, it was stated that when information was received it was checked and often found to contain errors. No amount of inspection will prevent problems arising – this quote will appear several times to illustrate the confusion between checking or inspecting errors out of a process and preventing errors arising!

COUNT THE TOTAL NUMBER OF 'F's IN THE PARAGRAPH BELOW.

The necessity of training farm hands for first class farms in the fatherly handling of first class farm livestock is foremost in the minds of farm-owners. Since the forefathers of the farm-owners trained the farm hands for first class farms in the fatherly handling of farm livestock, the farm-owners feel they should carry on with the family tradition of fundamental training of farm hands of first class farms in the fatherly handling of farm livestock because they believe it is the basis of good fundamental farm management.

There are 39 'F's. Very few people get this right first time. We also find there are many differences in standards between people. This is down to perceptual differences and illustrates the general Quality point that we all have different abilities and standards and no amount of Inspection can identify all the problems. Prevention is the only alternative.

THE COST OF PREVENTION

The third component of COQ is Prevention. The activities normally associated with Prevention include training, planning, forecasting, meetings, Quality Assurance, etc. The best way to remember the role of prevention is "One hour of planning saves ten hours of chaos".

It is sad to see that so little time, effort, energy and resources are devoted in today's organisations to prevention. The way of life in too many companies is 'crisis management' orientated. Firefighting becomes a way of life. Managers and staff get used to the culture and some actually start to enjoy it. Their time could be spent more effectively creating opportunities for the future and anticipating problems, rather than trying to solve yesterday's mistake.

PRACTICAL IMPLICATIONS OF REWORK, INSPECTION AND PREVENTION

How much of your time do you spend on work which could be classed as rework or 'doing work over'? Believe me, more than you think!

How much time do you spend each week correcting errors? How often do you have to go through a report and rewrite it? How often do you say to yourself: "That will do"? As you put the report away, you know you will have to do it again, but you think you might just get away with it this time.

How often do you write a letter and send it to the typing pool knowing that it contains inaccuracies which will need to be corrected?

TECHNOLOGY AND LAZY MANAGERS

Managers can become very lazy when new technology is introduced into a company. Fifteen years ago I was engaged in research into the human aspects of new technology. A number of us worked in a sample of organisations including companies in financial services and quasi-Governmental bodies which had recently introduced word processors, etc. Our group was interested in what had led to the decision to invest in the new technology. The answers were all productivity-based. However, our research suggested that there was no marked increase in productivity, and in some areas – the generation of documents above one page in length – productivity had fallen.

Prior to word processors, Managers spent time ensuring that the written communications were 'right first time', before sending them to the typing pool. They realised the problems that they would create with carbons, masters and copies, etc. Even lengthy documents like detailed reports were only typed two or three times. Rework was evident – but was necessary because it improved the content only. What we found when we looked at productivity after the introduction of WPs was that the number of drafts had radically increased.

Since the introduction of WPs, the number of average drafts for lengthy reports had increased from three or four to seven or eight. The material and content of letters and reports had stayed constant, but the ability to change documents easily created a great deal of flexibility and, with it, rework. Managers had not realised that they created problems for the typists. Their interpretation of flexibility had led them to be less structured and planned when writing text – believing they could change it at a later date. The constraints under which they had previously worked had been removed and the impact upon performance had been negative.

Managers believed this flexibility would improve the Quality of what they did, but it actually created rework for others. Knowing how easy it is to change a document created a casual attitude amongst managers. Secretarial staff were spending more of their time reworking the mistakes of others rather than becoming more productive. Although the aim of Office Automation was to increase productivity, in many cases this has not happened. Instead of the output of documents increasing, it has remained the same, but with more drafts being processed for each document.

CASE STUDY: The Personnel Department

In 1986 I worked with an American multi-national Telecom provider which had a number of Quality problems. As part of the Quality programme, I was taking the Personnel Department through a series of Management Development activities. We had linked Time Management with Quality Improvement. The seven members of the Department turned up for the training session, each with Time Logs which they had been keeping for some time.

Each staff member was asked to talk through the major activities in which they had been involved, and was asked to classify the items under three headings, ERROR, INSPECTION and PREVENTION.

On analysis, we found that, on average, the Department spent 54% of time **Reworking** errors and doing work again, 41% of time involved in **Inspection** activities, and 5% on **Preventative** action.

No wonder they hardly achieved anything. No wonder they came into work early and stayed late. Little wonder their morale was low!

The most surprising thing about the staff of the Department was that they knew they spent too much time in meetings and involved in routine paperwork, but they had never looked at the focus of the work using these three criteria before. We dug deeper to find out the cause of the problem!

LINE MANAGERS CREATING REWORK FOR SERVICE DEPARTMENTS

Whatever Personnel Managers say, it is extremely difficult for Personnel to become more proactive rather than a reactive service department. These departments exist to meet the needs of others in the organisation. In this case, the Department was working continuously with and reacting to Line Managers.

Personnel provided the usual Recruitment and Selection Services as well as Induction and Appraisal. The Personnel Manager was bright and had sought to introduce many new initiatives into the company. She had tried on many occasions to train Line Managers to understand the problems with Recruitment and Selection, and get them to appreciate the huge costs associated with either appointing the wrong person or attracting and short-listing the wrong group from whom to select.

RIGHT SECOND TIME

On many occasions, posts had been re-advertised and interviews held time and time again. It transpired that Line Managers were not spending any time at all preparing documentation for Personnel. They were using Job Descriptions which were years old and did not reflect the changing nature of some of the engineering posts. They were not taking care and being selective in using the material. The consequence of this behaviour was rework for others!

Some Line Managers were guilty of not training their supervisors in the use of the Disciplinary Code. Consequently, some staff were unfairly dismissed, which created costly administrative rework and other costs, such as compensation, for the company.

Generally, because the relationship between the Line and Staff function (Personnel) was poor, the Personnel Department was suffering. The only way to remedy the situation, and reduce the chances of spending all their time in the future reworking Line Management's errors, was to invest time in developing the right sort of relationship with the other Managers. This we could define as preventative action.

We originally set a target to double the time the Personnel people spent on prevention-type activities, and we knew that, in the long term, this would reduce errors, rework and inspection. Getting closer to the Managers and spending time explaining the problems the Department faced, the Quality of the service they could provide, if given detailed and accurate information, looking at company priorities and forgetting department differences and negative stereotypes, were all factors which helped reduce the amount of time spent on correcting rather than preventing errors.

We asked all those involved in the exercise to consider before they started a task:

"What is the best use of my time right now, and how can I ensure I spend time preventing errors arising in the future?"

This type of analysis helps focus upon key results areas in a different way. Thinking through your work in this way should help you spend less time firefighting and more time planning and preventing problems occurring.

ACTIVITIES ASSOCIATED WITH THE COST OF REWORK IN MANUFACTURING

Rework – or doing the same job twice

Retyping

Redesign and replanning

Recalls and expenses

Retraining

Reprogramming

Scrap

Excess inventory

Shortages
Reinspection – extra testing
Handling complaints
Forecast errors
Incorrect debit and delivery notes
Invoices matching with purchase orders
Lack of training in operational and supervisory areas
Failure to turn up for training courses
Failure to organise for absence whilst attending courses
Sample programmes not met
Poor communication
Downtime maintenance
No planned maintenance
Misinformation
Maintenance delay – cost of slow response
Morale
Housekeeping
Material handling damage
Failing to plan ahead
Not buying good quality material or good quality spares etc.
Misunderstanding in verbal communication
Incorrect labelling
Changes not communicated
Material availability
Failing to follow agreed action
Material movements not documented
Purchasing failing to appraise supplier
Wrong interpretation of correct information by designers
Time management
Inadequate spew of requirements
Orientation to short-term rather than long-term goals
Failure to react to causes of problems
Not maximising production rates
Non-effective monitoring of performance of people or plans
Not shutting down to maintain equipment
Lack of information flow
Accepting too many conflicting priorities
No identifiable mission
Time-wasting in all forms
Not learning from previous experiences
Poor quality equipment/materials

'Make it cheap'

Verbal communications – reliance on memory

Delays from suppliers trying to identify our needs

Not enough clear communication – up, down and across

Suppliers not meeting requirements

Design FMEA not effectively carried out

Late delivery of material means job has to be interrupted

Lateness attending meetings – repeating or waiting

Customer schedule changes

Material variation – no agreed spew

Inaccurate forwarded information due to time demands

Defective parts manufactured and included in finished product

Parts numbers and quantities do not match advice notes

Late deliveries – holding up production

Over-deliveries clogging up GI stores

Inadequate or missing process capability studies

Component production not synchronised

Raw materials not available at right time

Tool failures

Missing drawings

Progress-chasing

Parts right but wrong quantity

Parts wrong but right quantity

Parts wrong and wrong quantity

Parts and quantity right – wrong destination

Uneconomic use of raw materials

Excessive number of parts lost in set-ups

Non-feasible design

Lack of consultation between R&D and manufacturing

SPC charts not completed

SPC guesstimates

Failing to act on SPC information

Data from capability studies not fed to designers

FMEAs not completed at appropriate time

AQPs not performed or used effectively

Few real design standards

Agreeing impossible requirements with customers

Drawing specifications

Lack of adherence to Quality System

Cost estimating

Computer database not maintained

MAKING THE QUALITY MANAGER REDUNDANT

The oft-quoted statement: "The role of Total Quality Management is to make the Quality Assurance department redundant" is a myth, but, nevertheless, the major TQ thrust is to have the QA department spend more time preventing, rather than inspecting or correcting, errors. The impact of this action on the COQ is to reduce the overall costs of 'non-quality'. Resources can then be deployed from firefighting to prevention. The organisational culture should gradually change to reflect the 'error-free work' culture. This is the major shift in the Quality Cost formula.

MOVING FROM REWORK TO PREVENTION

Spending time Preventing problems so they will bring down rework is not easy. Don't expect this to be a straight swap, especially if the culture of the company is strongly orientated to firefighting.

On a diagram, the reduction in rework and inspection through an injection looks marvellous. But it is not that simple. When people are used to working in a set way – it is not easy to change them to spend more time on planning and prevention. In reality, we have to put in a great deal of prevention to start turning things around. At first we need ten hours of prevention to stop one hour of rework. It may appear uneconomical – but it is realistic.

A major concentration of prevention will change things most quickly. Don't assume that one or two training days for all employees, identified as prevention, will turn a company around. After training, teams have to be formed and special efforts made so that they can develop planning, forecasting, meeting, diagnosing, solving and preventing problems happening. The real commitment to TQ becomes evident by the resources devoted to prevention at the start of a drive.

TQ IS NOT COST-CUTTING

There is no short cut to reducing COQ. It can be achieved only through preventative measures. This means that the ideas for improvement must come from those with the knowledge and experience. In other words, TQ is user-driven. It is not imposed. TQ is not a cost-reduction or a productivity-improvement exercise. It is a major goal to get everybody to understand the COQ and its components, prior to and after, TQ. Once the workforce recognises that high COQ is creating an uncompetitive situation for the company, they will be committed to making TQ happen.

STRATEGIC GOALS AND TOTAL QUALITY

Reducing the COQ must be the organisation's priority, but it must not be a cost-reduction exercise. There must be plenty of evidence to suggest that there is a major investment in prevention.

Overall, companies will be aiming to create a low COQ. It means that the company is in a better competitive situation. Typically, the COQ associated with many companies in the UK is in the region of 20-40%. Reducing this huge cost can have a tremendous impact on the 'bottom line'.

For those of you not convinced, look at this simple example:

A small company with a turnover of £1 million per year makes an after-tax profit of 10%. Their COQ is a 'meagre' 20%. In other words, the profit in year one is £100,000 and the COQ is £200,000. If the company used its latent energy and resources and adopted a TQ approach, it could reduce its COQ significantly. Because of its size, it is able in the first year of TQ to reduce its COQ by 50%, a saving of £100,000. The result is outstanding! This has the same impact on the bottom line as increasing turnover by 100%. And to do this they usually would have to borrow large sums and deploy vast resources. But because this company adopted TQ, it cut costs, trimmed its slack and began doing things 'right first time'. The competitive edge is strengthened and its growth in the marketplace is assured.

IDENTIFYING COQ MEASURES

COQ measures are important within all areas of the organisation. People in the Service Sector tend to suggest that 'measures' are inappropriate and more suitable for manufacturing. This is not the case.

Every Departmental Manager or functional head must work with his team to identify key COQ measures which reflect a disproportionate amount of rework experienced within the section.

These need not be wildly sophisticated at first. They should remain simple. Manufacturing never have problems with coming up with measures, so let us address ourselves to the Service Sector.

Some examples may help to illustrate the measures. A Training manager had problems relating to measurement, claiming his work was difficult to measure. We suggested that he record the number of trainee days per month completed. Training on Health and Safety, Time Management and First Aid were all to be recorded. We wanted the Manager to keep fairly simple figures on two areas: planned and actual trainee days. As can be seen by the graph – the larger the discrepancy between the two, the bigger the problem. Although everybody was aware of this problem – no one had any data to demonstrate its severity. This data acted as a major push to work closer with Line Management. Through Pareto Charting the Training Manager was able to identify the major causes of the problem and take action.

In a similar fashion an accountant kept a simple record of expenses claims which were completed incorrectly. He also drew up a Pareto Chart identifying the mistakes most commonly made. He took corrective action, produced documentation on the most difficult sections and recirculated it to all managers. In time, this reduced the rework he experienced.

Sales Staff were concerned that their customers were not receiving the product on time. They carried out an analysis to identify the problem in production. It was not the fault of manufacturing.

Careful analysis identified the major hold-up being the R & D area. It was discovered that missing technical drawings in all areas were creating problems – 'missing' was later described as 'uncompleted'. These drawings were essential for tool design, inventory and purchasing, and production. If the most recent drawing was not available, staff worked off the previous generation of drawing, creating many timely delays and major errors. Our data helped to correct the problems with delivery. The most obvious reasons were related to computer downtime and CAD. There were insufficient screens for the workload required. A relatively minor problem, which could have been fixed with a small investment of £28,000, was creating rework problems for all departments and was costing the company at least £300,000.

Overall, COQ measures can help enormously in promoting TQ – but measures must be established and kept up to date.

COQ PUBLICITY IS CRITICAL

Collecting data and keeping it to oneself is not a good approach to TQ. The purpose behind using COQ measures is, firstly, to assess progress and, secondly, to publicise this to all your people. They must be aware of progress and be kept informed.

Graphical representation should be a predominant feature of any COQ campaign. Computers tend to print out data on A4, and A3 seems to be the biggest. Because it looks neat, managers pin up these graphs for publicity – but no one can see them. All areas should display COQ progress, monitoring at least five to seven measures per function. These should be placed in areas where people gather. The data should be understandable and readable at four metres. Go for big graphs. Keep them up to date. Move the location every ten days, otherwise people will become inured to them. Most of all, recognise that people who are involved in TQ want to monitor progress. If the news is good, they can celebrate. If it is bad, they will want to take corrective action of their own choosing. Monitoring and displaying progress is central to a successful COQ campaign

COQ PITFALLS

Although we have concentrated on one of the main reasons why companies pursue TQ and Culture Change, there are a number of pitfalls to avoid.

DON'T FOCUS ON NUMBER-CRUNCHING

Managers must ensure that they don't become obsessed with finding a definitive figure for the COQ. This obsession can become a number-crunching exercise, which can end in disaster. Collecting figures to prove a point is not always constructive, because the method of calculation may be based upon false assumptions.

Commitment to TQ is very much a matter of faith, although COQ is important. Being preoccupied with figures and trends coming down will do little to promote the co-operation required. Remember, TQ is chiefly concerned with changing the attitudes and skills of employees to 'right first time'. It is concerned with engendering a culture where prevention is the norm. Spending too much time on statistics can kill enthusiasm. But do remember that these figures are important for focusing upon specific progress.

COQ AND SALES TURNOVER

If you compare COQ with turnover, and turnover increases because of a new and unexpected project, does this mean that COQ diminishes? In fact, it may increase. Cost of Quality measures identify problems within a company. If the problems are not solved, why should COQ fall? As a company grows in business transactions, COQ will accelerate at least at the same rate. A company providing credit facilities to a major retailer when winning £50 million of business per year failed to correct its key problems which were inherent within the infrastructure of the business. Internal customers and suppliers were not working as a coherent unit for the external customer. Rework cost that provider of finance a great deal, and it therefore decided to eradicate it by committing to a TQ programme before its customer realised who was really funding the Rework.

We can create many problems when we equate COQ with sales and turnover. It might be appropriate to assess how much time each week you and your colleagues spend on work which can be categorised in terms of error and rework, inspection and prevention. Relate this to a financial measure later.

THE TRIVIAL MANY LEADING TO COQ

Don't trivialise COQ. When a document needs retyping don't assess its rework value. You are probably concentrating on the 80% of activities which contribute to the 20% of things which add to COQ. What we should be doing is working on key result areas, the 20% of activities which contribute to 80% of COQ. Develop the Pareto Principle to rework and waste.

COMPETING AGAINST OTHERS

Managers may use COQ in a competitive manner. They develop their own departmental COQ and then start competing with other departments and develop win-lose league tables. This is useless and self-defeating. Most problems in organisations which contribute to a high COQ are problems shared between departments. Because problems are so large, managers are loath to take ownership. Who wants the responsibility to solve a problem which impacts on other departments? Managers are busy enough anyway. COQ is a company responsibility. Co-operation rather than competition is the key to reducing COQ.

MEASURING LIKE WITH LIKE

When you measure progress over time, be sure you measure like with like. It is probable that your first assessment of COQ is not as accurate as your second, which could be developed after you have become involved in a TQ drive.

SET REALISTIC MEASURES IN ALL AREAS

Finally, when you set goals ensure that they are achievable and measurable. Develop yardsticks with which others agree. Don't impose your targets. Managers and staff are more committed to working towards their own goals than those picked for them. TQ must be user-driven.

SUMMARY

It soon becomes clear that COQ is a major issue for many service providers in Europe and the US. Rework activities often fail to be measured and even when they are, may not always fit conveniently into an internal costing system.

Rework is a hidden cost for which the customer pays. Rework can be incredibly demotivating for those who have to do it, and no amount of Rework or Inspection will create a quality service. Only a commitment to Prevention will really help us create a very positive culture focused upon doing things right first time.

The key issues for organisations for the next ten years are to measure COQ in Service areas and focus all attention on activities to prevent problems arising. This approach, known as 'fool-proofing' the process, will generate a healthy environment where internal customers and suppliers will work together as a cross-functional process rather than battling things out in the old fashioned functional setting.

Bullet Points

- Many service sector organisations are unaware of how much it costs them to produce Non-quality.

- Cost of Quality does not show up on Balance Sheets, Profit and Loss Accounts or Operating Statements – so they tend to be ignored.

- It could be costing a company as much as 40-50% of sales turnover to get things right second or third time.

- TQ is not the same as Cost Reduction.

- Measure the 'intangibles' in the Service areas first. This is where the real waste is evident.

- 85% of Quality problems originate in service areas.

- Cost of Quality is greater when there is a great deal of interaction between departments.

- Cost of Quality is composed of the costs of errors and rework, the cost of inspection and the cost of prevention.

- Rework and inspection costs can be reduced through an increase in activities and resources devoted to prevention.

- Rework can become the organisational norm characterised by firefighting and crisis management. Changing this culture requires a significant increase in preventative-type measures. This investment can decline as the drive for TQ intensifies, but the investment at the start should not be minimised.

- We seldom create rework for ourselves. We create it for our internal customers – those next in line who are dependent upon the Quality of service which we provide. Likewise our internal suppliers create rework for us. Managing this interaction between departments is what reduces company-wide COQ.

- Reducing rework can create a significant improvement in competitive position, but this will only occur in the long term and will only happen through expenditure of effort.

- All functions should identify COQ measures and keep up-to-date information on these.

- COQ measures should be displayed to promote Quality Improvement. Graphs should be accessible to all and large enough to merit more than a passing interest.

- COQ measurement should not focus upon number-crunching and exclude meaning.

- TQ is very much a matter of faith and COQ measures should be used initially to communicate progress and maintain enthusiasm.

- If sales turnover increases, so will COQ. Unless the underlying problems are resolved between departments, COQ will continue to rise.

- A win-lose mentality should not be created when displaying COQ. Some departments and functions will be more dependent upon the help and support of others to bring their COQ down. For some it will be easy to reduce COQ. Never develop a COQ league table – it will kill the enthusiasm of those who have a harder job to do.

- Try to measure like with like. Over time, the measure of COQ may tend to rise when everyone thought things were getting better. The COQ measurement may become more thorough and precise and the trend may indicate problems, when in fact all it indicates is the quality of the measure becoming more accurate.

- Set realistic targets.

Complete the exercise. It should give an interesting view of waste within your organisation.

WORKSHOP ON WASTE AND THE COST OF QUALITY

Every employee takes part in activities which may be grouped under the following headings:

1. REWORK: This means doing a job again – this may be because you were not provided with the resources, the correct information, etc. Or perhaps you or others did not have enough time to do the work right first time.

2. INSPECTION: This activity is basically about rechecking, spotting and inspecting errors in a process or product. You may have to do this before you provide the goods or service to other units.

3. PREVENTION: Identifying problems, finding the cause of the problems and putting them right once and for all.

ACTIVITY I

Now, consider what percentage of the day is taken up with each of these three activities.

a. Rework

b. Inspection

c. Prevention

ACTIVITY 2

Think of the activities associated with the following terms and list them under each heading.

a. Rework

b. Inspection

c. Prevention

TQ SUCCESS

Ciba Corning Diagnostics, world leader in the manufacture of high quality diagnostic equipment for measuring body chemistry, recognised a decline in demand for its product in the late 1970s. The reason for this was that customers were sending back equipment for repair. The cost of making things wrong was getting out of hand and impacting upon the company's competitive edge. Customers were turning to other sources of manufacture, namely the Japanese, who could provide products with zero defects.

Corning estimated that its Cost of Quality was amounting to 34% of turnover. Considering that Corning was making $1.2 billion dollars a year, 'non-quality' was costing a staggering $400 million.

Corning's Quality Drive over recent years has brought COQ down to single figures, while turnover has gone through the roof. This has improved its competitive edge and consolidated market share.

REWORK: WASTING TIME!

Below are a list of activities associated with unnecessary Rework. This information was generated by managers and supervisors while attending a Culture Change Workshop. It highlights the degree to which staff are requested to Rework processes which should have been provided right first time. Activities are grouped under departmental headings.

MARKETING DEPARTMENT

- Lack of briefing.
- Too many people involved in the process.
- Changes in directions and plans.
- Too much/Unnecessary stocks.
- Poor writing.
- Duplication of paperwork.
- Lack of company knowledge.
- Incorrect database.
- Inability to use database.
- Poor understanding of database.
- Hierarchy and knowledge.
- Communication barriers.
- Rushed decisions.
- Insufficient market knowledge.

- Lack of planning.
- Redrafting text.
- Replanning.
- Dealing with the same or repeat problems.
- Area Office problems.
- Not empowering people.
- No decision/rushed decision and frequent changes.
- Too many senior people involved.
- Unclear role and responsibility.
- Not giving full attention to problems.
- Hand-holding.
- Lack of technical expertise.
- Lack of training in Area Offices.
- Reactivating projects.
- Wasted time spent in meetings.
- Lack of agreed commercial channels.

OFFICE SERVICES: PRINTING AND STATIONERY

- Failing to check work before passing to Print Room.
- Lack of clear instructions require clarification.
- Wrong reference numbers quoted.
- Wrong forms used.
- Delay in receipt of requested items.
- No specific quantities of consumables requested
- No forward planning by departments – before they run out of stationery.
- Wrongly diverted and directed phone calls.
- Messages not passed on.
- Recipients of telephone messages do not pass on the message.
- Wrong format of Head Office Circulars adhered to.

OFFICE SERVICES, RECEPTION

- Callers dialling switchboard, returning call and asking for people by forename – message left did not clarify department or extension number.
- Monthly team-briefing and other team meetings when staff do not answer calls.

- Area offices going through switchboard rather than dialling direct.
- Lack of product knowledge to enable receptionist to put the call through to the right department.
- Lack of planning.
- Redrafting text.
- Replanning.
- Dealing with the same or repeat problems.
- Area Office problems.
- Not empowering people.
- No decision/rushed decision and frequent changes.
- Too many senior people involved.
- Unclear role and responsibility.
- Not giving full attention to problems.
- Hand-holding.
- Lack of technical expertise.
- Lack of training in Area Offices.
- Reactivating projects.
- Wasted time spent in meetings.
- Lack of agreed commercial channels.

SYSTEMS DEPARTMENT
- Poor requirement definition.
- Timescales not realistic.
- Duplication of effort.
- Poor contact with customers.
- Legacy systems.
- Lack of standards.
- External suppliers.
- Machine performance poor.
- Testing tools inadequate.
- Data prep keying.
- PC Reconfiguring.
- PS S/W Reconfiguring.
- Program recoding.
- Incident handling.
- Problem management.
- Complaint handling.
- Maintenance.

INVESTMENT ADMINISTRATION
- Lack of accurate and timely information.
- Changes in Datastream prices.
- Working system downtime (Sherwood and Datastream).
- Lack of information – Bank Statements.
- Job requirements to be clarified.
- Training deficiency in Lotus and Word Perfect
- Lack of time.
- Failure to prioritise.
- Amendments.
- External customers/suppliers.
- Recalculations of figures on Futures due to Broker delay.
- Lack of communication.
- Incorrect information – Cash Management.
- Database – checking system.
- Classification of stocks.
- Documents and working papers retained.
- Misinterpretation of information and regulations.
- Change in valuation (systems input).
- Copying data between systems.
- Input errors.
- Duplication of effort.
- Changes in Board Reports.
- Managers changing requirements and their minds.
- Report changes.
- Duplication of Blue Chip deals.
- Dividend Voucher incorrect from Citibank.
- Classification DTI/ABI and Accounts.
- Poor delegation of tasks.
- Collating information from other departments.
- External information incorrect.
- Inadequate checks on high priority work.
- Too many checks on trivial work.
- Materiality.
- Rerunning documents.
- Pick-up on development work.
- Rushed jobs.
- Job tasks to be clarified.

LIFE PROCESSING DEPARTMENT

- Recalculations.
- Lack of feedback from disgruntled internal customers.
- Direct debit: duplication of effort.
- Poor work and input from Area offices.
- Setting up new business.
- Procedures – forfeiture – early stage payments not continued.
- Writing poor new business.
- Telephone calls seeking clarification.
- Rework on data entry.
- Customers not understanding.
- Jargon in standard letters.
- Poor presentation/confused message in internal and external mail.
- Poor message projected.
- Misinterpretation of requests.
- Control of files and papers.
- User department does not have control of files.
- Wrong input, companies, banks, departments.
- Don't see each other as customers.
- Rushing jobs – firefighting.
- Lack of knowledge.
- Lack of facilities.
- Computer downtime.
- Lack of systems.
- State clear objectives.
- Ineffective planning.
- Poor attitude leads to checking.
- Lack of training.
- Lack of information.
- Pressure for speed.
- Poor handwriting.
- Careless processing.
- Inaccurate input.
- Lost papers.
- Poor equipment.
- Poor attitude.
- Resistance to change.

- Failure to listen to instructions.
- Poor presentation.
- Incorrect information.
- Half a story.
- Lack of incentive.
- Poor communication.
- Not focusing upon the job in hand.
- Interruptions.
- Lack of initial planning.
- System failures.

INSPECTION AND OVER-CHECKING

Below are a list of activities associated with unnecessary Inspection. This information was generated by managers and supervisors while attending a Culture Change Workshop and highlights the time devoted to the degree to which staff are requested to check and test whether a service has been provided right first time. Activities are grouped under departmental headings.

SYSTEMS DEPARTMENT

- Data preparation verification.
- System testing.
- User acceptance testing.
- OSA testing.
- Service status reporting.
- Inadequate documentation.
- Code walkthroughs.
- Reading journals.
- PPFs.

INVESTMENT ADMINISTRATION DEPARTMENT

- Cash forecast.
- Review Board Papers.
- Citibank (4 steps).
- Manual input checking.
- Comparisons.

LIFE PROCESSING DEPARTMENT

- Recalculations.
- Lack of feedback from disgruntled internal customers.
- Direct debit: duplication of effort.
- Poor work and input from Area offices
- Setting up new business.
- Procedures – forfeiture – early stage payments not continued.
- Writing poor new business.
- Telephone calls seeking clarification.
- Rework on data entry.
- Customers not understanding.
- Jargon in standard letters.
- Poor presentation/confused message in internal and external mail.
- Poor message projected.
- Misinterpretation of requests.
- Control of files and papers.
- User department does not have control of files.
- Wrong input, companies, banks, departments.
- Don't see each other as customers.
- Rushing jobs – firefighting.
- Lack of knowledge.
- Lack of facilities.
- Computer downtime.
- Lack of systems.
- State clear objectives.
- Ineffective planning.
- Poor attitude leads to checking.
- Lack of training.
- Lack of information.
- Pressure for speed.
- Poor handwriting.
- Careless processing.
- Inaccurate input.
- Lost papers.
- Poor equipment.
- Poor attitude.
- Resistance to change.

- Failure to listen to instructions.
- Poor presentation.
- Incorrect information.
- Half a story.
- Lack of incentive.
- Poor communication.
- Not focusing upon the job in hand.
- Interruptions.
- Lack of initial planning.
- System failures.

INSPECTION AND OVER-CHECKING

Below are a list of activities associated with unnecessary Inspection. This information was generated by managers and supervisors while attending a Culture Change Workshop and highlights the time devoted to the degree to which staff are requested to check and test whether a service has been provided right first time. Activities are grouped under departmental headings.

SYSTEMS DEPARTMENT

- Data preparation verification.
- System testing.
- User acceptance testing.
- OSA testing.
- Service status reporting.
- Inadequate documentation.
- Code walkthroughs.
- Reading journals.
- PPFs.

INVESTMENT ADMINISTRATION DEPARTMENT

- Cash forecast.
- Review Board Papers.
- Citibank (4 steps).
- Manual input checking.
- Comparisons.

- Exception reporting.
- Spreadsheet input.
- Typing.
- Prints.
- Additions.
- Datastream check.
- Contract notes.
- Settlements.

LIFE PROCESSING DEPARTMENT

- Check calculations/letters.
- Check input from banks.
- Rereading mail/rehandling mail.
- Hierarchy slows down the process.
- Unnecessary check of minor details.
- Double checking.
- Is there a better way to do this.
- Continual appraisal of the job.
- Aware of expected standards.

ACTIVITIES ASSOCIATED WITH PREVENTION

Below are a list of activities associated with Prevention. This information was generated by managers and supervisors while attending a Culture Change Workshop and highlights the activities where an investment in time should be radically increased in order to reduce COQ in the long term. Activities are grouped under departmental headings.

LIFE PROCESSING DEPARTMENT

- Job knowledge.
- Training.
- Understanding whole picture.
- Company knowledge.
- Technical skills.
- Correct people for the job.
- Staff morale – feeling part of the team.

- Good planning.
- Communication.
- Standard setting.
- Flexibility and willingness to change.
- Feedback of errors.
- Management skills.
- Meetings skills.
- Time management and objective setting.
- Telephone/complaint handling.
- Communication skills, especially with the bereaved.
- Design and development.
- Planning and co-ordination.
- Briefing meetings.

MARKETING ACTIVITIES

- Planning time devoted to specification prior to briefing.
- Listening to upward information.
- More verbal – to complement written communication.
- Conflicts with house style requires consistent standards.
- Provide more + – feedback.
- Checking information from printers.
- Knowing who has to see what and why.
- Dealing with invoices.
- Checking the chain – who has done/seen what.

SYSTEMS DEPARTMENT

- Formal reviews.
- Clarifying terms of reference.
- Training/objectives/standards.
- OSA/Service Level Agreements.
- Program testing/SWT.
- Report production/writing.
- Documentation.
- Training.
- Change control.
- Performance Management.

- Capacity planning.
- Service level management.
- Faulty materials (from external suppliers).
- PC configuring.
- Project planning.

CHAPTER 4

Cultural and Behavioural Change

There has been a major confusion about Total Quality since its first introduction into Europe. For corporate change to happen it must be complete and sustainable and focus upon working with the living fabric of the organisation – its culture. This chapter focuses upon the behavioural dimension of change, highlighting how the confusion between systems and culture has arisen, addressing the issue of resistance to change, and suggesting how these can be addressed.

Certainly when managers are first confronted with the whole concept of TQ, some tend to perceive it as another 'system' which can be grafted on to an organisation. When companies are first exposed to BS 5750 and the ISO 9000 series they tend to relate the Quality business to a prescribed 'system'. A great number soon learn that this is not the case – but others persist in the belief that achieving set standards or accreditation is what TQ is all about.

When the DTI first launched the Quality Programme in the UK in the 1980s there was a great deal of emphasis given to the application of systems. Most of the case studies in glossy brochures and on video tape were based upon accreditation to BSI standards. When standards and systems had been given such hype, it is not surprising that people actually started to believe that TQ was simply about standards.

This misconception persists even today. Early in 1989, I gave a presentation to a group represented by a professional body. The one-day conference was entitled 'Total Quality Management'. I was shocked to find that two out of four speakers were asked to speak on achieving BS 5750! It is no different today seven years later. Conferences and one-day workshops still persist in using the Total Quality banner and often provide little more than a mechanistic view to achieving a set quality standard. Of course, standards are important but culture is more so. I refer to 'standards' rather than accreditation because my belief is that setting and achieving performance standards are an umbrella term for improvement, with 'accreditation' to set systems being a sub-set of the process.

Standards setting and getting are critical to quality improvement, but they should not be at the expense of successful change and improvement of the culture. Standards are the framework for many Quality systems. Forty-seven thousand companies presently hold accreditation of ISO 9000. We know that achieving this high standard gives many of their 'customers' confidence to either continue or start doing business with these companies. Accreditation undoubtedly may well help to improve their competitive edge of the business – but it is only one step on the road to Total Quality.

Many TQ practitioners think that the 'systems vs culture' approach to quality improvement has created problems that are all focused upon winning the commitment to change. Commitment to a culture change requires far more than commitment to achieving a set accreditation.

In the early days, because BS 5750 was given such prominence, the attention of CEOs was focused upon a 'system' for improving things. What was sold was a commitment to improve how the QA Department managed and controlled processes. Effectively, Quality was sold as residing with the QA Department. Hence the lack of interest by the service sector in TQ. All the publicity was focused upon the production environment. Consequently, there was a general lack of understanding and this was manifest when it became time to appoint a champion to fight the quality cause within the organisation.

In many companies the reaction of CEOs was to make Quality professionals totally responsible for TQ Drives. How could TQ become a dominant part of the culture in all functions and all departments when the over-riding message given by senior officers was that quality resided in the manufacturing areas within the business? Overall, in the early days, there was a great deal of inconsistency in the message for Quality Improvement which has resulted in many initiatives never improving or delivering the promises to companies which were once thought possible.

Government Departments and various Institutes involved in the profession of QA put too much emphasis on QA to the detriment of shaping a vibrant culture. This was in contradiction to the messages given out by the Quality Gurus. All the time Deming, Juran and Crosby focus upon the importance of the whole organisation. Tom Peters was presenting the case that Quality was a service issue and companies needed to adopt a more holistic approach to change.

Once, when working with a major brewery, my belief was the QA Manager should be the last person who should be made responsible for the new Quality initiative. The HR Director became the champion for Quality, integrating our efforts to change the culture with a major Customer Service drive.

What is important is that those who drive the quest for quality should have developed behavioural and people skills. They should be adept at managing corporate change from senior levels and be firmly grounded and trained in HRD & OD (Human Resource Development & Organisation Development) practices. Compare the training of these specialists with the rigorous training completed by most QA professionals. Most have not been equipped with change management skills and do not operate at the very top of the business. And for those QA professionals who do project these skills, I would encourage them to take responsibility for change, but not under the name of Quality Assurance. The further we can move from the QC/QA tag, the easier will implementation of change become. There is a great deal of expressed nonsense that, unless we possess specific Quality training, we will not understand the dynamics of implementing Total Quality.

THE QUEST FOR QUALITY IS OVER WHEN YOU HAVE ACHIEVED A 'SYSTEM'

For some companies, achieving BS 5750 can create a belief that their quest for Quality is over. Too many documents and certificates adorn reception areas testifying to 'standards', but unfortunately these standards are not always maintained on the shopfloor. Strong supporters of the systems approach will immediately reject this claim. But there are companies where accreditation for standards is not always reflected in actual work behaviour.

CHEATING THE CUSTOMER

Working with an engineering company some years ago I saw the Quality Manager of one of four factories doctoring the SPC data on several production lines. This was a common practice – devised to fox the customer. He would carefully plot SPC charts and have these ready for inspection when the customer's quality professional called every four weeks. He further falsified data for submission for accreditation for BS 5750. Clearly, this manager recognised the power and importance of controls and standards in helping others make informed decisions about the company, but failed 100% to live by the spirit inherent within the procedures and control systems.

This created further problems when the concept of Quality was taken down to the shopfloor. Because of witnessing managerial practices focused upon 'fooling the customer', winning commitment at this level of the organisation was extremely difficult.

In summary, the 'systems'-only argument is one which has raged since the advent of TQ in this country in the mid-1970s and still has not been resolved. However, for an holistic approach it is important to consider the Nine S's (original Seven S's) approach. Athos and Pascale and Peters and Waterman were perhaps the first to use the Seven S's analysis in describing this approach to organisational change which will be expanded upon now.

THE ORIGINAL SEVEN S's APPROACH

There are certain approaches to organisational change which work. These can be broken down into the Hard and Soft S's. Hard S's referring to the logical, technical, observable tools, techniques and methodologies for change, and the Soft S's referring to the more creative, intuitive elements of the culture and that which is driven by people. We have added both Symbols and Synergy to the original Seven S's to give a greater understanding of what we mean by organisational culture.

Hard S's
- Strategy
- Structure
- Systems

Soft S's
- Symbols
- Staff
- Skills
- Style
- Shared Values
- Synergy

STRATEGY

Focusing upon business strategy is critical for any business. If a company does not know where it is going or there is some ambiguity among the top team, there can be some major problems for the business as whole.

Often, when I have started working with a company on a TQ drive my attention has been diverted towards helping the company develop a strong 'Strategic Planning Process' for the business. Without a direction, focus, targets and objectives, no TQ drive will ever be successful. No amount of investment in TQ or Culture Change will help improve the business if it is being blown around like a rudderless ship. Strategic Planning is a critical and current issue for many organisations and it surprises me how many times we have to address this issue before engaging on a drive for TQ.

The goals and objectives issues frequently arise when conducting a Cultural Survey. Responses to the question "Can you with some degree of certainty explain key business goals and objectives?" are not always positive and when we compare the results from the Top Team with those of their Direct Reports and different functional areas, we understand there is an issue which needs resolution. It goes without saying that if the TQ drive continues without creating a coherent strategy for the business, it will not be long until the drive falters.

CULTURAL SURVEY AND STRATEGIC DIRECTION

The selection of questions from a cultural survey highlight the issue of how well strategy and objectives are understood. All figures are in percentages. SS refers to Sales Staff, SM to Sales Managers, OS to Operational Staff, OM to Operational Managers, TS to Technical Staff and TM to Technical Managers. D refers to Directors. The company in this example took immediate action to rectify the situation of confusion highlighted by the Cultural Survey. Its energising CEO took full responsibility and committed to a programme to establish core objectives and core values.

CULTURE REVIEW QUESTIONNAIRE

Are goals and objectives communicated to you (tick one response).

		SS	SM	OS	OM	TS	TM	D
a.	By accident	38	29	40	11	40	17	0
b.	In a planned way	62	71	60	89	60	83	100

Can you with some degree of confidence (tick one response) describe the longer term goals and objectives of your Function (rather than your specific team)?

		SS	SM	OS	OM	TS	TM	D
a.	Yes	0	43	45	67	67	67	80
b.	No	100	57	55	33	33	33	20

Can you with some degree of confidence describe the longer term goals and objectives of the organisation? (Tick one response).

		SS	SM	OS	OM	TS	TM	D
a.	Yes	31	71	63	67	67	100	80
b.	No	69	29	37	33	33	0	20

It really concerns me that so many organisations can pursue a murky image or vision rather than tangible objectives for the business. What concerns me most is talking with Directors of some businesses about strategy. Depending on who I speak to, I develop radically different pictures of where the business is going. There should be a great deal of effort in establishing a strong strategy and it does not finish here, because the strategy has to be well communicated throughout the business.

There have been instances when companies have developed a strategy for improvement but disclosed the strategy to only a few senior people. It is like hiding it in a black box. Strategy is confined to a certain few officers and never filters down, even to the Direct Reports of the top team.

How can these top team Direct Reports, responsible for managing the vast numbers of people in a business, focus their energies to get results when the top team does not take them into its confidence? There are instances though, as in Mergers and Acquisitions activity, which require strict confidentiality. But generally speaking we should be able to cascade our overall plan for improvement throughout the business. Those companies who keep the plan a mystery will never glean the contribution of their staff. So there are two issues: Has your business developed a coherent strategy for doing business in the future; and has it communicated it effectively to those who are expected to get the results?

At this juncture you may want to 'score' your organisation 'out of ten' on its ability to form and communicate meaningful strategy throughout the business.

But let's be optimistic and assume this is done well – on what other areas do companies need to focus their attention?

STRUCTURES

It is now understood that flat structures are really important for a business. They generate customer responsiveness by getting rid of the insulating layers which keep the customer perspective from filtering through to those at the top. Also, flat structures can promote cross-functional working by getting people to work horizontally. They also promote empowerment by getting rid of 'over-management and control' – but still many companies have too many layers. A company will never reap the rewards of TQ if it still has more than four layers in its structure – most businesses, however large, should aim for three layers.

Critics of flat structures query that a manager can manage large numbers reporting to him. My answer is simple and direct. You only manage the difficult people because you will have trained the rest of your staff to stretch their skills and experience. You will have developed a self-managing team with people working on projects and appraising their performance as a contributor to projects rather than just reporting to one manager in one function.

When contemplating structure, where should Quality Improvement lie? I think we can forget it residing in QA or QC. It must reside at the top of the organisation in an area where change and improvement are the norm rather than the exception. This does not always mean the HR section.

PERSONNEL MASQUERADING AS HUMAN RESOURCES

It is a good idea to have an executive other than the QA manager lead a drive for improving the culture and service delivery: don't just jump to the HR department solution. I have worked in companies where the HR function was very advanced, the key responsibility for change lay with the HR Director and change was fast and effective. However, in other companies the practice and understanding of organisational change portrayed in that department has been sadly lacking.

Carefully consider the options of who should front and control the drive for TQ and, if necessary, bestow responsibility on those who deal mostly with Service delivery even if it is Sales or Customer Service. But don't gravitate to HR just because you think it may know a little about people. Remember the quality of its policies and practices is probably what has shaped the culture up to now!

SYSTEMS

Systems improvements are a great driver for change. As companies grow we find that systems, protocols and procedures have to be installed. Establishing the right degree of 'control' is very important. Too much control will stifle staff, and too little will create ambiguity and Rework. Systems and protocols only exist to provide guidance and a way for the organisation to achieve its objectives. Customer-focused procedures are critical for any business and these should be applied rigorously as long as they deliver service excellence. But an over-emphasis on Systems, Procedures, Protocols, to the detriment of effective teamwork across functions will stifle growth and innovation. Blind adherence to Quality Systems without growing the people will generate only short-term objectives.

> **BUREAUCRACY IS THE ENEMY OF SERVICE DELIVERY**
>
> We heard recently of an organisation accredited with ISO 9000. It was asked by its key customer if it could supply components almost immediately on a 'one-off' emergency basis. The customer did not want frills, just the components. Urgently. The supplier said it could not deliver to order because it would be going against its own quality procedures. The customer pleaded and asked again, saying that this was a special 'one-off' occasion and it needed the components for a special order for an overseas client – who was also willing to pay for any rework and replacement components.
>
> It was desperate for the product – it did not care about quality! It was one of those rare instances when action was required and keeping to procedures was to be ignored. It would be bad practice for the supplier, but essential for the customer to win new business.
>
> The supplier of the components did not comply with the request. The supplier did the right thing for 'internal control' but neglected good 'customer service'. The company's inactions led it to losing the customer which comprised 30% of its business – all because it would not bend. Blind adherence to a bureaucratic quality system is no way to run a customer-focused business.

ASSESSMENT OF THE HARD S's

The Hard S's approach to improvement is sound and sensible. When companies recognise there are quality issues within their businesses, many tend to focus upon the **Hard S's** approach as a solution. I would argue that many companies only adopt a partial commitment to the Hard S's with little or no commitment to implementing changes through the Soft S's. For instance, many companies commit to developing powerful Systems to run their key processes, but fail to commit to a long-term Strategy. Others let Structure determine Strategy – when we all understand that first we set Strategy and then plainly Structure must be led by and follow business Strategy. There is plenty of scope for analysing the performance of implementation of effective change using this model of Hard S's. You may want to question how well equipped is your organisation to master and implement 'best practice' in the Hard S's.

The Hard S's are sold very convincingly in structured MBA programmes and are the core components of the high level development in most business schools within Europe and the US. There is scope for improvement, especially in implementation of ideas, but overall, the commitment to change and implementation is undoubtedly focused upon the application of the Hard S's. Yet real change only comes about by adopting a balanced approach to both the Hard and Soft S's. The Soft S's will be explained in the next section.

There needs to be at least equal focus upon the Soft S's: those aspects which appear less tangible but which create significant improvement for the business. Probably the most common reaction in the Western companies to improving Quality is to focus only on the Hard S's and neglect the Soft S's because they are more difficult to manage. A traditional management education does not inculcate the skills in Managers to manage their introduction. Generally speaking, until recently, most organisations have tended to focus upon the **Hard S's, Strategy, Structure and Systems**, for doing things. It is a good start – but not good enough!

Organisations which are truly excellent and strive to improve Quality in everything they do include IBM, Motorola, Digital, Rank Xerox, Corning Glass, 3M, Dow Chemical, Toyota, Matsushita, Mitsubishi, Hitachi, ICL, Pedigree Pet Foods, Hewlett Packard, etc. They all use the **Hard S's approach** – but complemented by the **Soft S's**.

These companies recognise that the **Hard S's** are highly structured and tend to reflect our strengths as managers. We can all analyse, conceptualise, plan, develop systems and critical paths for making things happen. The **Soft S** approach requires that all these things be done – but recognises that the soft side, that side which relates to people and their actions, the roles that they play, has a large part to play in creating significant Quality improvement. Improvement does not come only from Strategy, Structure and Systems. It does not come from the Hard S's *per se*. Improvements in Quality, movement in flexibility and creative ideas come from People and this perspective is best illustrated in the Soft S's.

Let's look at the **Soft S's** and see how we can use them to create a TQ culture.

SYMBOLS

When first examining and understanding an organisational culture we tend to focus upon the way it is communicated to its constituents or onlookers. We process information visually, by what we see. We use our auditory senses to listen to and judge what we hear about an organisation. We also use our intuition, our kinesthetic senses, to get a 'feel' for the organisation. Sometimes we find it difficult to express these feelings, our first impressions. The 'feelings' are formed quickly through our non-logical sense – our intuition – and they are real and usually accurate.

However we perceive an organisation and what it stands for, we do make judgements. Usually these judgements are made quite quickly based upon the 'symbols' which reflect the organisation. Symbols can relate to personal experience or hearsay, what we have heard about the business, and they are usually quite tangible. Once we have understood the 'symbols' reflecting a business we then focus only upon data which confirm the prejudices we have formed – either positive or negative.

Car parks and allocation of spaces, the way we are greeted by staff either face to face or on the phone, the location of offices, their layout and design are all examples of organisational 'Symbols' which can be used deliberately to influence the perception of those who will interact with or observe that organisation. Often when symbols are negative they have evolved by accident or default rather than by design.

Recognising that 'symbols' really do affect how people respond to an organisation is something of which many senior officers are unaware, yet by creating the appropriate positive symbols, culture change can emerge overnight. If it is sustained and consistent with other organisational practices, a positive view of the organisation will develop. To illustrate the reverse, a leading company in insurance services spent a great deal of money on logo-patterned carpeting for its Reception Area, but failed to invest in improving tangible customer service to those who would never visit the much-vaunted refurbished Head Office – its customers. Obviously, the expenditure was heavily criticised by staff and customers alike.

Many companies devote and invest tremendous resource and time in developing the right 'perceived' image for the company, using TV commercials. The same company still fails to deliver to customer requirements. Clearly, there is a major mismatch between the 'image' it wants to create for the company and the real image of what the company finds important. Symbols are incredibly powerful in shaping the culture and in the next chapter the issue of Symbols is explained in some depth.

It should also be remembered that the top team can significantly influence the internal and external image of the business by paying attention to the Symbols projected by the organisation. Spending time isolating the key variables which create an impression of either positive or negative feeling for internal and external customers is time well invested by the top team. That is why so many companies commit to the process of Modelling. So the action to take is to examine the core components of the effective corporate culture and the symbols used by other successful companies and then use these as a flexible template for improving Service Excellence.

STAFF

Change first starts with self. No change was ever effective which did not focus upon changing how people think about and carry out their work. Effective and speedy change happens only when it is driven with the consent and the creativity of the people who own the processes and the culture, yet there is still scant attention paid to the application of change through the Soft S's. People are often no more than an afterthought for those who drive and run the business.

There is surely no argument that people are the company's most valuable resource. How often have you seen this statement in a company's Annual Report? Yet the reality is that all too often we fail to consider just how much we can get from our staff. And, to be brutally honest, we don't usually treat them well enough to command 100% commitment from them. If we treated staff well, gave them opportunities, gave them control, the opportunity to develop and be trained to their full capability – then we would marvel at their performance. There is sufficient research in the applied behavioural sciences examining the impact of organisation structure on technology, organisational performance, job satisfaction, alienation and labour turnover, to fill a library. This research suggests that we get the staff we deserve. If we develop our staff, commit to mutual trust and empower them, superlative performance will result. If we focus upon control and run a very structured, non-trusting, bureaucratic business, we will get mechanistic people uncommitted to going that extra mile, beyond that for which they were employed.

So why is it that we have failed to take account of the people side of the business? It has a great deal to do with failing to equip our managers with the capability to motivate, captivate and create a strong team spirit in our staff. If all we focus on is technical improvement, it is not unusual to understand that technical managers promoted for their capability for working with things fail to understand, comprehend and motivate others to stretch beyond their current capabilities.

Failing to commit to our people – except in corporate exhortations, such as the Annual Report – is also witnessed when we fail to train them to learn, think and improve their performance while working for us. We can sometimes fail to commit to mastering skill development and creating a positive learning environment.

SKILLS

Providing training in attitude, skills and knowledge is critical if we are to expect our staff to be as lively, innovative and knowledgeable as our major competitors. We need to improve significantly the training experiences of staff at all levels, provide more resources and give people the opportunity to 'get on with it' – rather than stand in their way.

In too many UK organisations, the commitment to skill development is very poor. Working with one business I was surprised to find that some of the supervisors had not attended a Training event, internal or external, for over 11 years. As one supervisor asked: "Have things moved much over the last 11 years?"

By committing to improving the skills of our people, we automatically improve their self-esteem, which should be our principal goal. We must understand that self-confidence and stretching people out from their comfort zones is the only way we can improve performance. The HRD strategies available to achieve this are numerous but applied only among the leading businesses. Too many organisations claim they cannot afford to invest in skill development. I would argue they cannot afford not to!

Finally, on Skills development, too much training focuses upon technical skills to the detriment of organisational skills. Training is also organised often on people only 'knowing' more at the end of the event and when training focuses upon this there can be a major problem. That problem is that training is designed so that people will 'know' rather than be equipped to 'do' more. I believe we should concentrate solely on helping people 'do' more through skill acquisition, not just be able to recite or recall information. This means helping people implement and practise their organisational skills essential for improved performance. Sadly, this is an area which is most in need of investment. We need to think more about the process of training and inculcate a strong 'learning environment' if we want staff to retain and improve their skills (see Chapter 12).

THE PERSONAL SKILLS TEST FOR TRAINING

There is test I like to apply when talking through skills development. Imagine the organisation in which you are currently employed as your business. The success of your efforts in managing the venture will impact upon your personal bottom line – either positive or negative! Ask yourself to what development activities would you personally commit to provide your staff with the core skills to excel? How would you design development sessions? What criteria of performance improvement would you choose? What trainers would you use and which would you reject? How would you evaluate development Workshops and how would you reward those who practised a commitment to accelerated learning?

If the answers to these questions differ from your current practice – ask what action can you take to equip your people with the core skills to lead to significant improvement in their performance and their self-confidence?

STYLE

This is probably *the most critical of all the Soft S's*. Here we are suggesting that the management or leadership style of those driving TQ through the organisation will determine the rate at which Total Quality is accepted. (Style and Leadership issues are examined later but I will make brief comments on what I think is important.)

Staff focus upon looking for congruency between what you say and what you do. Style of Leadership is critical to success and I say that we need Quality of Management before we get Quality Management. Given the choice between investing in Leadership or Quality I would have to commit to Leadership, for without Leadership there is no Change.

leadership

Most companies do not understand it just yet, but they will be forced through the challenge of the marketplace and their competitors to equip themselves with the Leaders to take them into the early years of the next century. Too many companies are staffed by senior people who do not display Leadership or, more importantly, understand how vital it is for improved performance.

Many companies will experience a Leadership crisis within the next few years because Leadership is a skill which has remained undeveloped in many businesses. A focus upon product knowledge or technical expertise in our senior staff has left a vacuum in those core skills which underpin successful Transformational Change. Only by focusing upon improved Leadership skills will marginally performing organisations secure their future.

Simply stated – the success of an organisation is achieved through those who manage others. The people who manage the majority of staff report directly to the top team, yet the provision of development for these people in Leadership skills can be minimal.

It should be the responsibility of every top team Director to equip himself with Direct Reports who have the ability to master and implement change through their people. Direct Reports need to be equipped with Transformational Skills to develop, motivate and ensure that cross-functional teamworking should be – business as usual. That is the challenge for organisations for the next ten years – to start with some rigorous programmes on real Leadership and Transformational Change skills.

SHARED VALUES

All organisations are driven by Values. If the business is effective and successful, the Values are stated, positive and customer-focused – often modelled upon best practice. The less successful businesses are probably driven by Values which are unstated and which undermine the whole concept of Customer Service, Values which exist by default and have probably been created by negative managers whose behaviour has created more fear than positive accomplishment.

There you have it! All organisations have the ability to create a Value System to drive and illustrate the behaviour which is expected from all who manage others. Many top teams fail to understand the concept of Values and therefore take no action to install the most positive and customer-facing Values in their business. My belief is if the top team fail to create and, more importantly, live by strong positive Values to drive their business – they will fail.

When a top team commits to highlighting the core Values by which they want their business to prosper, they are stating that these are the principals they want their managers to live by, and the Values will help in a major way to understanding and differentiating the managerial or leadership behaviour which is encouraged from that which is not. Most organisations have significant improvements to make in creating positive Values and the top teams of these companies would be surprised at how quickly this process can create results.

Overall, the purpose of stating and 'sharing and owning' Values is to create a new organisational culture where Quality of service is valued. This means we have to examine the culture, identify the predominant value systems and adapt and if necessary rebuild the Culture, with a forward-thinking, preventative element which is geared to continuous improvement. (This is the focus of Chapter 10.)

SYNERGY

There is little to say about Synergy except that there should be a continuous drive for integration with the Hard and Soft S's. Failing to understand that a complete focus upon Hard S's only will yield short-term sterile results is important in understanding why TQ often does not work. A balance between Hard and Soft S's must be achieved and here the aspect of Synergy is important.

Synergy explained as $2 + 2 = 5$ is succinct and still accurate. A coherent and equal emphasis upon Soft and Hard will yield the results we desire and a strong culture to take us successfully beyond the year 2005.

Organisations which take equal cognisance of the blending together of the Hard and Soft S's will stand a much greater chance of making Total Quality a dominant force within the culture. Those companies who rely more on the hard S's will have tremendous difficulty in establishing success in the long term. They will also find it a difficult task to get staff to take it seriously, for the simple reason that the senior officers will be using a mechanistic solution to solving a human problem.

BEING SELF-CRITICAL AND WANTING TO IMPROVE

The key to Total Quality rests within each of us. Quality does not happen because of just applying a particular technique. Utilising Hard S's solutions such as Failure Mode Effect Analysis, MRP, JIT or Taguchi Methodology will not create Total Quality. How each of us commits to the technique and how we work with others to make it work determines our success.

In order to succeed at anything, we need to be self-critical and challenge how we do things. If we fail to question our assumptions and the Values we hold – we will probably never improve. Sometimes there is too much focus on looking for the fault – or a scapegoat – or what causes non-quality rather than seeking and implementing solutions. More time can be spent allocating blame rather than setting up preventative measures so the problem never recurs. This highlights a negatively driven culture where staff and managers move away from taking risks.

FEAR OR BLAME CULTURE

If we spend time allocating blame, how can we expect people to be self-critical and talk about possible improvement? (In Chapter 12, the focus is upon staff being open and trusting in training workshops, picking upon a problem in their immediate area of work where progress can be made and doing something about it. Here they should be encouraged to take corrective action – to stop non-quality – or take preventative action so that the problem never arises again.) It is extremely unlikely that staff will be open and trusting in a fear-driven culture, where admission of working in a non-TQ manner is an almost certain guarantee for displacement elsewhere.

Perhaps this attitude is most prevalent in meetings where managers and supervisors are present, not just to transact business, but to 'cover their backs' and their department. Here functionalism rules, and there is little apparent commitment to cross-functional process. 'Loyalty' is to the department. People are forced to feel and display 'loyalty' to their function. This is encouraged through the presence of strong norms. Anyone going against these strongly held values, norms and behaviours is classed as disloyal. It is Managers who maintain this culture and the more they do so, the less likely it is that TQ will take root in the business. Killing the negative 'fear- or blame-driven' culture is imperative if culture change is to develop.

PEOPLE ARE BOSS WATCHERS!

Everyone watches everybody else and, in particular, most people are Boss Watchers. They watch to see the consistency between what the Boss does and says. If Managers fail to lead by example and demonstrate efforts to become self-critical and improve their personal performance, it is unlikely that their Direct Reports will buy into the new behaviours. If Managers stop doing things which hurt the company and other departments, then there is every chance that others will become sold on the idea of Total Quality.

Even before we get started to build a new positive culture – some effort should be made to unfreeze the old culture. Commitment to change, whether it be to losing weight, to quit smoking, to get 'fit', to lead a stress-free life – is only actualised when a person is open about the way he or she is currently living. In other words, they verbalise a need to change the way they do things.

People can change only when they are ready to reject their present behaviour as being undesirable or harmful. If they feel their behaviour is not creating harm to themselves or others, there is little incentive to change. For instance, the successful treatment of alcoholics only starts when they admit dependency. People only give up smoking when they want to, when they realise the high health risks and costs of failing to do so.

Any change requires commitment. But changing is not easy. It is not easy because once we have acquired a habit it is difficult to break.

If these 'personal things' are difficult to change, how easy is it for us to change the really difficult things like the way we manage, the way we talk to people, the way we prioritise, the way we solve problems etc.? It appears to be extremely difficult. It is perhaps the biggest reason why TQ initiatives don't provide the results for which we hoped, because we don't understand and master the process of change necessary to create a Total Quality company. We need to look realistically at changes which are necessary and work through a plan for successful implementation.

WORDS AND WORKSHOPS CHANGE NOBODY

Running training sessions and projecting the TQ ideal is interesting and satisfying, but never easy – because it involves changing the behaviours of those who manage the organisation.

When we look at implementation, we often find that there can be disagreement about the likelihood of certain actions happening and in particular a new culture growing and becoming dominant. Some people, but not all, may be pessimistic in outlook, look back at the organisational behaviour over time and come to a quick conclusion that change is never going to happen. If people focus on change *not* happening, it won't!

During training workshops some pessimistic souls have taken us back to the 1970s and painted pictures of MBOs, Quality Circles, Participative Management and Team-Briefing as being good initiatives which were introduced in the organisation, but failed for a host of reasons. These issues cannot be ignored. It is clear that the organisation has had a major problem in installing these new ways of working. It is clear these initiatives have not been sustained because they did not have support. It is obvious that there has been a key failure in the past to implement the concepts fully. These issues need to be debated openly and fully so that we can learn how to implement change more successfully.

INFLUENCE RATHER THAN CONTROL

In Training Workshops I have always believed that each of us has to influence, discuss and reason with those attending. No one can run a successful Training Workshop without dealing with and answering objections to new ideas. Many of these objections may come from participants who have never witnessed the 'new way of working' or the 'new culture' but rather have been exposed daily to the 'old negative culture'.

Workshops should be so designed as to challenge, to persuade, discuss and debate the key issues for improving the culture, and positive methods to do this by airing feelings and concerns, discussing anxieties and debating them in open forum is the only way to introduce

Total Quality. Admission of past mistakes in implementing change is extremely healthy and demonstrates to staff that the organisation is serious about introducing Total Quality.

In a 'Blame-driven Culture' it is not unusual to spend 75% of the time in Workshops discussing and debating with participants the barriers and the solutions to managing change successfully. This is time well spent because it focuses upon the process of improvement. Failing to discuss issues and keep to a mechanistic timetable, when there are clearly cultural issues to debate, creates a belief that the 'consultant' is there to present a case and do little else. This reinforces the old culture: things being done 'to you' rather than 'with you'.

WHAT PERSONAL CHANGE DO YOU WANT?

A key point is, how much change do we create in training sessions? Some produce little in terms of tangible results (reasons explained in Chapter 12), apart from a verbal commitment to "think about things" and to improve "something" within the immediate work environment. Clearly, these Workshops have been poorly designed.

But, how can we expect the 7-8 hours of a training day to create the 'inspired action-man' who will reject the 'old behaviour' and become Total Quality orientated overnight? Is this unrealistic? No!

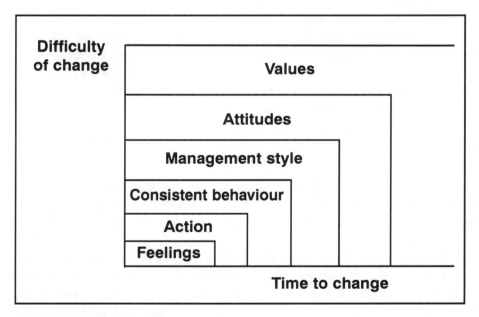

Fig. 5 Case: Fear of being open

With reference to the diagram, there is a strong relationship between difficulty of changing those things about ourselves and time taken to change. The more difficult the change, the longer it takes!

For instance, it is relatively easy to get people to 'feel' good about change and in particular Total Quality. It makes good sense and is not founded upon ivory tower conceptualisation. TQ trainers should be able to make people feel good about the concept. They can go away from the training session with a warm glow, an inner commitment to the words and arguments – but unfortunately this doesn't mean that change will take place. Change happens when people do things differently. Taking people beyond the 'feeling' stage requires some form of self-direction to do something, to get and to see results. Getting people to do 'one thing' differently is not so easy. Agreeing to apply a concept in an area and report back later on progress should not be so difficult in theory, but, believe me, it can be in practice.

CASE STUDY: Fear of Being Open

Members of a management team agreed that they would each develop five to seven Cost of Quality measures within their immediate work areas. They were all based in manufacturing and should have found it comparatively easy. They were provided with handouts of how to develop COQ measures. Six weeks later, only 40% reported back with the measures. Why was there a 60% failure rate? They found too many reasons/excuses not to provide the data! "Too busy", etc. In effect they did not want to do it. Why? It transpired several months later that they were concerned about how the data would be used and who at corporate headquarters would see it.

Getting people to do not just one thing right, but to adopt the new behaviour as a consistent way of working traditionally, took a long time. But now training design can get people to change aspects of themselves at a much faster rate than was previously thought possible.

In cases where managers and staff have a positive 'role model' upon whom they can model their own behaviour, someone who leads by example and reinforces good behaviour – then the chance of success is also high. The absence of a 'role model', and adverse or critical style portrayed by Senior Staff, will do little to embed TQ within the Culture. Staff will also leap upon this information to prove that TQ will fail.

Overall, we need to remember that people are Boss Watchers. If the boss says one thing and does another – there is ambiguity. Be aware that this will be noted and word will spread. Information or expressed opinions which confirm prejudices regarding change reinforce belief in the continued existence of the 'old culture' and will make TQ no more than a nine-day wonder .

Consistent behaviour is one thing, but changing management style, attitude and values is something else. We need time to change. People do not change as quickly as we would like them to, so we need to develop conditions to promote change. We need to be able to help them through the key stages in the Transition. This is easier said than done – but it can be completed speedily when the correct training skills and inputs are focused entirely on helping people change and transform their organisation. But a failure to create a readiness for change will delay the benefits of TQ from ever taking hold.

RESISTANCE

In order to facilitate the transition to Total Quality, we must examine the reasons why people resist change. Let us explore these and suggest possible solutions.

FEAR

The first thing which people do when they hear of change is to personalise it and ask, "How is this going to affect me?" Unsubstantiated rumours, which are neither confirmed nor rejected, add to a situation where the worst possible scenario is perceived. Simply by talking with people about the likely outcomes is sufficient to put them at ease. We must consider carefully before sending out messages. We need to communicate the same message without deviation. Develop briefing sessions which dot the i's and cross the t's. Remember, communication should be measured by what is received, not what is sent.

PERCEIVED LOSS OF CONTROL

When change comes about there is a perceived loss of control. Prior to changes, people perceive they have some security in what they do. Change does mean doing things differently, creating new knowledge and information which will have to be learned and applied. It is to be expected and not unusual that some people will be concerned. What we need to do is to specify what changes will take place and how this will impact upon work and staff. Even if we don't know the full extent of changes over time, we should be able to point to a few non-threatening examples which we can communicate to others. We need to put a great deal of planning into preventing people problems arising and this means addressing what others could perceive to be threatening conditions. By doing this in advance of any meeting or communication we can help others take control of the change by explaining how the transition can become seamless and a positive challenge.

PERSONAL UNCERTAINTY

This is best summarised as: "Can I live up to the expectations of others? Am I competent to do the new things?". Here the anxiety is internalised. People have heard grand phrases, examples of organisations committed to Total Quality and the behaviour displayed by managers and staff alike. Staff are exposed to new ways of working and they hear of unbelievably improved performance which they consider will be hard to achieve. They hear of Empowerment, Re-engineering Teams, Continuous Improvement, Cross-functional Working, Self-managed Groups, Leadership and Corrective Action Teams – the list is never-ending. So it should be no surprise that employees worry that they may not be able to live up to your expectations of them. It would only be natural to have some self-doubts.

The solution here is to inform: how long the change will take, the likely consequences, the gap between present performance and future expectations, and the actions the organisation is taking to help staff at all levels rise up the learning curve. Above all, gradual change is an important factor which must be reinforced. People cannot change in a day – so why frighten them into believing that they need to?

IT MAY MEAN MORE WORK!

It most certainly will! Companies do not become world leaders and renowned for Quality without a great deal of expenditure of effort from their staff.

There will be times when Total Quality will appear to be backsliding. For every two steps forward – you may slide back two-and-a-half. If Total Quality were so easy, we would have done it years ago – so don't build up unrealistic expectations. We all know we have to pursue preventative-type activities in order to get things right first time. Doing so reduces rework in the long term. There is not a straight substitution of preventative activities for rework.

Initially, we have to put 10 times more effort into the **preventative** activities to reduce **rework,** for the simple reason that rework has been in the culture for so long that it is difficult to change. We do need to expend 10 times more energy, at least initially, to remove old practices. The old culture and its procedures, departmentalisation and demarcation lines will reject the collaborative preventative approach – so the 10: 1 ratio is not so unrealistic.

PAST RESENTMENTS

"I'm not working with the guys from Personnel – they are too interested in scoring points" or "The Marketing people really let us down on the customer tour – they did no preparation at all." "Manufacturing work well on a day-to-day basis – but they really don't have an appreciation of the problems we have in our Preventative Maintenance Programme." Prejudices, resentments and misgiving about others in the same company are historical and yet still live on in too many organisations.

What concerns me as a promoter of Culture Change and TQ is that there is frequently a lack of trust between units and departments – a concern that working with 'others', even within the same company, may inhibit our effectiveness. There are too many negative stereotypes often founded upon events in the past. It is time to change those memories or use them to help us reframe how we will work together in the future.

What is most worrying is that this departmental/functional or location stereotyping is counter-productive. The organisation exists to meet the needs of all – and only a team effort will bring prosperity and security for everybody. If we could break down these false, destructive and negative barriers and practise more horizontal management, ie. spending time working on cementing lateral relations – then we may be able to benefit from TQ. Failing to work with others, inventing and reinforcing negative stereotypes, does nothing for TQ. Utilising the negative energy in a positive way is a sure method of making the change to TQ.

FLAVOUR OF THE MONTH

This is a very common attitude and difficult to defeat if an organisation has been known for its short-term commitment to a variety of programmes. What happens is that a new fad creeps into management circles and, without proper appraisal, assumptions are made, packages and videos purchased and everyone is hit with the fad. Unfortunately, this does not last long. It may well have worked if it had been given a chance, more resources and time, but it failed. And, when the change is evaluated, we find that we may have only achieved success in the short term, because the change was not sustained.

In some companies, TQ has been treated as Flavour of the Month and thus has very soon been rejected and discredited.

THE DEATH OF TQ

When I first wrote this book in 1990 I forecast that TQ would be dead in many companies by 1993. I was not wrong. Those companies who have driven the concept and made it work have prospered. Those who used TQ as a two-letter acronym and put little support behind it have a few folders on their shelves to remind them of the Training Workshops – but TQ has not impacted on the performance of the company or become a positive element of their culture.

We are quite concerned that if sufficient people do discredit TQ, because they fail to give it a chance, treat it as a current 'flavour', give little support and resources when required, then TQ will never work for them. This is particularly sad because Culture Change is the only known process to significantly enhance corporate performance. There are no panaceas which can aid an organisation to Transform. TQ, through changing and building a customer-driven culture, is the only known antidote for poor quality Service delivery.

It isn't TQ that does not work, it is the process of managing the implementation of TQ which fails in too many initiatives. Poor reputations for ineffective change strategies spread quickly and *the* major opportunity for improving the competitive edge of many companies will not have been given a fair chance.

The only way to avoid this is to plan, plan and plan again and work through your people. Communicate these plans, the visions and the practicalities to all your people.

IT MAY GO AWAY IF I IGNORE IT

Suffice to say that this is a natural reaction from those subject to the 'flavour' approach. This phrase is destructive, because the attitude of the person is so geared to failure. The only way to resolve this is to lead by example. Failing to do so will confirm the negative prejudices.

UNWILLING TO 'TAKE OWNERSHIP' AND BE COMMITTED

This is a very strong attitude sometimes experienced at middle management and supervisory levels. They have been the meat in the sandwich for too long. They have had to be able to meet the strategic needs of the business and deal with the detail lower down the corporate ladder. Couple this with the conflicting demands they endure.

In particular, they may have to satisfy the conflicting demands of senior management, "design and deliver it on time – but it has to be the right quality", while at the same time being in the unfortunate position of having their resources reduced through 'cost-reduction programmes.' These examples of conflicting goals, together with dealing with problems from the shopfloor, can be an unbearable burden – especially when the dominant culture is to 'absorb conflict' rather than pass it up the management hierarchy.

Middle Managers and Supervisors can see it as just one more chore – knowing commitment to real change is skin-deep. The actions needed to clear this image are obvious and revolve around being the first to demonstrate real change.

> **CASE STUDY: Total Quality and Cost Reduction**
>
> Recently I spent some time with the Total Quality Manager of a computer manufacturer. I happened to notice that his department was adjacent to the Cost Reduction Department. He told me an amusing story.
>
> Apparently, both departments would appear to use the same strategies for achieving aims which were inconsistent with each other. For instance, the Cost Reduction Department will recommend that head count be reduced in a key manufacturing area. The person who goes does much of the cleaning up – keeping workstations fresh, tidy and free from clutter.
>
> Six months later, the same person is brought back as a 'preventative measure' to aid manufacturing, taking pressure off assembly workers. Clearly, someone somewhere should be co-ordinating things – this should be settled once and for all – nobody appears to be taking ownership!

IT'S YOUR RESPONSIBILITY

The most common time to hear this is when those in control of Service areas suddenly realise that Total Quality might have something to do with them. They quickly get hold of the QA Manager and ask him to pay a visit. This comprises five minutes listening to the QA Manager, then passing the responsibility to others.

Failure to be self-critical and look at what can be improved in the Support or Service areas of some manufacturing businesses will ensure that Quality remains a production, rather than an organisational, issue.

I have witnessed this very behaviour by a Finance Director who focused blame for poor Quality on to the shopfloor. He focused all his energy on taking photographs of overflowing scrap bins, noting disorderly tool-handling and damaged tools, exposing dirty and incomplete drawings, highlighting poor housekeeping and so on. He made little attempt to be self-critical and appraise the quality that he provided to his internal customers. He portrayed the 'it's not my fault' behaviour extremely well.

Here it is obvious that not all the Management Team have got the message. Those in charge of non-manufacturing areas project the difficulty of identifying waste and the subsequent measures required for monitoring progress. Hands are thrown up in horror. Faces are wrinkled at the very thought that they have a responsibility for Quality improvement. Heads shake with disbelief that waste can occur in areas other than manufacturing. These behaviours can be particularly pronounced in Accounts, Marketing, Sales, Data Processing, and Research and Development HR, and any area which provides a service to others in the business.

The answer to the issue of responsibility lies in collecting data at the Cultural Survey and Audit stage so that this can be used to convince Leaders of Service functions that they have a part to play in promoting Total Quality.

"FIRST YOU CHANGE, THEN I WILL"

This is a variant of "You put your hand in the fire then I will" and is sure to lead to non-activity. It is founded upon the belief that if someone is strong enough to oppose the action required – this will create the stimulus for *total inactivity*. Just to be safe – to avoid being branded a Luddite – different members of the management team may take it in turn to reject proposals and being identified as the instigator.

If allowed to continue, people fail to turn up for meetings and physically withdraw from the process. This adds to other meetings being attended by half-hearted people who have physically arrived, but who have psychologically withdrawn their commitment. Witness the number of times that those attending turn up with half the promised information and suggesting that data collection was too difficult or that "real work" business pressures got in the way. These are all are fine excuses for doing nothing – excuses, not reasons!

There is a simple solution to this problem – the CEO fires the first person who fails to do what he has promised. A bit extreme you may say – but what else would move such a comfortable culture?

It must be remembered that top team members are only in the position to safeguard and grow the business. Having top team members who are uncomfortable with change which is in the best interests of the company should be encouraged to work elsewhere.

"They will find out that what I have been doing over the years is wrong. I could be penalised."

Very rarely is this verbalised, but it is evident. Moving from a culture based upon CYA (Cover Your Ass), where blame is the norm and punitive actions are a day-by-day occurrence, is not easy. Moving from a culture where people are fired for doing wrong things – ie. providing inaccurate data and incorporating this in a key process – to a culture where problem identification and risk-taking is actively encouraged, can be alien to some Managers and Supervisors. They cannot believe that it is possible to change from one to another culture. What makes matters worse is that when they behaved in the old ways – which are now perceived as wrong – they were rewarded. So who can blame them for their concerns? Why should they believe there has been a real change in substance?

Consider as well in recent times, when redundancy is common, that few (managerial) staff are going to orchestrate their own 'end' by admitting to generating non-quality actions.

Trust is the only way of resolving this problem. This takes time. Knowing that resistance is evident and indeed is normal, is important for both internal and external change agent. Change is not easy – but at least an appreciation of why people resist change gives us all scope to erode these 'elements of resistance' before Total Quality is introduced.

SUMMARY

We have made some effort to project the importance of the soft side of the organisation and, indeed, change will not take place until actions have been taken to recognise this. This leads us to the terms 'Organisational Values and Culture' which may mean little to many people. They seem to conjure up the image of woolliness and intangibility. People speak a great deal about managerial values and organisational culture, but find them hard to define. Select any ten people within an organisation and ask them to write down statements or phrases which reflect the managerial values and the culture of the organisation. In many cases you will get ten disjointed views.

What does this tell us? That those who manage the organisation do not see it fitting or of value to promote a common view of how its employees can do things. It also tells us that by some magical process, the spirit of co-operation is created throughout the company and somehow comes together at the right time. This might have been acceptable in the 1970s when, in all honesty, most companies did not need to be 'Quality' conscious – because price was more important. Things have changed and companies need to consider organisational culture and values as being the real issue for change in the next century and beyond.

Bullet Points

- Highly customer-focused, team-driven cultures are founded only upon improving the values and behaviour of all staff in the business.

- A Total Quality culture cannot be created by adherence to an accreditation system.

- Quality systems can be a route which companies take to implement Total Quality, but is only a small step in the process.

- Total Quality is a philosophy of getting things right first time, every time. It has to be owned by everybody within the organisation – whether departments are service or manufacturing based.

- The Nine S's is a good approach to implementing Total Quality.

- Don't rely too much on the Hard S's to the exclusion of the Soft.

- Strategy, Structure and Systems will give the basis for a Total Quality approach – but they are just the framework upon which to build.

- Total Quality comes from people. Creativity, flexibility, teamwork, participation, continuous improvement and Leadership are critical. Without the right Symbols, Staff, Skills, Style, Shared Values and Synergy, Total Quality will never deliver the benefits to the organisation.

- Rejecting the culture which allocates blame and promotes fear is the right way to build a customer-focused culture.

- People are Boss Watchers. They recognise that deeds and actions of their Managers reflect their degree of commitment to change.

- Change is not always easy – it is difficult enough giving up personally damaging habits – asking people to change the way they manage and work with others needs an investment in time and some new thinking.

- Be patient. Necessary change can become easy.

- Be aware that some resistance to change is natural. This is not to mean it is desirable – but accept it – diagnose the reasons for it, and do something positive to help people through their personal Transformation.

- A reality of life is that some people fear change. Work with them and persuade them towards a positive future.

- Change may mean a temporary loss of control – especially for those in Supervisory and Managerial positions. Take them with you. Communicate and inform frequently. Learn to listen attentively to their concerns and address them.

- Living up to Total Quality is not always consistently easy. Examine the concerns and the training needs of staff at all levels and address them now.

- Total Quality will mean more work, at least an investment in time.

- Nothing good ever came by chance – certainly not the cultural transitions we desire. Additional time and resources must be found to make things work.

- Bury old resentments between functions and personalities. Total Quality is about building a compelling future. Destroy the past and reject the old stereotypes. Reframe the best as a platform for improvement for the future.

- Total Quality should be here to stay. At some time it may appear to be 'flavour of the month', but overall 100% success is founded upon 99% perspiration and 1% inspiration.

- Once a company is committed to Total Quality, it will not go away. It's there to stay and will become an enduring part of the culture. Remember what it can do for you and your people, and progress it every day – even by only a small percentage.

- At first everyone has doubts about the role he can play in the change process. But persevere – value your contribution, however small. Seize TQ as an opportunity to make things happen – all the things you would want to do if you were the Chief Executive of your organisation.

- Remember, everybody has a responsibility to create change. It does not matter where you are in the structure – you can do something to make your company more competitive and become a better place to work.

- Reject the old idea that 'you change before I do'. It is negative and self-defeating. Replace it with 'I am learning new things faster and faster and changing and improving all the time'.

- Every day try to find one reason to make Total Quality work. You may be surrounded by some who find ten ways to make it fail!

- Do what you can in your own way to reward people for their successes. Avoid the negative attitude of finding fault. Project the belief that TQ is about putting things right.

- Assess the culture and values of the organisation. Do your utmost to build on the good positive parts of the culture and work on destroying the negative culture.

CHAPTER 5

Shaping a Total Quality Culture

What is organisational culture and why is it important in promoting Total Quality? Culture sums up the 'way organisations function'. It has been defined as "the way we get things done around here". If we want to promote TQ we have to go some way to promoting a culture where people feel free to contribute their ideas, where involvement in problem-solving and decision-making is the norm. Culture is the set of beliefs, values, behaviours and norms which make an organisation tick.

We all can tell a good culture from a bad one or a positive from a negative one. Most of us have walked into organisations and quickly came to conclusions about how things are achieved. We create an instant picture of what we see and feel. Perhaps the time when we focus upon a culture is when we visit a company for the first time either as a customer or as a potential employee. We quickly form impressions about the business from a very short exposure to it.

As a customer we quickly identify what is important to the company from how people greet and talk with us. There are usually plenty of artefacts around the business which may indicate what behaviour is acceptable and that which is not.

Another quick way to be exposed to a culture, at least at a fairly superficial level, is when people attend for a job interview. Most get a good idea whether it is the sort of place they can work or not. It is intuitive, somehow like a sixth sense, and we form impressions very quickly on what the company stands for and how it goes about achieving its targets through its people. Having formed our first impressions we proceed to focus our attentions on the judgement we have already made. People do tend to trust their intuition and feelings to make decisions rather than relying solely on their objective senses.

We can usually tell:

- If the organisation is a pleasant place to work.
- Whether it values customer service.
- How it achieves its results.
- What is important to the business.
- How well information is communicated.
- How staff manage.

CULTURE AND ARTEFACTS, SIGNS AND SYMBOLS

The observable and tangible aspects of an organisational culture are examined through its artefacts, those things which stand out and indicate certain ways of working. These are signs or symbols which the organisation displays either consciously or not. Recognition of the impact of 'symbols' of culture to outsiders, would certainly lead to consideration of a Cultural audit!

THE LOCAL AUTHORITY PLANNING DEPARTMENT

When working with a Planning Department and visiting their offices shared in common with other Council departments – I was greeted by probably the least customer-focused person ever. I was told to wait for my appointment with no indication of where to wait, but duly took a seat in the outer Reception area, much used by the public who visited the department. I marvelled at the decor – a ceiling with several polystyrene tiles missing through which I could see the inner working of electrical components as well as corpses of a variety of insects. None of the seats matched. The ash tray was full to overflowing – at 8.45 am!

I brought the state and impression of the Reception Area to the attention of the Director of Property Services and he asked that I spend some time in the building assessing the physical, visible parts of the culture. With an Instamatic Camera I took pictures which were presented at our next training Workshop, highlighting the importance of creating a good impression. In glorious colour were four dead rubber plants supported by two pieces of 2x4 battening, other plants growing in an interesting mixture of soil and cigarette ends, Notice boards invisible under torn and ancient news bulletins. It could be clearly seen which boards were tidy and up to date and those which were not. Toilets and public areas were also examined. These photographs were central in focusing attention on the possibly trivial, but most observable, elements of the culture. If this was how the organisation presented itself to those to whom it delivered service, what did it tell us about the attitude of the employer to staff and public alike?

Because the Building was in a large public domain and the Reception area was owned by no one single department, the buck was passed, little effort was expended to improve appearance. It was certainly the case that staff were accustomed to the poor surroundings and worked despite this – but it did highlight the impression of a lack of care, gained by clients.

Artefacts, symbols and company culture can be summed up in terms of office design, display of messages, architecture, posters, messages to employees, allocation and proximity of car parking spaces, office decor, open door policy, etc.

To examine culture and its impact upon people, consider how people are dealt with at the reception area of a company. How friendly do employees appear to be? Do receptionists use titles frequently or less often? Do they project the informal first name approach? This tells us much about company culture.

When phoning a company, the speed and tone of response of people answering the phone, the concern for accuracy when taking messages, all say something about their concern for you – the customer.

In particular, the behaviour of 'customer-facing staff' also tells us a little bit about how they are treated as employees. If their manner is gruff, direct, insensitive and focused upon transacting business without making this a pleasant experience – there is a good basis to belief that the way these people are managed is very similar. It's true the quality of 'customer relations' which a customer enjoys is only a reflection of 'human relations' within the organisation.

Other symbols of culture include: the cleanliness of staff eating areas, up to date notice boards, safety reporting and posters, etc. – they all portray a picture of what is important and is encouraged in the business and that which is not. The interesting point is we can all pick up the cultural vibes very quickly. It is difficult to hide a poor or negative culture. And it is surprising that many senior officers in organisations are totally unaware of them and the impact they have on their staff and their customers. If the managers truly had an awareness of the poor image they portrayed – they would suppress it.

CHANGING THE SYMBOLS TO CREATE CULTURAL CHANGE

The first thing a good friend of mine did when he became plant manager of a US-owned, UK company was to create change. He said that everybody was waiting for him to do something – as an indication of how things were going to be from this time on. He decide to change the car parking allocations.

All the customer and visitor spaces were to be adjacent to the Reception, not a quarter of a mile away from the entrance. This, he said, "was to ensure that our customers recognise themselves as being important". The second thing he did was revolutionary! He located all the senior officers of the company at the far end of the car park, approximately a four-minute walk to the Reception area. There were to be no exceptions.

When I asked him why he did this, he replied: "There is a good chance that the Managers may bump into some of their people on the way in and out of work every day – it will give them the opportunity to talk, they always claim not to have the time during the day".

In this example the new manager was clearly trying to send several messages about culture to his new staff and this shows how it is possible to create significant change in an environment by influencing just one or two things.

THE CULTURE BREAKER: KICK THE SHERRY HABIT

Neil Roden, the newly appointed Training Manager in a financial services company, decided that enough was enough in terms of organisational culture. He had recently taken responsibility for creating change to promote team development in what had been a very stable and traditional business with little change in the 1960s and 1970s until the late 1980s. There had been plenty of indication that the culture suited a bygone age. The old culture was strongly autocratic with a heavy dose of departmentalitis. He and others were in charge of turning it into a thriving, breathing, entrepreneurial environment – where teamwork and motivation were key values. He looked at the culture and one sign seemed to say it all. 'Sherry at lunch-time.'

Now this guy was not a killjoy, but he asked himself: why did managers drink sherry at lunch-time? It was a sign of the old culture, part of the organisational heritage which is fine for a Christmas Party, but not to be encouraged in a business which was experiencing severe competition. Should managers drink at lunch-time while on training courses – ensuring that the afternoon could be spent sleeping in some form or other? The Training Manager clearly believed that replacing sherry with soft drinks was reasonable – and a way to tell managers that things were changing.

The soft drinks were provided. This small change created so much anger in management circles that he is still renowned as the guy who killed an 80-year-old tradition. This one action won him the nickname of "Rambo". It was only a small start – people became aware that he meant business and that the company were being serious about changing for a new approach to "doing things". Neil's attitude toward the importance of forging a performance culture is evident in all the positions he has taken up since then – currently a major mover and shaker and HR Director of a prominent bank group.

DISORGANISED FACTORY FLOOR

Consider going on to a factory floor where we find that 'housekeeping' is less than perfect, where everybody is running around in a mad frenzy, where the great majority of staff are involved in chaotic firefighting. This tells us about how the organisation is run and what is important in the enterprise.

First impressions tell us a great deal and are usually a good impression upon which we can make judgements. These are only the superficial, the outward signs of what is important, but they tell us a great deal about how we manage.

A SOCIAL EXAMPLE

Consider for one minute a social, not a business context. You are attending a restaurant in town with your spouse. Your first impressions as you walk through the door are that it is poorly lit, wallpaper and decor are past their best and rancid smells permeate the building. Those outward signs of the culture and atmosphere of the restaurant tell us much about the likely care and attention which the 'owner' will lavish upon us during our meal.

Now, there are always exceptions to the general case – but how many of us would stay to sample the cuisine? I guess very few. This example is not so different from the organisational experience.

The culture indicates certain behaviours and suggests particular values which guide behaviour. These are the assumptions which we make about a company and they are the visible signs which employees pick up and live with.

RICHARD AND THE COKE CANS

Richard Tinkler was in charge of TQ within an engineering company. I had noted on my trip of the factory floor that the workshop floor was littered and that there were a great many empty soft drinks cans in the 'work in progress' bins. Richard took photographs and displayed them on the notice board with the message, "Coca-Cola Plant". It seemed to do the trick and send the message to the staff that the state of their environment was fundamentally their responsibility.

Interestingly, whenever he wanted some of the manufacturing and Quality Control people to take an interest in the work we were doing, he would orchestrate a walkabout past the scrap bins – carrying his camera. For some reason, from then on his presence would create an interest among his fellow managers which would then help them focus their attention upon waste and Quality improvement.

CULTURE, MANAGEMENT STYLE AND ASSUMPTIONS

Management style is driven very much by the 'assumptions' we make about how things should be done and the culture and values which underpin them.

We all know bad, negative or weak cultures when we experience them. But they are not always the same thing. A strong culture can also be negative and drives for results through fear. There are also very positive cultures which establish little because they lack focus and direction.

So what should we look for in a Culture?

- Is it performance-driven or is it in need of a kick start?

- Is it negative, punitive and fear-driven? If it is – it will achieve results for the wrong reasons, people will do things to avoid the unpleasant things in life.

- What positive elements exist within a culture? Can we use the positive compelling aspects of reward and recognition to drive improved performance.

- Who are guardians of the culture and do they support and create a culture or do they fail to take responsibility and let it evolve by accident?

These are all questions which a targeted Cultural audit can uncover which is central in making lasting change growth.

Be certain – Cultural change is the secret to implementing TQ. First make some attempt to decide on changes which are required within the culture. This means measuring and quantifying the culture. What is it that you can change about those things which project a lack of concern for Quality and what actions can you take? Change those things to convey the TQ message, reinforce your changes with consistent effort, and lead the process by example.

CREATING A CULTURE

Most Corporate cultures have been around for a long time and are not easily changed. Founders of companies create the original cultures. The beliefs of the founder and the senior management team are translated into rules and systems, norms and style of managing which are either covertly or overtly encouraged. These are passed on to people who join the company – whether the values which underpin the culture are consciously driven or hidden.

TURNOVER AND CULTURAL LOSS

One problem which cultures suffer from is people leaving the company. The higher the turnover at certain levels, the more the culture needs to be reinforced. Working with a nationwide sales organisation we were not surprised to find a turnover of 25% for the sales executives per year. Bearing in mind the 'Demographic Time Bomb' (the shortage of good quality staff) and the difficulty of attracting good people into the South East of England, the company decided to do something about their culture. They realised that for staff to stay in the company, they needed to feel there was a place for them now and in the future. Through the use of assessment centres, succession planning and career development, the company managed to formulate a development plan for each of its people. It rejected the idea of just 'throwing money' at the problem and offering higher salaries for jobs. Changing the culture to be caring and developing staff helped in the retention of staff who would have been attracted to their competitors.

Time and time again what is important to staff is not security of tenure. What we find more important is that staff feel they have the skills and experience to be valued highly in the job market by other potential purchasers for their services. Being 'valued highly' provides far more security in the long term than maintaining a dead-end job with a dead-end company who just don't happen to move deadwood on. Sooner or later they may have to! So, what is important for business Leaders to understand is that 'investing' in developing the career and potential of their staff is the biggest single investment you can give to ensuring the organisation retains the best staff in the company.

Where turnover is the highest in the company, the levels of people who tend to move on and the reason for moving can help us isolate key areas for change. The purpose, to strengthen the company by changing personnel policy to build a loyal and committed staff.

So what about the culture that exists between functional units within a business? Some would say that it is not unusual for the culture in Sales and Marketing to be quite high in comparison with other units because of the nature of self-motivation required to perform well in the function. So what of other functions where the personal drive for advancement or recognition may not be so evident?

WIN-LOSE CULTURES BETWEEN FUNCTIONS

Working with a service company, we witnessed an event in a training session which said much about company cultures. Representatives of the Credit Control Unit and Marketing were present. It was evident there was a lot of negative stereotyping between the units.

The Credit Control unit was very strict about how work was carried out. There were strict demarcations between jobs, and work was very serious. The Marketing Unit were noisy and always seemed to be partying. There was a mutual dislike between the units, and the company had to take action – because it was creating problems for customer service. There was no commonality in the culture between the functions. They were housed in the same building on the same floor, but there was little involvement between unit members. Clearly this was a case where unit heads had to take some responsibility for making things happen. They came up with a simple strategy – get each of their senior staff to make a point of meeting with someone different from the other unit each week. The meetings would take 15-20 minutes with the purpose of exchanging information about each other. These sessions grew and people started to meet informally to view each other differently, but not at a fast enough rate. So we organised a short training session which would have a huge impact on the culture of both functions and, more importantly, improve relationships between functions.

We organised sessions with about six members from each function present. Simply we asked each group to complete the following tasks:

- Describe the characteristics of my unit and colleagues.

- Describe the characteristics of (the other) unit and their staff.

- Describe how the other group would describe our group – and why would they describe us this way?

This was an opportunity to bust through the negative stereotypes between the two groups. Obviously, the Marketeers saw themselves as flamboyant, focused and achievement-orientated. The Credit Control people saw this group as shallow, opinionated and arrogant. Likewise, the Credit Control people identified themselves in a positive light and the Marketeers described only the negative side. Then we focused upon real events and how these formed the misperceptions between the functions. No holds were barred. People were asked to justify their judgements of others. Soon it became clear that the apparent negative characteristics of the other group were essential for that group to perform their role successfully!

In less than two hours we had each group valuing the importance of the contribution of the other group to the overall company-wide effort for customer service. We destroyed the negative stereotypes which were responsible for major win-lose relationships. By focusing upon behaviour and attitudes founded upon false evidence and prejudice we managed to get two groups working together. Everyone in both teams went through the experience and it took us no more than three two-hour sessions. The teams started to work together, rather than in spite of each other, and the negative relationships which had separated the two teams from working together in years was now destroyed. This simple example emphasises that Culture Change can happen in an instant and will do if you focus upon changing perceptions, attitudes and behaviour.

TRADITIONAL CULTURES

Many traditional companies portray the old culture which is not exactly geared up for TQ. Symptoms include poor layout and design of office and manufacturing areas, dirty and uncared-for staff facilities, poor lighting and environmental conditions, etc.

This can be further reinforced by managerial behaviour which is erratic and geared to achieving only short-term results. Here, ends are more important than means and punitive measures are the major way of getting things done. Tie this in with outmoded procedures, a commitment to repair instead of preventative maintenance, a 'that will do' attitude and the story and the culture start to unfold. This is a pretty negative culture. You can bet that people won't hang around at the end of the day.

Things do not always appear so obvious. Talking recently with Rose, a woman employed as a temporary secretary, she told me that she was not looking forward to returning to one of her clients for a short-term project. This company had a really poor name for man management and when secretaries from her agency were offered assignments there, many refused.

Rose, the secretary, told of being in the secretarial pool for five weeks, during which time very few people talked to her at all, including managers. Her first contact with management was an interesting one. She was at her workstation when approached by a manager who thrust a typed document at her, and without looking at her said, "Are you RB (her initials)? Correct this and bring it back to me straight away". No introductions or social niceties, nor even common courtesy. Need more be said about that prevailing culture?

CULTURES ARE CREATED BY HEROES AND ANTI-HEROES

Culture can be good and bad, but its growth or continuation is dependent upon the stories which pass around about the people who propagate the culture and are often described as 'legends'. Often these legends are stories about critical incidents which have taken place in the company. These 'legends' become part of the folklore of the company. The more frequently they are told and retold, the more credence the legend obtains. Eventually, this reinforces the belief about the company culture that this is "how we do things around here".

Legends tell people in the company what is acceptable behaviour and what the culture will permit. Legends also feature people as the key movers in the stories. People and their actions demonstrate what is okay and what is not. Cultures can't exist without people doing things. Those who make stories live can be described as Heroes and Heroines – but only in as much as the stories are positive. If the stories are negative then we have an anti-hero – and we all know too many of them!

Stories originate and spread throughout the business at great speed. For instance: "Did you hear about John Lynch and the way he closed the sale with Websters? It was textbook stuff, it got the company right off the hook and the commission was the highest anybody has been paid". These stories and legends abound. Even if the hero leaves, the story continues. Stories like this are legion in really positive companies. They are told and retold always with a positive message. But what about the other side of the coin? We can all think of stories which reflect the company in good light, but there are other stories which reinforce the belief that people are working in a negative culture – where no one cares. These legends spread rapidly too.

"Have you heard about Ian's latest scam, he tried to get all those drinks at lunch-time put on the food bill. Will that guy stop at nothing? He cheats the company all the time."

This story can always be bettered by others in the immediate vicinity who either reinforce the negative elements of the story or introduce another 'legend' which puts Ian in a bad light.

BELIEVING THE WORST!

This can be really dangerous for companies. When customers and suppliers are treated to these revelations about managers, this can create an extremely bad impression. Sales take months to materialise and can be lost in seconds if customers discover issues of lack of integrity within a company.

The grapevine can be very powerful in helping shape or destroy a culture by what is expressed about key people in the business. Even if stories are only are half true, there are many of us who will not be sufficiently open and objective to reject what we have heard. There will be a tendency to use 'selective perception' and look for data which confirm what we have been told.

It is imperative that companies examine the culture they project, because the culture and legends which support it are transmitted to others who make business decisions about the company.

The type of culture also gives us an indication of whether TQ will be successful or not and where it may fail.

CULTURE AND THE JAPANESE

Anyone who has taken a trip around a Japanese company committed to the TQ concept will immediately note an open and trusting climate, where teamwork and interdependence is encouraged. How else could they win the commitment of their people to generate literally thousands of new ideas for making things better?

On a recent trip around a Toyota plant in Japan, it was hard to believe that people could *not* get involved in continuous improvement. A visit to Kawasaki Steel told a similar story. How was it that the environment was so clean, that newly drawn posters proclaiming up-to-date quality improvement were tidy and free from dust, and the area for coffee and lunch breaks was as pleasant as a modern office in any hi-tech company?

The Japanese have no special advantage over us in their country. Many, however, continue to claim that it is impossible to create the TQ Culture in Western companies. The culture, they say, is something unique to Japan.

ORGANISATIONAL CULTURE CREATING PERSONAL VALUES

When Ciba Corning Diagnostics was implementing its educational programme reflecting Total Quality, a story was told of a married couple who were working together in the same company. The husband worked in the manufacturing operation and the wife in an administrative role. The training really impacted upon this couple. The strength of the training and, in particular, the emphasis placed upon changing values became so powerful that the couple were inspired to re-evaluate their life together so as to help each other achieve their full potential in all areas of life.

The values inherent in TQ acted as a catalyst for the couple who had clearly never given much thought to their 'value systems' before then, to work through how they were going to spend their time productively and positively in the future, whether at work or in their leisure time. This illustrates that much of the educational and developmental content of the programmes for improvement have a great deal to contribute to how people work, live and enjoy their time together. What started out as a business intervention clearly had advantages for social relationships. These and many other stories characterised how the TQ Drive at Corning created change in the way people did things not just in their work but in their Total Life.

INDICATORS OF CORPORATE CULTURE

A group of managers brainstormed the factors they thought important in indicating the predominant culture within a company. The results are below.

Atmosphere – did it feel good, was it a nice place to work?

Ethos – the way things were laid out.

Spirit or teamwork.

Warmth and friendship.

Ideals – company messages and how they were displayed.

Management Style – what people did, not what they said.

How they talk to you, the tone and manner of communication.

Listening to us – is there evidence?

Attitudes to employees portrayed through notice boards.

Involvement – did people incorporate the ideas of others?

Ambience – was it a nice place to be?

Telephone Response.

Promises not kept – especially between departments.

Events – was there evidence of a corporate get-together?

Criteria for selection/appraisal – was it a pleasant experience?

Type of Communication.

Negative rumours and the failure to address them.

Reception – staff entrances and goods inwards and outwards.

Stereotypes of departments – what is projected by opinion leaders?

Answering the phone – was there a concern for helping?

Tidiness in all areas.

Clutter in non-manufacturing areas.

Participation – is there encouragement for people to participate?

Belonging – did they feel at home?

Motivation – the process – was it carrot or stick?

Shared corporate values – were they known by all and displayed?

VALUES: THE BUILDING BLOCKS OF CULTURE

This takes us to the building blocks of culture, the value system which predominates within any organisation. Not many people give much thought to the key values – but they are critical in helping to manage change, only if people live up to them.

What are values? They are stable, long-term beliefs that are hard to change. Values cannot be proven or disproven – but they can be refuted or substantiated by the actions of key people in the organisation. They define what is 'right' or 'wrong', 'good' or 'bad', 'correct and incorrect'. Values are often hard to articulate in words, but do have a great deal of influence in how we behave and how we run our organisation.

Organisational Values constitute the 'culture' of the organisation, the set of beliefs that people share about what sort of behaviour is 'correct' and 'incorrect'.

When these organisational beliefs conflict with individual personal values, people are likely to psychologically distance themselves from the organisation – there can be a fundamental rift between staff member and employer. Here there is a failure to share the same beliefs and ways of doing things. The response by many in such cases is reflected in withdrawal by the member of staff. Here the presence of the nine-to-five attitude, the 'us and them' syndrome, 'the work to rule mentality', the 'not invented here' attitude, resistance to change, aggressiveness in labour disputes and sheer bloody-mindedness are the most obvious examples!

If staff do perceive a conflict of values – they can usually accommodate this – but fail to be committed to the goals and aspirations of the organisation in the long term. They will see the role they play in the company as simply a means to an end and, at this stage, their commitment will diminish.

CULTURE AND PEOPLE

The observed behaviour of people can be deceptive. Although on the surface, people may tend to project the nine-to-five mentality, show little creativity in their work and fail to come up with suggestions, it does not mean they are not capable of doing so. It means they choose not to. Many people who attend work are imaginative and display enthusiasm when working on projects they enjoy – but do they express it when they work for you? Often these people will throw themselves into activities which interest them and give them a level of satisfaction. On the whole, the vast majority of people are imaginative, keen to contribute, creative, flexible and enthusiastic. What can we do to cause these behaviours to happen while they are working for us? And the really important question is why are these behaviours more common outside the work environment than inside? What have we failed to do to motivate workers to display the same creative talents in worktime as they do outside of work?

VALUES: YOU HAVE TO LEARN TO VALUE YOUR PEOPLE

A reason these behaviours may not be displayed when working in an organisation is that the 'culture' inhibits and counters the initiative which people want to project.

A culture opposed to development, a culture which treats people only as a resource, which needs to be controlled at all times, where the method of reinforcing behaviour is punitive, is an organisation which is on the slide downwards. Absence of vitality, trust and genuine value for human beings is tantamount to organisational suicide.

> *To promote the value system which underpins Total Quality, is for managers to have to learn to do one thing well. They have to learn to genuinely value their people as they do their own family and themselves. Learning to value people, looking at them as people, not employees, or hourly paid or blue-collar workers, but people, is a major step. Looking at your people from the neck up, not from the neck down, is a good starting point.*

VALUE STATEMENTS

Value statements reflect our intentions. But they do not create a change in behaviour on their own. This can only be achieved through marrying managerial behaviours to specific value statements – and this does not happen by accident.

We may need to spend time thinking through the values which are important to us as an organisation. Having these statements posted up in the reception area is not sufficient. Time and effort has to be expended to make these 'managerial behaviours' the norm by which all supervisory staff measure their ability to manage people.

We should devote time to making these values explicit to ourselves and others. Consistently coaching our managers in these values will provide us with standards which are understood by all within the organisation.

TYPICAL COMPANY VALUES

VALUES ON GROWTH AND SUCCESS

'The principal reason for the organisation's existence is to create added value for the company and provide staff with stable employment.'

We can achieve this by:

Anticipating and meeting the requirements of the customers.

Maintaining a competitive position by utilising the talents and capabilities of staff.

Rigorously adhering to standards and communicating these to our people.

VALUES ON SAFETY

'Our aim is a safe and hazard-free working environment.'

We can achieve this by:

Developing safety rules, procedures and education in advance of current legislation.

Following rules on safety and preventing accidents arising.

Thinking safety, to train and reinforce the 'safety first mentality'.

Protecting our people, our customers and visitors, and the environment in which we work.

VALUES ON JOB CONTENT

'It is our objective to provide everybody with a satisfying job and the opportunity to improve skills and develop.'

We will achieve this by:

Promoting job satisfaction through the redesign of work.

Consulting and involving our people in job changes and the introduction of new technology.

VALUES ABOUT CORPORATE AND COMMUNITY RESPONSIBILITY

'We will lead, act as an example to others and be a responsible member of the local community.'

We will achieve this by:

Participating in community affairs.

Pursuing the interests of the community.

Promoting confidence in our actions by communicating openly and actively with the local community.

VALUES ON COMMUNICATION

'To provide accurate, reliable and valid information to our people and ensure that we listen to the opinions of others.'

We will achieve this by:

Ensuring that our managers' key responsibility is to promote effective communication horizontally within their responsibility and across boundaries with other functions.

Educating and informing everybody about our plans for the future and how we intend to achieve our objectives.

Recognising, encouraging and valuing people who promote effective communication.

Being honest and telling people what we think, rather than what we want them to hear.

Understanding there are many views on subjects, and valuing different perspectives, opinions and viewpoints on subjects.

Generating teamwork and working together.

VALUES ABOUT ETHICAL STANDARDS OF BEHAVIOUR

"The methods by which we achieve results.'

We will achieve this by:

Promoting honesty.

Ensuring that when there is a conflict between interests, personal and company – all perspectives are examined.

VALUES ON PEOPLE DEVELOPMENT

'The person who fails to develop and go forward – takes one step backwards.'

We will achieve this by:

Providing our managers with the responsibility for the development of their people.

Keeping our people up to date with changes in job design and the acquisition of job skills and knowledge.

Providing our people with the opportunity to develop through a staff development programme.

Recognising and rewarding our people who take responsibility to develop new ways of working.

VALUES ON QUALITY

'It is the policy of the company to provide customers with defect-free goods and services, on time every time, without defect, error or omission.'

We will achieve this by:

Ensuring that all our people are trained in Quality management.

Promoting teamwork and taking preventative action.

Developing a climate of involvement and joint problem-solving with all staff from all areas.

Value statements can be of two varieties, Values which are projected externally towards the community, our customers and suppliers, and those which are projected inwardly and relate to the management of people. These internal Values are implicit to promoting Quality of product and service throughout the company.

Overall, it is necessary for the senior team to recognise that TQ really is a cultural change requiring significant change in behaviour reflected through our values – those things which we hold most dear. If the Values are important to us, we find that they guide our behaviour. In other words: "We value what we do and we do what we value". Can there be a better philosophy to work to?

The level of consistency between "what we value and what we do" will only come about through example. "How can we possibly expect others, lower down in the organisation, to promote TQ if we have not done as much as we could to create the right climate and culture for change by exploring our values?"

ORGANISATIONAL PERFORMANCE AND STRONG CULTURES

In studying the performance of eighty companies, Deal and Kennedy found that the more successful companies were those which had strong cultures. The strong culture was categorised thus:

- Had a widely shared philosophy of Management.
- Emphasised the importance of people to the success of the organisation.
- Encouraged ritual and ceremonies to celebrate company events.
- Had identified successful people and sung their praises.
- Maintained a network to communicate the culture.
- Had informal rules of behaviour.
- Had strong values.
- Set high standards for performance.
- Possessed a definitive corporate character.

PETERS AND WATERMAN: *IN SEARCH OF EXCELLENCE*

Peters and Waterman in *In Search of Excellence* identified eight organisational characteristics which tended to be a major feature by the excellent companies. Hands-On Value-Driven was the characteristic which most closely reflects the importance given to organisational culture as such. The Hands-On Value-Driven culture is broken down into ten 'beliefs' which reflect that culture.

- A belief in the importance of enjoying one's work.

- A belief in being the best.

- A belief that people should be innovators and take risks, without feeling that they will be punished if they fail.

- A belief in the importance of attending to details.

- A belief in the importance of people as individuals.

- A belief in superior Quality and Service.

- A belief in the importance of informality to improve the flow of communication.

- A belief in the importance of economic growth and profits.

- A belief in the importance of 'hands-on' management; the notion that managers should be doers, not just planners and administrators.

- A belief in the importance of a recognised organisational philosophy developed and supported by those at the top.

Charles Handy in his books *Understanding Organisations* and *Gods of Management* makes constant reference to Organisational Culture. He has developed a working definition which enables us to examine culture from a tangible perspective.

ORGANISATIONAL ANALYSIS

This analysis helps us stand back and assess the success and operation of our organisation and in particular the organisational culture. It is a useful exercise to take some time off and assess success, the organisation's strengths and weaknesses, and take appropriate action. A useful diagnostic model to use is his questionnaire based upon the work of Roger Harrison.

Handy suggests that we can classify organisations into a broad range of four cultures. The formation of 'culture' will depend upon a whole host of factors including: company history, ownership, organisation structure, technology, critical business incidents, environment, etc.

The four cultures he discusses are Power, Role, Task and Person. The purpose of the analysis is to assess the degree to which the predominant culture reflects the real needs and constraints of the organisation.

Handy uses diagrammatic representation to illustrate his ideas.

THE POWER CULTURE

He describes the Power Culture as a Web. He suggests that this reflects the concentration of power of a family-owned business, which can either be extremely large or small. The family operation with strict responsibilities going to family members, responsibility given to personalities rather than expertise, creates the power structure of the Web. Examples to which he refers include the massive institutions in the US, run as a small family business at the top and known as 'robber barons'. Power is concentrated in a small area, the centre of which is the wheel or the centre of the web. Power radiates out from the centre, usually a key personality, to others in the family who further send information down to either departments, functions or units. The important point to note is that because power and decision-making is concentrated in so few hands, the strategists and key family members create situations which others have to implement. It is difficult for others outside the 'family network' to influence events. (*Dallas*, the long-running TV saga, displayed this culture with the Ewing family of oil tycoons.)

The ability of the power culture to adapt to changes in the environment is very much determined by the perception and ability of those who occupy the positions of power within it. The power culture has more faith in individuals than committees and can either change very rapidly and adapt, or 'fail to see the need for change' and die.

THE ROLE CULTURE

The role culture has been typified as a Greek Temple and has often been stereotyped as portraying bureaucracy in its purest form. The apex of the temple is where the decision-making takes place, the pillars of the temple reflect the functional units of the organisation which have to implement the decisions from the apex. The strength of the culture lies in specialisation within its pillars. Interaction takes place between the functional specialism by job descriptions, procedures, rules and systems. This is very much an organisation culture run by a paper system. Your authority is not based upon personal initiative – but dictated by job descriptions.

Co-ordination is by a narrow band of senior staff. This is the only co-ordination required, as the system provides the necessary integration.

Handy states that the job description is more important than the skills and abilities of those who people the culture. Performance beyond the role prescription is not required or encouraged.

The authority of position power is legitimate. Personal power is not. This reflects Weber's pure theory of bureaucracy. System effectiveness depends upon adherence to principles rather than personalities.

Handy suggests that this culture is appropriate in organisations which are not subject to constant change. These cultures function well in a steady state environment, but are insecure in times of change. The role culture is typified in Government Departments, Local Authorities, Public Utilities, and the Public Sector in general. This sort of culture finds it extremely difficult to change rapidly. The role culture is typified by rationality and size. You will have experienced this culture if you have ever worked with a large state enterprise.

THE TASK CULTURE

The Task Culture is characteristic of organisations which are involved in extensive research and development activities. They are much more dynamic. They are constantly subject to change and have to create temporary task teams to meet their future needs. Information and expertise are the skills that are of value here. The culture is represented best by a net or lattice-work. There is close liaison between departments, functions and specialities. Liaison, communication and integration are the means whereby the organisation can anticipate and adapt to change quickly.

Influence in this team culture is based upon expertise and up-to-date information where the culture is most in tune with results. The dangers for this culture exist when there is a restriction in resources when it could become more 'power or role' orientated.

THE PERSON CULTURE

The Person Culture is characteristic of the consensus model of management, where the individuals within the structure determine collectively the path the organisation pursues. If there is a formalised structure, it tends to service the needs of the individuals within the structure. Organisations which portray this culture reject formal hierarchies for getting 'things done' and exist solely to meet the needs of their members. The rejection of formal 'management control' and 'reporting relationships' suggest that this may be a suitable culture for a self-help group, a commune, etc., but is not appropriate for business organisations.

DIAGNOSING ORGANISATION IDEOLOGY
Roger Harrison

Organisations have patterns of behaviour that operationalise an ideology – a commonly held set of doctrines, myths, and symbols. An organisation's ideology has a profound impact on the effectiveness of the organisation. It influences most important issues in organisation life: how decisions are made, how human resources are used, and how people respond to the environment. Organisation ideologies can be divided into four orientations: Power (a), Role (b), Task (c), and Self (d). The items below give the positions of the four orientations on a number of aspects of organisation structure and functioning and on some attitudes and beliefs about human nature.

Instructions. Give a "1" to the statement that best represents the dominant view in your organisation, a "2" to the one next closest to your organisation's position, and so on through "3" and "4". Then go back and again rank the statements "1" through "4", this time according to your attitudes and beliefs.

Existing
Organisation
Ideology

Participant's
Preferred Organisation
Ideology

1. A good boss is:

_____ _____ a. strong, decisive and firm, but fair. He is protective, generous, and indulgent to loyal subordinates.
_____ _____ b. impersonal and correct, avoiding the exercise of his authority for his own advantage. He demands from subordinates only that which is required by the formal system.
_____ _____ c. egalitarian and capable of being influenced in matters concerning the task. He uses his authority to obtain the resources needed to complete the job.
_____ _____ d. concerned with and responsive to the personal needs and values of others. He uses his position to provide satisfying and growth-stimulating work opportunities for subordinates.

2. A good subordinate is:

_____ _____ a. compliant, hard working, and loyal to the interests of his superior.
_____ _____ b. responsible and reliable, meeting the duties and responsibilities of his job and avoiding actions that surprise or embarrass his superior.
_____ _____ c. self-motivated to contribute his best to the task and is open with his ideas and suggestions. He is nevertheless willing to give the lead to others when they show greater expertise or ability.
_____ _____ d. vitally interested in the development of his own potentialities and is open to learning and to receiving help. He also respects the needs and values of others and is willing to help and contribute to their development.

3. A good member of the organisation gives first priority to the:

_____ _____ a. personal demands of the boss.
_____ _____ b. duties, responsibilities and requirements of his own role and to the customary standards of personal behaviour.
_____ _____ c. requirements of the task for skill, ability, energy, and material resources.

Existing Organisation Ideology	Participant's Preferred Organisation Ideology

—— —— d. personal needs of the individuals involved.

4. People who do well in the organisation are:

—— —— a. shrewd and competitive, with a strong drive for power.
—— —— b. conscientious and responsible, with a strong sense of loyalty to the organisation.
—— —— c. technically effective and competent, with a strong commitment to getting the job done.
—— —— d. effective and competent in personal relationships, with a strong commitment to the growth and development of people.

5. The organisation treats the individual as:

—— —— a. though his time and energy were at the disposal of persons higher in the hierarchy.
—— —— b. though his time and energy were available through a contract with rights and responsibilities for both sides.
—— —— c. a co-worker who has committed his skills and abilities to the common cause.
—— —— d. an interesting and worthwhile person in his own right.

6. People are controlled and influenced by the:

—— —— a. personal exercise of economic and political power (rewards and punishments).
—— —— b. impersonal exercise of economic and political power to enforce procedures and standards of performance.
—— —— c. communication and discussion of task requirements leading to appropriate action motivated by personal commitment to goal achievement.
—— —— d. intrinsic interest and enjoyment to be found in their activities and/or by concern and caring for the needs of the other persons involved.

7. It is legitimate for one person to control another's activities if:

—— —— a. he has more authority and power in the organisation.
—— —— b. his role prescribes that he is responsible for directing the other.
—— —— c. he has more knowledge relevant to the task.
—— —— d. the other accepts that the first person's help or instruction can contribute to his learning and growth.

8. The basis of task assignment is the:

—— —— a. personal needs and judgement of those in authority.
—— —— b. formal divisions of functions and responsibilities in the system.
—— —— c. resource and expertise requirements of the job to be done.
—— —— d. personal wishes and needs for learning and growth of individual organisation members.

9. Work is performed out of:

—— —— a. hope of reward, fear of punishment, or personal loyalty toward a powerful individual.
—— —— b. respect for contractual obligations backed up by sanctions and loyalty toward the organisation or system.
—— —— c. satisfaction in excellence of work and achievement and/or personal commitment to the task or goal.
—— —— d. enjoyment of the activity for its own sake and concern and respect for the needs and values of the other persons involved.

10. People work together when:

—— —— a. they are required to by higher authority or when they believe they can use each other for personal advantage.

Existing Organisation Ideology	Participant's Preferred Organisation Ideology	

—— —— b. co-ordination and exchange are specified by the formal system.

—— —— c. their joint contribution is needed to perform the task.

—— —— d. the collaboration is personally satisfying, stimulating, or challenging.

11. The purpose of competition is to:

—— —— a. gain personal power and advantage.

—— —— b. gain high-status positions in the formal system.

—— —— c. increase the excellence of the contribution to the task.

—— —— d. draw attention to one's own personal needs.

12. Conflict is:

—— —— a. controlled by the intervention of higher authorities and often fostered by them to maintain their own power.

—— —— b. suppressed by reference to rules, procedures, and definitions of responsibility.

—— —— c. resolved through full discussion of the merits of the work issues involved.

—— —— d. resolved by open and deep discussion of personal needs and value involved.

13. Decisions are made by the:

—— —— a. person with the higher power and authority.

—— —— b. person whose job description carries the responsibility.

—— —— c. persons with the most knowledge and expertise about the problem.

—— —— d. persons most personally involved and affected by the outcome.

14. In an appropriate control and communication structure:

—— —— a. command flows from the top down in a simple pyramid so that anyone who is higher in the pyramid has authority over anyone who is lower. Information flows up through the chain of command.

—— —— b. directives flow from the top down and information flows upwards within functional pyramids which meet at the top. The authority and responsibility of a role is limited to the roles beneath it in its own pyramid. Cross-functional exchange is constricted.

—— —— c. information about task requirements and problems flows from the centre of task activity upwards and outwards, with those closest to the task determining the resources and support needed from the rest of the organisation. A co-ordinating function may set priorities and overall resource levels based on information from all task centres. The structure shifts with the nature and location of the tasks.

—— —— d. information and influence flow from person to person, based on voluntary relationships initiated for purposes of work, learning, mutual support and enjoyment, and shared values. A coordinating function may establish overall levels of contribution needed for the maintenance of the organisation. These tasks are assigned by mutual agreement.

15. The environment is responded to as though it were:

—— —— a. a competitive jungle in which everyone is against everyone else, and those who do not exploit others are themselves exploited.

—— —— b. an orderly and rational system in which competition is limited by law, and there can be negotiation or compromise to resolve conflicts.

—— —— c. a complex of imperfect forms and systems which are to be reshaped and improved by the achievements of the organisation.

—— —— d. a complex of potential threats and support. It is used and manipulated by the organisation both as a means of self-nourishment and as a play-and-work space for the enjoyment and growth of organisation members.

INDIVIDUAL AND GROUP PROFILES

Sums of Ranks

	a. Power Orientation	b. Role Orientation	c. Task Orientation	d. Self Orientation
Existing Organisation Ideology				
Participant's Preferred Organisation Ideology				

Tally of Lowest Scores of the Group Members

	a. Power Orientation	b. Role Orientation	c. Task Orientation	d. Self Orientation
Existing Organisation Ideology				
Participant's Preferred Organisation Ideology				

This instrument was developed by Roger Harrison, Vice-President for Overseas Operations, Development Research Associates, Homestead Farm, Mountain Bower, near Chippenham, Wiltshire, England, and 16 Ashton Avenue, Newton, Massachusetts 02159. The author would be interested in receiving normative data from readers.

---

*Fig. 6 Diagnosing organisation ideology (Source: **The 1975 Annual Handbook for Group Facilitators**)*

APPROPRIATE CULTURES

Handy's typologies of organisation structures suggest that we should try, whenever possible, to match the culture with the external demands and constraints on the organisation.

DIFFERENT OPERATING UNITS REQUIRE DIFFERENT CULTURES

One factor that must be borne in mind is that different operating units within the organisation require different structures. Some Units or Functions will be operating in a steady state environment, where there are very few changes and the future is reasonably predictable, whereas others are subject to a great deal of change not just in what they do – but how they do it. Consequently, it is desirable to have different approaches to managing and different 'cultures' in different units. The characteristics which determine the culture of departments and functions total four in number and are undernoted.

A **Crisis/Breakdown** environment refers to decisions which have to be made speedily and which impact upon the long-term effectiveness of the organisation. A culture to reflect the strategic side of things which requires constant change, direction and re-evaluation must be 'power orientated'.

A **Research and Development** environment is one currently requiring constant change. The process of creating innovation is also important. Experts have to be taken from key areas, and moulded together to reach a project objective. The Task culture is one geared for this activity.

The **Steady State** environment typifies the repetitive duties in which all organisations have to engage in order to remain efficient. This may include accounting procedures, selection, recruitment, salary and wage administration, inventory control, maintenance, etc. A culture based upon the predictability and procedural approach of the Role Culture would appear to meet the needs of the function.

The **Policy-making** environment refers to the creation of long term-plans for the company. If Policy-making is perceived as an interactive process – the Task Culture seems the most fitting. Secrecy and security may tend to make this culture prone to the Power orientation.

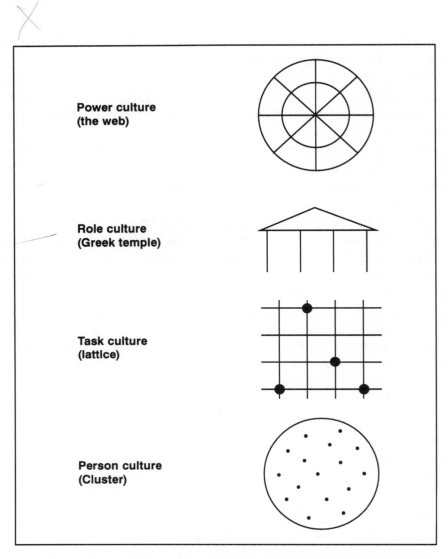

*Fig. 7 Handy's four organisational cultures (Source: **Understanding Organisations**, 1993)*

What Handy suggests is that different units which pursue different activities should adopt a culture which reflects their needs. For instance, book-keepers working in a Steady State climate, where the certainty of the work they do is predictable, will probably function best in a Role Culture. A Task Culture would be inappropriate, because the systems and procedures which exist are sufficient for the purpose.

A research unit will require to project a Task Culture, but would not work effectively with a Power, Role or Person Culture, and, likewise, policy-making in a Person Culture is time-consuming and divergent.

In other words, organisations should try to develop appropriate cultures for various aspects of the organisation.

In a large organisation, managing cultures is difficult, especially for those people who have to interact with other units having differing cultures. Imagine the likely problems of a QA Manager, from a Role Culture, trying to get the Chief Accountant from a Power Culture to discuss the implementation of TQ in a Task Culture manner! Clearly we need to think about what sort of culture we need to operate in and the predominant culture in other areas.

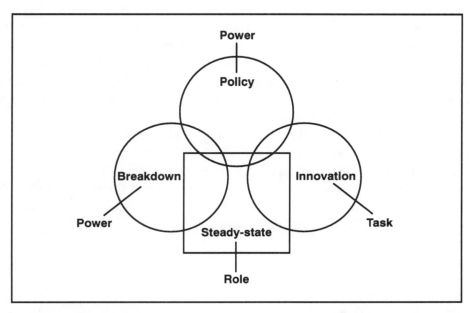

Fig. 8 Relationship between function and culture (Source: **Understanding Organisations**, *1993)*

LEARNING TO MANAGE HORIZONTALLY!

Managers must understand the 'culture' concept and how it impacts upon their performance. It is critical that we learn to cope with people from different cultures. (The management of differences is pursued in Chapter 11.)

We should be spending more time getting ourselves to understand different cultures. A Quality initiative may well work in a Steady State environment like 'financial management' but the same initiative could die in a marketing or sales unit where cultures change rapidly. We need to concentrate resources on managing across boundaries rather than top down through functions. The real waste is always identified between boundary personnel – the internal customer-supplier link. Pursue this approach and TQ can be implemented very quickly.

TRANSITION MANAGEMENT AND CULTURAL CHANGE

Knowing what Culture is desirable, engendering the key Values – reflected by consistent Managerial Behaviour – will not, unfortunately, create the TQ change you want. You have still to manage the transition from one state to the other. Change takes time and, as we saw in Chapter 4, can promote a great deal of resistance in people.

Understanding the changes which employees go through, their likely behaviours, their perceptions of situations and the support they need to manage and move on are complex.

Elizabeth Kubler Ross was interested in how people came to terms with change. Her research involved the investigation of the stages and behaviours displayed when coming to terms with terminal illness. Similarly, other researchers have spent time exploring how people come to terms with radical changes in their life, including divorce, alcoholism, bereavement, redundancy, etc. We have a great deal to learn from the research undertaken. Much of it is applicable to organisational change and, in particular, Total Quality.

Let us not minimise the effect of TQ on an organisational culture. It is a radical change strategy which is geared to changing the culture in the long term. The fact that TQ is 'people-driven' and requires a self-critical approach with particular relevance to management style suggests that there will be a great deal of resistance. Although Chapter 4 described the symptoms of resistance – it is necessary to examine the major stages which people go through when involved in significant organisational change.

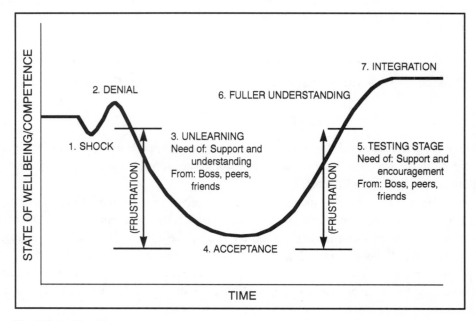

Fig. 9 Transition Curve

STEPS IN TRANSITION MANAGEMENT

It is important to examine the sequence of steps and the major stages in any transition. With reference to the Transition Curve, it is clear that over time most people can come to terms with change. Time and support seem to be the deciding factors. On the vertical axis of the Transition inset is 'Competence'. Let us call this the ability to master and manage the key activities of the job, coping with the unforeseen and managing people to get results.

Let's assume no change at all – or at least controllable change. Most people seem to prefer working in a stable environment. It is comfortable, most problems can be foreseen and stress can be controlled. However, introduce change and what happens?

With reference to the Transition Curve, Managers experience Shock [1]. There is a downturn in their competence and comments include:

"Why did the company decide to promote TQ now – we haven't even got over SPC yet?"

"If you ask me, it will never happen, we have taken on too much with new technology in the laboratory area – we'll never find time for it."

"For sure it will mean more work – I just hope we have the resource to do the job well."

Typical characteristics of shock reverberate throughout the structure. Thankfully, man is a logical creature and he progresses to the next stage, that of Denial [2]. You will note that competence, the ability to do the job and cope with ambiguity, increases, or so it appears. This false competence is fuelled by the belief that nothing is ever going to happen. People get together and reinforce this.

"TQ is too big – they would never introduce it into this company. Just to train the staff in this region would require at least thirty trainers. The company will never spend the money."

"Listen, TQ is just flavour of the month – just keep your head down, say the right things. . . and we'll be into a new fad by next year."

This stage of false competence, reflected in the Denial stage, does not last too long. When the messages of TQ cascade down the hierarchy, when Costs of Quality measures are identified and data collected, when training takes place and the senior officers go away to their workshops, there is a realisation that TQ is going to happen soon. And it will be involving everybody.

People experience Unlearning [3] . On the one hand they are coming to terms with the reality of change, they may be stressed. They certainly will be uncertain about the role they will play, how things will be in the future, how their job will change, what new skills they require, what predominant values will be displayed and so forth. They need to unlearn the old ways and move to the new. But this is not so easy. There is a genuine fear. Failing to communicate the intention and the practice of TQ to all will further reinforce the negativity of change.

At the same time uncertainty is the order of the day – there will be frustration doing things differently. Eventually, with support, help and realistic visions of the future, people go through the Acceptance stage [4]. They have now stopped going downhill and start going uphill. They are trying to learn the new ways. They have accepted that change has to take place but now they have different problems. They may not know how to change. Unless people have been shown "how things are going to be" – how can they practise these new behaviours? How do they get and interpret feedback?

It is all very well telling people that TQ is about getting things "right first time", but leaving them with a slogan, with a passion – but without a system and road maps – is sheer lunacy. Expecting that people can make their own way, learn all they need to, and practise behaviours is unrealistic. Here we can see that if Managers fail to plan, communicate, involve and listen to their people prior to the roll-out of TQ, then a management team can create real problems for itself. From 'Acceptance' [4] to the Testing Stage [5] is a natural progression. Organisations must provide the resources, the workshops, the training and counselling for staff who find it difficult to make the transition. Encouraging and adopting the right Leadership behaviour (see Chapter 6) is imperative to building a cohesive group of managers who are willing to tackle uncertainty. During the Testing stage, managers will make mistakes, but they should be encouraged to persist in their efforts. Behaviour will be similar on the shopfloor. The company which takes time out to brief all its managers, and ensures that this process is pursued 'throughout the structure' will benefit from real success. Companies who don't communicate will have a difficult time moving people along the transition curve. Eventually, through trial and error, support and Leadership – all staff should progress to Fuller Understanding [6] and Integration [7].

ADJUST YOUR MESSAGE – DEPENDING ON WHERE THEY ARE!

Knowing where people are on the Transition Curve is important. But that is not the end of the story. Different people at different levels will have a different perception of TQ. While the senior officers have progressed to the final stage, Integration, others will be well back at Shock [1], Denial [2] and Unlearning [3]. If the senior officers have little understanding of the dynamics of change, they will not realise the impact their public announcements and assertions will have on others. Working out where your audience is on the Transition Curve is critical before sending messages about how marvellous TQ really is. People will see and experience only fear, frustration and a request to look for new ways of working. To address this imbalance, your relative position on the Transition Curve must be appraised in comparison to others, ie. – those whom you manage. This concern for people and involvement is a reflection of the most caring behaviour exhibited by any senior team. This was demonstrated by many companies who took their TQ Drive seriously; including Corning Glass (Ciba Corning), Dow Chemical Co. and Borg Warner Chemicals (UK) among others.

Failing to take account of the Transition Curve, where your people are, how they feel, their perceptions of the senior teams' performance, backed up by incidents and behaviours to confirm this or reject this, are activities all companies should find time to pursue.

SUMMARY

Don't underestimate the power of the organisational culture. It can take you up and it can take you down. Managers have total control of what it says about your company. Ensure it says something that is strong and positive – not weak and flimsy. Too many managers fail to focus upon building a strong and sustainable culture. This chapter has highlighted what is important in creating the foundation for that culture. It has also highlighted diagnostic tools which can help you decide where you are along the change path. You have numerous different ways of evaluating the culture that you want and, if you refer to Chapter 4, you will be able to examine the behavioural issues as well. Finally, we spent some time looking at the changing which people experience when moving through change. We have to understand where they are in order to make sense of their behaviour and their responses. It is important to look at the process of change and ask yourself what you can do to shape the corporate culture to make it vibrant, positive and customer- and team-focused.

Bullet Points

- A Culture is the set of values, behaviours and norms which tell people what to do, how to do it, and what is acceptable and unacceptable.

- Artefacts, signs and symbols are the overt displays of culture. They can be conveyed consciously or unconsciously – but they are still received and understood by everybody.

- Change things first which underpin a negative view of the organisation. These can be quite small – but their existence may say a great deal about your priorities.

- You can never create TQ in an organisational culture which is negative and punitive.

- Choose your culture and create it through example.

- The wrong culture creates people who are switched off, demotivated and who want to get even – can you blame them?

- Make your culture People-Orientated. Recognise that developing a culture in which people can thrive and grow is the route to Quality Improvement.

- Flexibility, creativity and continuous improvement come from a culture where people are treated as being more important than capital and technology.

CHAPTER 6

Leadership for Beyond the Next Century

"Ninety per cent of Culture Change initiatives in the UK will fail because they do not have the backing of the senior management team. The senior team in many cases does not realise that it has to change the way it manages, including its style. Many think that public exhortation of the TQ philosophy is their only responsibility to staff. They confuse words with action. When TQ dies because of their failure to lead by example, they move on to the next 'managerial gimmick' hoping that it will give them the success they crave but for which they have failed to work."

EXCELLENCE: LEADING THROUGH VALUES

We have just completed a series of advanced five-day programmes on Leadership for a major US-owned financial business. This company continues to win business from rivals in the UK. This is because of the quality of the staff and the Leaders they create. It is anticipated that business will double by the year 2000. More than 130 managers, who lead 2,000 staff, have been through this intensive and demanding programme. It incorporates advanced Leadership techniques, creating and implementing positive Team Values, mastering Culture Change and assessing personal impact using an advanced 360 degree appraisal tool. Prior to attending the programme they were briefed and came prepared to improve performance. During the Workshop they revisited the company to conduct Focus Groups so they could take action to improve the culture. They had feedback on their Psychometric profiles and they worked cross-functionally on major projects to significantly improve the culture of their business. All groups fed back their proposals to their Directors who gave their unreserved support to take ownership for continuous improvement.

QUESTIONS

How would you rate the Leadership training provided by the average company in comparison to this case above?

How would you rate their ability to master and implement change in comparison to their competitors in Europe?

Leadership and Commitment is the foundation of an effective TQ initiative. Without it, even the most carefully designed programme will never work. In some situations, Management Teams fail to understand the level of commitment required to make TQ a living, breathing, reality.

This is understandable, especially when a Management group is exposed to TQ for the first time. Many can get swept along on the wave of enthusiasm and forget about the hard work required over a fairly lengthy period of time. The ideas and methodology of TQ are simple to understand and assumptions are made about the ease with which these ideas can be put into practice. 'In all honesty, if TQ was that simple, many companies would have done it years ago.'

LEADERSHIP AND COMMITMENT

Leadership and commitment go hand-in-hand. Leadership is the key issue in promoting commitment, a fact recognised by a major American-owned chemical company. When I was introduced to the UK Management Team, I found that they wanted to follow the example of their parent company and pursue Total Quality from the same perspective. Their initiative, developed in the States some years ago, was referred to as TQL or Total Quality Leadership.

The Team met for a two-day workshop. Some had already been exposed to the TQ concept, but the Operations Director was keen to ensure that everybody was on the same part of the learning curve. The timetable is undernoted to illustrate the importance of the issues which were debated.

TOTAL QUALITY LEADERSHIP WORKSHOP

Day 1

0900	Introduction and Objectives
0910	The Drive for Total Quality
0930	Costing Quality Workshop
1100	Cultural Preconditions for Total Quality
1300	Lunch
1400	Four Principles of Total Quality
1410	Case Study: Meeting Customer Requirements
	Appraising the Internal Customer
1515	Case Study
1600	Leadership Style and Psychometrics
1800	Workshop closes

Day 2

0900	Case Study: Effective Implementation
	Creating Total Quality Leadership and Managing
	Resistance to Change
1100	Assessing Readiness for Total Quality. Appraising
	Organisation Culture
1300	Lunch
1400	Action Planning: Implementing Total Quality
1800	Workshop Closes

In the two-day session the Management Team wanted to explore the key issues. In particular they wanted to examine: Preconditions for TQ; Creating TQ Leadership Behaviour; Managing Resistance to Change; Assessing the Readiness for TQ through appraising Organisational Values and Culture; and Action Planning.

PRECONDITIONS FOR TQ

Few companies consider the preplanning stage and fail to grasp that TQ is a Strategic issue. TQ must be the central strategic theme for the company for the years ahead. Customer Care, Just in Time, SPC are all sub-sets of the TQ process. We can introduce these aspects of corporate Quality separately, but they will not work as well as if they had been introduced as part of a TQ-managed strategy led by a strong group of Senior Managers.

Customer care will not work without a TQ organisation. SPC, especially in service areas, will not work if the company fails to take the right corrective action.

CASE STUDY: The Death of SPC

A small engineering company had introduced SPC. Some areas were implementing the recording process through charting. The QA manager demonstrated the commitment to SPC by careful recording, although there appeared to be little corrective action taken. SPC died in three months. The reason: the operatives could not see the point of filling in charts when no corrective or preventative action was being taken. The organisation's culture was not committed to prevention and, therefore, it stood little chance of creating effective change.

CASE STUDY: Getting to Know You

When working with a Management Team on a Leadership initiative we agreed to set an action plan for change. The Management Team recognised that they had neglected Supervisory Team-Building over the years.

The Managers would keep an up-to-date diary of their progress with supervisors. We wanted to appraise progress. Their task was simply to programme into their diary each day for a month, the names of any two out of twenty supervisors. Their specific role was to talk with each supervisor for ten minutes per day, a total of twenty minutes. The purpose of the discussion was *not* to be related to day-to-day work, but to highlight areas for long-term company improvement.

The results were poor. Most managers started off with good intentions, but as the weeks went by the commitment to the task died. The reason given and agreed by the team was 'lack of time and firefighting'. Overall, the Team was composed of a good group of managers but their failure to work through a simple 'management by numbers' exercise demonstrates the difficulty in trying to make a larger change initiative work.

Likewise, companies interested and apparently committed to driving TQ through their organisation admit to having difficulty with other change initiatives. . . although in reality they continue to do so.

Examples include flexibility training and briefing groups. The responses:

"Well of course TQ is different, all our managers are committed. . . although briefing did not work. . . the staff wanted that to fail."

Shopfloor supervisors tell a different story:

"Briefing was never given a chance. . . it all started off well, but after two months the briefing notes were just pinned to notice boards without comment or feedback, and no one really wanted to hear what we had to say."

The major point which comes from this discussion is if we can't introduce a briefing system based upon the simple elements of communication, how are we going to introduce TQ, which is concerned with major changes in culture and management style?

There are other issues which need to be considered including: Organisational Structure and Redesign, Communication effectiveness, TQ and Strategic Planning, etc.

"The route is simple. Don't run before you can walk. TQ is far more complex than some other change strategies and requires a great deal of commitment and planning."

CREATING TQ LEADERSHIP BEHAVIOUR

"Leaders are born not made" is a statement which has little credibility with most managers. Provided strengths and weaknesses are assessed objectively and managers are given the opportunity to develop, most will learn and acquire these skills.

There is a general assumption in the UK that if you can do your job well enough, you will eventually gain promotion to a managerial position. Some promotions to these dizzy heights can create problems for those who are ill-prepared. We all know of engineers or technicians, who were 110% effective at their technical specialism, but, when promoted out of their sphere of competence, made lousy managers. There has to be recognition that there is a serious problem, and managers have to be trained to manage and lead.

TQ CANNOT ADDRESS THE NEGLECT OF YEARS

Some time ago I was working with an organisation who finally committed to put all their managerial group through a strongly structure-led approach to Total Quality programme staged over a two-day period. The focus of the programme was on examining the core elements for change and the key quality tools which could be used in problem-solving. The programme was extremely successful and managers left the Workshop with a new vitality and some very useful approaches to introducing TQ. The good news filtered through to the Directors and they decided to examine how we could extend such training throughout the whole company. All the Directors, except one, were in support of the programme and his one objection boiled down to the fact that "TQ training was thorough and effective, yet managers and supervisors attending the workshops still could not lead, manage a team, communicate with feeling or motivate a work group"!

We were quick to point out that the two-day programme focused upon techniques for TQ implementation and that just two days' exposure to quite a varied programme could not make up for years of neglecting to provide managers and supervisors with the basic skills just to do their job.

Clearly, anyone thinking that two days' exposure to a concept without equipping managers with core skills is sufficient, needs to rethink his training objectives, outcomes and strategy. For organisations who have failed to invest in rigorous Leadership training it is best for the company to forget about TQ for a while, and invest in Leadership Drive – pursuing TQ when the correct Leadership behaviour is in place. Sending unfocused lost souls along to TQ Workshops with a wide remit of returning well equipped to deal with Culture Change, Quality Tools, Personal Development and Team Skills plus the ability to juggle is expecting too much of even the most talented consultant. Managers put under pressure to somehow acquire these skills without proper guidance and development will only increase their tension and anxiety when trying to learn and will create ambiguity in the minds of others about what TQ is all about. Is TQ about learning everything about management and leadership and change? Who knows? But many companies believe these skills and others can be acquired in a blink of the eye.

CASE STUDY: Afraid to Attend Workshops!

Some time ago supervisory maintenance staff from an engineering company attended a TQ seminar. Some of the staff were fairly anxious – thinking they must have done something wrong to be on a training programme. They soon settled down when they realised that effective change and learning cannot take place in a climate of fear. However, one chap remained nervous throughout the session and took me on one side when I gave out case studies for analysis. He told me he had great difficulty in reading and would not be able to contribute to proceedings. This chap had been employed for fifteen years in a supervisory position and he couldn't read! His managers did not know of his problem. What surprised me was how he could understand the instructions for stripping down equipment when he couldn't read. More importantly, how did he manage to conceal this fact from his colleagues and boss? Perhaps a more pertinent question is. . . how was it that his direct manager had no knowledge of his condition?

If we are not aware of the learning deficiencies of our staff, how are we going to develop them to pursue a genuine competitive edge to our business?

WHAT IS LEADERSHIP?

I don't think anyone can disagree that Leadership in any TQ initiative is imperative. But what do we understand by Leadership and does Leadership mean the same thing to different people? Bennis in his book *Leaders: The Strategies for Taking Charge* claims that "academic analyses have given us over 350 definitions of Leadership. Literally thousands of investigations over the last 75 years. . . have not created a clear understanding of. . . what distinguishes. . . effective leaders from ineffective ones. . . ".

Much has been written on Leadership and Management Style. We can study the early works of McGregor, Blake and Mouton, Reddin, Adair, Likert, and many others to examine their thoughts and theories. We could literally write a very large book just on Leadership alone.

As an example, McGregor suggested that the beliefs and attitudes we hold about workers will create a dominant Leadership style. Simply explained, two extreme models of Leadership Style were developed which McGregor named Theory X and Theory Y. For instance, the X manager was far more directive, had little trust in people, believed that strict control systems needed to be in force in order to achieve results. Correspondingly, the Y model was based more upon a democratic and participative approach – believing that people sought recognition and responsibility in their work

---

Assumptions about human nature which underpin McGregor's Theory X

1. Work is inherently distasteful to most people.
2. Most people have little interest in work, are not ambitious, have little desire for responsibility and prefer to be directed.
3. Most people have to be coerced, rewarded or punished to gain their commitment to organisational goals.
4. Most people have little interest in, or capability for, contributing towards the solution of organisational problems.
5. People are motivated only by reward or punishment.
6. Most people require constant control and are often threatened with sanctions to achieve organisational objectives.

Assumptions about human nature which underpin McGregor's Theory Y

1. Work is pleasant and is as natural as play, if the conditions are favourable.
2. Workers have discipline and self-control to achieve organisational objectives.
3. Workers are motivated by things other than rewards (money) and punishment (sanctions).
4. The capability for contributing towards solving organisational problems is widely spread throughout the workforce.
5. People are motivated by things other than money. Motivation is a psychological process and involves recognition, esteem, social worth and group belongings etc.
6. It is natural for people to be self-directed and creative at work, if the conditions allow.

Source: McGregor's Theory X/Theory Y Model

The Theory Y or human relations approach has gathered ground since then and Blake and Mouton and others have developed their own variant based upon the premise that people are important and we need to utilise their talents in order to achieve results.

COMMITMENT: DISTURBING RESEARCH EVIDENCE

There can be no doubt that people are our most valuable resource and managing them by utilising a style to involve them is critical – especially in a TQ Drive. Bennis quotes important research findings which should give us all cause for concern – especially for the way we manage people. Research was carried out in the US with non-managerial workers.

It was claimed that;

- Fewer than 25% of all job holders said they were currently working at full capacity.

- 50% said they do not put effort into their job over and above that which was required to keep it.

- 75% said they could be significantly more effective than they presently are.

- 60% believed that they did not work as hard as they used to.

There is no reason to doubt the authenticity of the research. There is no reason to doubt that similar results are in evidence in Europe. And there is no reason to doubt that this is characteristic of some managerial staff within your business. What this tells us is that if we are being serious about TQ we have to really learn to manage people. What is most important is that TQ requires an additional contribution from Leadership within the structure. TQ creates a climate of 'improvement', but this has to be driven by a special breed of staff who understand how to motivate, get the most out of and develop people. This is called Leadership.

Commenting on the data above, it is of interest to ask:

- Why do people feel as they do?

- Why are people alienated from work?

- How do we cause them to take a fresh direction?

- What action can we take to motivate them?

These are all Leadership secrets which are known and understood – but not practised in many companies. There are too many instances when a failure to lead is an everyday occurrence in too many organisations.

Later we will be looking at the recent important contribution to 'Leadership and Management Style' made by Kouzes and Posner. But just now it is important to examine what Leadership is really about.

We take the term 'Leadership' very much on face value and if we asked a group of people to define it, we would probably generate a long list of desirable characteristics. Let's have a look at what the credible researchers say about Leadership, examine their viewpoints and consider how we can generate real Leadership behaviour in our organisation in the 21st Century. Having a passion for TQ is no longer sufficient. We need to inculcate, at every level of management and supervision, a real desire to 'lead by example'.

LEADERS AND MANAGERS: WHAT IS THE DIFFERENCE?

Warren Bennis and Burt Namus in their book *Leaders: The Strategies for Taking Charge* suggest that empowerment – the ability to generate enthusiasm, vision and communicate this to our people – is critical in any Leadership role. They start to draw the distinction between managing and leading. "Managers do things right. Leaders do the right thing."

This is an important distinction between Managers and Leaders. But they were not the first in the field with this view. Wortman's research distinguishes between Operating and Strategic Managers. His argument is that senior managers should think strategically in the long term whereas in reality managers are those who make things happen on a day-to-day basis. There may appear to be too many 'Operators' and too few 'Strategists'.

He suggests that too many managers are too concerned with day-to-day matters, something which concerns much of Goldratt's writing in *The Goal*. Managers are too concerned with achieving short-term goals, ie. maintaining productivity at any cost, keeping inventory at too high a level, reducing costs and agreeing short-term decisions which are working against the long-term mission of the organisation, etc. This short-sightedness can create major problems when we consider the difficulty of creating a TQ culture which challenges and rejects the short-term approach.

LEADERS SHOULD BE CHARISMATIC

Wortman contends that Leaders should be charismatic, flexible and inspiring – especially with regard to those they manage. Leaders must be able to inspire others to create and manage change, to take responsibility and, above all, to take risks. Moreover, this charismatic stance is not like a bolt from the blue, a magical process, it can only be achieved through people. Involving, participating and actively listening to others is the only way we can create genuine improvement in everything we do. He further contends that there is a fundamental difference in personal characteristics between the 'operator' and the 'strategist'.

Zalenznik, a researcher with similar views, argues that leaders and managers differ in many different ways and he draws this out looking at four dimensions: attitudes towards goals, conceptions of work, building relationships with others and the sense of self.

Managers enjoy working and relating with people, achieve much of their esteem and recognition from such activities and work to maintain control, whereas Leaders are visionary in outlook, risk-lovers and independent.

TRANSFORMERS AND TRANSACTORS

This important dichotomy is reinforced by Burns, except he calls Leaders 'Transformational' and Managers 'Transactional'.

Transformational Leaders are independent, visionary and inspirational, driven by long-term goals, visions and objectives. They provide a mission for others to follow. They expect the same high standards from their people. They are real change-makers!

They have a clear view of what they want to achieve and are less concerned with the detail than getting what they want. They are interested in 'ends rather than means'.

Transactional Managers, on the other hand, are especially good at achieving short-term results, foster teamwork and work in a practical manner.

Clearly, Transformational Leaders and Transactional Managers need to work together. Teamwork is imperative, but what is of concern is an organisation which fosters the growth of one type to the exclusion of the other.

Leadership characteristics	
Transformers	**Transactors**
• Visionary, inspirational	• People and task centred
• Forward planning	• Short-term orientation
• Intuitive and creative	• Practical, concrete, tangible
• Active	• Passive
• Change orientation	• Maintain stability
• Challenging	• Clarifying

Whether an organisation is peopled by Leaders or Managers will determine its success in implementing a major cultural change. Transformational Leaders are especially good at creating new initiatives, stimulating action and loyalty and getting all to row in the same direction.

Transactional Managers are better at administering a system and making sure things happen on a day-to-day basis.

Leaders and Managers develop different approaches to getting results. They both make things happen by managing others. They adopt different approaches, but ostensibly focus upon the same five areas: giving direction, motivating, rewarding and recognising success, developing and meeting the needs of their people.

The important point to make is whether Leaders or Managers, what they do with their people will determine the success they achieve.

DEVELOPING BALANCE BETWEEN TRANSFORMERS AND TRANSACTORS

Whatever the behaviour of these Leaders or Managers, the outcome can be the same. But a structured integrated outcome can only come from those in positions of power assimilating the talents of both sets of Managers and Leaders. For success in TQ both sets of individuals are important. Bearing this in mind, how much time do senior officers in corporations give to exploring the desirable Leadership or Management Style which they want their people to project?

LEARNING BY COPYING THE BEHAVIOUR OF OTHERS

In many cases, senior staff should consider developing a Leadership programme prior to embarking upon TQ. In some cases, people rising through the organisation adopt a style which is modelled wholly on the style of their manager. This stereotype is the only example upon which to model behaviour. If a key senior manager has risen to high rank using one style exclusively, very few middle or junior managers will adopt a style which is at variance with this, recognising that certain styles are associated with success.

PASSION AND SYSTEMS

The conclusions we can generate from such important research has much relevance to Leading a TQ initiative. To paraphrase Tom Peters, there is a problem with 'passion and systems'. An organisation composed almost completely of Transformational Leaders may incite the 'passion without the system', and organisations peopled by Transactional Managers will develop the 'system without the passion'.

But where does this leave us? What type of management style or leadership style do we encourage? In all honesty, there are too many organisations which adopt the Transactional Manager Model. People are rewarded for achieving short-term perspectives, progression to senior levels is determined by managers who 'do things' rather than those with vision. In too many cases, rewards and recognition are bestowed on those who get the results we need today – not those who create opportunities for tomorrow.

Many organisations are now considering and applying Human Resource Policies to inculcate the vision and creativity of their staff and the organisation, but these are too few and far between. We need senior people to create change and demonstrate the examples which others follow. But at the same time we need people to follow through. Overall, we seem to have plenty of the latter but none of the former.

CASE STUDY: Why Bother Creating Change!

A large public sector organisation decided that it would take its high-flying graduates on a Workshop to encourage innovation. Much of the training was of the outward bound variety. Focus was on Leadership and Team-building rather than the traditional Administrative focus. At the end of the two-week session participants were asked to generate a Personal Action Plan for change. They were asked to 'bash the bureaucracy, change things and make them happen' – even if it did create chaos. They were told they had to be revolutionary, challenge the obvious, take action, and report back in three months' time.

One young man, Martin, went back to his job with lots of ideas, and one day during the coffee break he looked down from his eighth floor office on to the car park, which was next to a railway station.

He noticed over a period of a week that there were always at least ten car parking spaces free. He went to his Area Manager and told him of his idea. Because of the location of the building, in a busy city centre, he knew he would be able to rent the excess spaces to nearby offices. He was certain he could charge a fee of at least £500 per year per space. His idea was rejected.

Martin was not one to give in so easily – so he went to see his Divisional Manager – who again rejected the idea without thought or discussion. Martin – still enthusiastic and knowing he had to report back having put his action plan into action – decided to rent out the parking spaces, anyway. He approached a group of accountants adjacent to his place of work who accepted the offer and forwarded a cheque for £8,000. Martin promptly set off for the Accounts Department and found to his horror that there was no mechanism for paying in the money or for paying in any such revenue!

Martin had not realised the organisational turmoil he would create. He left within four months to go to a lively US company where people who challenged the obvious were encouraged and rewarded.

The moral of this tale is that there is little point developing the entrepreneurial vigour of staff if there is no concession to making good ideas work. Martin wanted to create change and build upon the foundations of the old culture. The old culture rejected his idea – and this was reinforced by the attitude and management style of the organisation.

Clearly, this organisation fulfilled its own wishes, as it is now peopled totally by Managers to the exclusion of Leaders.

George Bernard Shaw summed up the situation between the 'reasonable and unreasonable men' thus:

> *"The reasonable man adapts himself to the world: the unreasonable one persists in trying to adapt the world to himself. Therefore all progress depends upon the reasonable man."*

ACHIEVING RESULTS THROUGH OTHERS

Leaders and Managers have one thing in common, they achieve results through others. Kouzes and Posner have developed some original research work which has direct relevance to getting the most from and with people. Bearing in mind Quality improvement, flexibility and involvement come from our people, then it's wise to start comparing our performance against 'what we could do'.

Kouzes and Posner were interested in studying the behaviour of the manager who achieved something quite extraordinary. They studied a large number of 'high achievers' and found that the stories of success which were told were seldom those found in textbooks. The research revealed a pattern of events leading to incredible success. What were the conclusions? They were that 80% of the time managers engaged in activities which fall under five headings. The incredible reality is that these factors are what differentiate the high-flyer from the also-ran! All these activities are to do with 'doing things with people'.

CHALLENGING THE PROCESS

Leaders are pioneers – people who seek out new opportunities and are willing to change the status quo. They recognise that failing to change creates mediocrity. They innovate, experiment and explore ways to improve the organisation. Most importantly, they realise that not all good ideas come from themselves. They realise that others 'close to a problem' are probably more able to come up with a sensible solution. They recognise that listening is probably more important than talking. Leaders are also prepared to meet whatever challenges may confront them. This involves looking for new ways of doing things and experimenting and taking risks.

Leaders also recognise the way they manage people is a testing and training ground for potential Leaders. Risk-taking is encouraged. Mistakes are assessed as formalised 'learning experiences'.

INSPIRING A SHARED VISION

Leaders look toward and beyond the horizon. They look to the future with a dream of what might be. They envision the future with a positive and hopeful outlook. They believe that if people work together – they can achieve the impossible. Leaders are expressive and attract followers through their genuineness and skilful communications. They do not deceive. They show others how common interests can be met through commitment to the overall goal. Leaders who project this approach look at the future, share and discuss it with their people and work towards their dream.

ENABLING OTHERS TO ACT

Leaders know they are rewarded for getting others to achieve their results. They know they cannot do it alone, they need to generate enthusiasm and commitment in others, to be persuasive, to develop relationships based upon mutual trust. They get people to work together – towards collaborative goals. They stress participation in decision-making and problem-solving. They actively involve others in planning, giving them discretion to make their own decisions – even if this means they make mistakes. Risk-taking is encouraged. Leaders ensure that people feel strong and able to do a job. This behaviour involves getting others to work with them and giving discretion to others.

Leaders 'empower' others to become Leaders in their own way – not just to do as they are told. This requires an ability to manage ambiguity and take responsibility for others.

MODELLING THE WAY

Leaders are clear about their business values and beliefs. They have standards which are understood by all. They stand up for what they believe in. They communicate this to their people. They keep people and projects on course by behaving consistently with these values and modelling how they expect others to act. Words and deeds are consistent.

They make us believe that the impossible is within reach. Leaders also plan and break projects down into achievable steps, creating opportunities for small wins. They make it easier for others to achieve goals by focusing on these steps and identifying key priorities. This means they describe and 'model' how things should be. This often means setting examples and behaving in ways which reflect their values and beliefs.

ENCOURAGING THE HEART

Leaders encourage people to achieve difficult targets. They persist in their efforts by relating recognition with achievements. They visibly recognise contributions to the overall purpose and give frequent feedback. They let others know that their efforts are appreciated. They communicate the success of the team and celebrate small wins. Leaders nurture a team philosophy and go out of their way to say thank you for a job well done.

They manage to sustain efforts and encourage others to put even more effort into what they do.

Overall, these five basic behaviours differentiate an effective leader from his poorly performing counterpart.

Having a model to work with is extremely useful – but real progress with a Management Team comes from comparing performance with the Model. An exercise based upon this model is an extremely useful way of comparing performance, and to make it doubly powerful it is possible to introduce the perception of others with regard to leadership behaviour.

CASE STUDY: Learning To Lead

A Senior Management Team agreed to undergo assessment of the 'Leadership style' utilising a learning instrument based upon Kouzes and Posner's original work. All eleven managers completed a questionnaire based upon self-perception of the five key areas. Also six managers, working for each of the Senior Staff, completed a similar questionnaire – this time based upon their perception of their managers' capability in these five areas. The results were averaged and fed back. We found in 30% of cases there was an agreement with style, but in 70% of instances we found there was fundamental disagreement and this was narrowed down to two areas, 'Enabling Others to Act' and 'Encouraging the Heart'. The shock of examining the impact of Leadership behaviour from the subordinates' viewpoint was critical. All the Management Team went away with specific things to do to project the image of the effective Leadership Style.

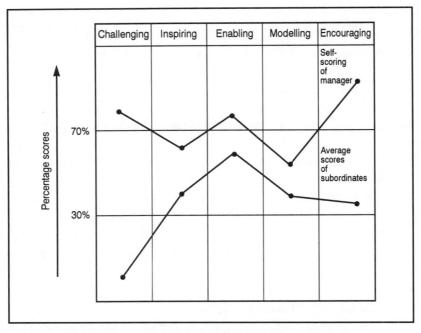

*Fig. 10 Learning to lead (Source: **The Leadership Challenge**, 1987)*

TEN COMMITMENTS OF LEADERSHIP

1. Search for challenging opportunities to change, grow, innovate and improve.

2. Experiment, take risks and learn from both successes and failures.

3. Envision an uplifting and ennobling future.

4. Enlist others in a common vision by appealing to their values, interests, hopes and dreams.

5. Foster collaboration by promoting co-operative goals and building trust.

6. Strengthen others by sharing information and power and increasing their discretion and visibility.

7. Set an example for others by behaving in ways that are consistent with your stated values.

8. Plan small wins that promote consistent progress and build commitment.

9. Recognise individual contributions to the success of every project.

10. Celebrate team accomplishments regularly.

---

*Extracted from Kouzes and Posner's **The Leadership Challenge**, Jossey Bass 1988.*

For a TQ initiative to work it has to be led from the top. The greater the commitment from Leaders, the stronger the vision projected and reinforced through behaviour, actions and deeds, the faster TQ will become the dominant culture.

PSYCHOMETRIC TESTS AND TQ MANAGEMENT STYLE

The Leadership issue is critical to a successful TQ Drive and for this reason some pioneering companies have been adopting a number of approaches to assessing Leadership among their staff. The Management Team and Middle Managers of a client company went through a series of Psychometric Tests (Myers Briggs, 16 PF, OPQ Concept 3, 5, and 4.2, 5.2, as well as Firo B), the purpose of which was to address managerial style inadequacies and deal with them positively.

The Managers were keen to get involved. They drove the initiative and most benefited from the experience. We were also able to assess resistance to change in some areas. We were thus able to take preventative action, ensure that new ideas were fully discussed with individuals who were more resistant, and ensure that plans were monitored. This was also an important Management Development activity for the staff involved. The Management Team benefited from the experience, in particular with reference to their Leadership behaviour, how they work in teams (Quality Improvement Teams, Corrective Action Teams), how they interact with others, motivate, organise and coach.

This is a similar approach used with a major finance house currently pursuing TQ through cultural change. The ten senior staff of this £1 billion company have been through the process of self-development through psychometrics. They have taken this opportunity to assess current style and to develop one more in keeping with the needs of the future. The principal reason for this initiative is that 65 managers under their control also need to think through a change in style in keeping with a 'team-driven' environment and this, in turn, will impact upon their teams. This company recognises that no one down the line will change unless he sees his superiors leading by example.

What is important in today's organisations is that managers can manage and lead. There appears even today to be plenty of managing but not much LEADING. Assessing personal strengths and weaknesses is critical in order to bring around change quickly.

"In simple terms, Organisations get the people and Leaders they deserve. If they fail to invest in developing a coherent managerial style, understood by all, with rewards commensurate with actions, they cannot create a meaningful transition to TQ."

FAILURE TO LEAD CREATES RESISTANCE TO CHANGE

Never minimise the resistance factor in organisational change. People at all levels can find ten good reasons for making TQ fail, but not find one to make it work. This state of mind exists because these individuals probably report to a manager lacking in Leadership skills and failing to inspire vision.

With such a poor role model, it is not surprising that some people crave stability and security. Once they have learnt a job they don't want to have to relearn new things and do things differently. If they are managed poorly, they will never move beyond their comfort zone.

Increasingly nowadays, people are realising the need to improve and change just to maintain present performance levels. Going back in time, Alvin Toffler in *Future Shock*, and Charles Handy in *The Age of Unreason*, reflect the same message as Tom Peters in *Thriving on Chaos*, that things are changing so rapidly only the more successful companies which are peopled by visionary Leaders are those which will continue to master their environment, grow and prosper. Clearly, there is a problem for the organisation peopled with deadwood – who fail to master the process of Leadership and to thus achieve their results through others.

Installing TQ is relatively easy if you have the right people to lead the process. Organisations need to address the factors which lead to resistance and these are all governed by the quality of Leadership we employ. Conquer these and a TQ culture will exist.

"Managers who adopt a 'corporate change drive' through Leadership behaviour will succeed while others are still listing reasons why they cannot change! Where there is ambiguity in the preferred Management Style there is uncertainty in the minds of those Leading us into the future."

LEADERSHIP AND ACTION PLANNING

This is the key. If the Management Team fails to come up with a structured approach to TQ, it is unlikely that it will work.

I am not suggesting that the Team, without support and a framework, can generate its own TQ plan. It needs to be supported and guided through the key stages and sequence of activities which lead to the creation of a TQ culture.

As consultants we develop a critical path outlining the approach a company can take. During the diagnostic phase, the Senior Team and ourselves work closely together assessing progress. The areas which need clarification include:

- What aspects of the culture will cause Leadership to progress quickly with the business?

- What action must we take now to develop a positive role model of Leadership to which others can aspire?

- What is inherent in the culture which will hinder us in the process and how can we remove this quickly?

- What action can we take to ensure that the culture will quickly highlight the more tangible aspects of Total Quality?

- Choosing and recording Cost of Quality indicators.

- Agreeing tangible milestones to assess progress.

- Ensuring that all TQ objectives are achievable, measurable and compatible with company objectives.

- Deciding upon the structure and commitment of action planning within the structure of supervision and management.

There is a great danger at this level that the Directors or Senior Managers running the TQ Drive can 'pass the parcel' to others lower down the hierarchy. Being committed to doing as well as talking is paramount. If there is a failure to reflect words with actions, others will feel, see and witness the failure to be committed.

If the Senior Team feels it doesn't have the time or resources to devote to this stage and passes it down to other levels it is in effect saying "TQ is not my responsibility".

If the Senior Team really is committed, demonstrate this by doing what it tells others to do.

WHAT IS COMMITMENT?

Commitment is an essential element of a TQ Drive. Commitment must exist at every level. It is a duty, an obligation, a responsibility to make TQ work. It is adherence to plans, principles and procedures. Beyond all these things it is a 'personal statement', a guarantee, a pledge, a promise, and an undertaking not just to talk about, but to promote TQ and act in a TQ manner at all times.

Commitment is:
'Doing what you say you will do.'
'Ensuring that your behaviour and actions mirror your statements on TQ.'
'Ensuring that others are involved in the process.'
'Ensuring that staff are *sold* rather than *told* to get involved in TQ.'
'Ensuring that TQ is not flavour of the month, but a commitment to get things right first time – always.'
'Leading by example.'

Not being committed is reflected in:
'Talking not doing.'
'Finding ten excuses not to do something.'
'Being cynical.'
'Failing to seek involvement and rejecting personal responsibility.'
'Blaming others.'
'Assuming that others should do it first.'
'Thinking that TQ affects others but not yourself.'
'Failing to live up to promises or agreements.'
'Doing nothing but that for which you are paid.'
'Failing to be self-critical.'

SUMMARY

The major thrust of any TQ initiative lies fairly and squarely with the Management Team. If it succeeds, it does so by the Team's efforts. If it fails, it does so because the Team has allowed it to fail. Leadership in any company is critical to success. But more than this, Leaders should be critical of their own performance. They should look for feedback and take action to make things happen. They should not expect TQ to materialise out of thin air, be created by a magical process or be the responsibility of somebody else down the line. Leadership will determine whether the drive for TQ is successful or not. Remember you just cannot have too much Leadership in your company, for without Leadership there is no change!

Bullet Points

- Eighty per cent of TQ initiatives will fail because of a lack of commitment to lead by example. Ensure that your company is in the 20% of success by developing strong Leadership.

- Leadership and Commitment are inseparable. If there is are major doubt about Leadership, if commitment is failing, then stop TQ – you can't do TQ twice. No one believes you the second time.

- TQ is about creating cultural change – which means changing everything we do. This also means changing how people manage.

- 'Leaders are made not born.' Companies create the Leaders they deserve. If little attention has been spent on developing a consistent style – take two steps back, correct it before you get involved in TQ.

- No amount of TQ training will undo the years of neglect and failing to train managers in the basics and how to manage.

- Leadership is about people. Leaders create a devotion for and from their team. Leadership based upon the hard 'bottom line results' model has its limitations – as does shouting at people. People are sophisticated – they need to be motivated and feel involved as part of a team.

- Research suggests that people are unprepared to put as much into their job as they used to. Let's change this. People are unprepared to put effort into the job if the conditions are not favourable. To create favourable conditions we need Leaders who care, whose deeds and actions reflect their values and who are prepared to get into the heart of people management and produce the conditions and empower people to create change.

- Leaders should be charismatic. They should be liked. Although being liked is not a condition of Leadership – if you are, you have more power.

- Leaders should inspire others to manage change, confront the impossible and think the unthinkable.

- We should train our Leaders to cope with ambiguity, stress and change.

- Encourage Transformers. Organisations without Leaders who challenge the way they do things don't learn or grow. We need unreasonable men, innovators and mavericks to create the quantum leap to TQ.

- Ensure that the balance is right between Transformers and Transactors.

- There is no recorded research indicating that too many Transformers lead a company to failure. There is a plethora of research which tells us that unimaginative, safe, risk-averse Management Teams kill initiative, chase off their best managers.

- Enjoy creating Transformers. Challenge the way things are done. Success comes from challenging the old and producing something new.

- Clarify what is desirable management and leadership style now. Imagine a bright young graduate asked you: "What do you need to do get on in this company?" Make sure you have the 'role model' in mind.

- If you don't have a Role Model of the desirable Leader for your company – how do you create the vision in others to progress and achieve?

- You need passion for change and systems to make things happen. On the whole, we have enough Systems – or at least they are easy to create – we need Passion for change and improvement and this is only evident through Leadership.

- Develop Human Resource Policies to create real Leaders. Make sure Policy is seen in practice.

- Lead and achieve through your most important resource – your people.

- Challenge the way things are done and seek continuous improvement in everything, at every level and across functions in your organisation.

- Inspire others and create a vision which is tangible and achievable for those who rely on you to make the future a reality.

- Enable others to do what you want. Give them resources, time and support.

- Model the way you want others to behave. Lead by example.

- Encourage people to achieve results. Find people 'doing one thing right and tell them why they did well'. Reinforce behaviour in a positive fashion. Celebrate success and recognise achievement and share success.

- Assess the style of your Management Team. Look at their strengths, discuss weaknesses and take corrective action. Ask about the impact of your style on those you manage. Listen to what they say – even if you don't like what you hear. Change the way you do things.

- Learn to realise that most of us resist change. We like the stable and predictable. Learn, and encourage others, to love change and come to realise that this is business as usual.

- Decide what the Management Team want to happen in terms of changing their Leadership behaviour. Do it and monitor progress.

- Ensure that Commitment is reflected in Leadership behaviour.

CHAPTER 7

Pitfalls to the Implementation of Culture Change

KEY ISSUES: PITFALLS AND DISASTERS

This is the last chapter in this section dealing with the critical issues in 'Managing the Transition to Culture Change'. We have already established that TQ is a behavioural change which is concerned with assessing and preparing the way for 'cultural change'. This cultural transition can only be achieved through Leadership, which is 'where management ends'.

We now can explore in a more general way the possible Pitfalls and Disasters which stand in the way of Total Quality. The issues for consideration fall within two areas: preparing the way for Total Quality and Implementing it (Implementation is the focus of Section 4 of the book). Preparing the ground is determined very much by the relationship which exists between those internal to the organisation, who have to live with the problems of TQ, and the role of the external change agent or consultant. This is not to say that companies cannot implement TQ without the help of an outsider – but many companies take this option because they have a reservoir of experience upon which to draw – which should complement the enthusiasm and the skills of those within the company who are there to facilitate change.

ATTITUDES: THE ROLE OF THE INTERNAL CHANGE AGENT

During a discussion with a company creating a TQ drive, one of the senior managers asked the likely qualifications of a TQ manager internal to the organisation. Before receiving an answer, another senior manager mentioned that one particular director, who was not renowned for his contribution, would be retiring in the next year and this would give him something to do!

Clearly, this sort of attitude has never created significant change in the way organisations function. I prefer to think that this statement was naive rather than serious. However, the situation is real and does create some concern. We need to consider seriously the criteria used for the appointment of internal managers to champion TQ.

We know that the prerequisite of an effective TQ initiative is that the Senior Management Team or Board take full ownership of the drive and 'lead by example'. So much is founded upon this important criterion that we can tend to forget the other factors which ensure that TQ is not just another 'quick fix'.

Management Teams are fully aware that a TQ Drive must fit the needs of their individual organisation and must be tailored to its special circumstances. Organisations can get so carried away with the inherent wisdom of TQ, together with the simplicity or 'good sense' of the concept, that they fail to take account of the important issues relating to implementation.

IF TQ WAS SO EASY – WE WOULD HAVE DONE IT YEARS AGO

Implementing TQ is not easy. We are asking managers to rethink the way they do things. We ask them to be critical and identify waste in their immediate areas of work. We encourage all staff to be open and trusting and forget all about the 'history and politics' associated with the way they have previously functioned. Can we change so easily?

If firefighting and reactive management are the normal ways of life, it is naive to believe that to change the culture and achieve the transition to Total Quality would not be difficult.

LEADERS WHO CHANGE THE CULTURE

What we require are Transformational Leaders, who are not shy, who can create change and who are, when necessary, capable, willing and prepared to be viewed as unpopular in order to force the key issues. Some would say that is why we employ external consultants, but here lies an inherent danger. How can we be sure that when the Consultancy team leave the organisation, TQ will not leave with them? How can we ensure that TQ really is a breathing reality when the overhead projectors have been packed away and the dust settled in the Boardroom?

Clearly, there is only one answer, to ensure that 'champions' or 'heroes' exist within the structure who are keen and enthusiastic, who believe that TQ will give their company a competitive advantage and ensure that the long-term benefits of TQ are not simply words written on paper. It is a major concern that managers should take responsibility for promoting TQ inside their company, take over the role and responsibilities of the external consultant.

RESPONSIBILITY FOR LEARNING

Many consider this issue and take their responsibilities seriously. In other words, external consultants recognise that they owe clients a duty to create a team of facilitators who continue the message. The really successful initiatives are those where the internal TQ Manager actively projects TQ within and outside the organisation.

THE TQ MANAGER SHOULD BE GUARDIAN OF THE CULTURE

Obviously, the Manager responsible for Culture Change will vary radically depending on the size and sector of the organisation. Companies or organisations who are primarily Service-orientated will require just as assertive an individual as a production business. The skills for creating change will be the same, but the focus upon the tools and techniques which underpin TQ may vary considerably. For instance, the manager working in a finance business may have to have developed skills in working and facilitating change and focus more on the less demanding analytical problem-solving approaches.

The manager in a manufacturing business probably will have to develop some expertise in JIT, MRP and Taguchi Methodology. What is important to both individuals is that they can assert and project the importance of quality and communicate this every day.

THE LAW FIRM

When working with a successful law firm, Lindsays WS, I was first introduced and worked well with Nora Kellock, the Partner responsible for Quality. A large legal practice based in Edinburgh with a very positive reputation was committed to becoming the first firm in Scotland to achieve a strongly focused Quality culture, evident not just in their responsiveness in general terms to their clients but also acquiring BS 5750. They established both goals and certainly outshone many of their competitors, particularly in their commitment to change.

Generally speaking, lawyers are not renowned as the most change-orientated people and they do have a reputation for being fairly independent in their thinking. Having the positive and strong attitude of the internal facilitator, Nora, to promote Quality within the business and to translate TQ terminology into actions with the energetic Managing Partner, John Eliott, it soon became apparent that the 14 Partners who ran the business would personally commit to the Drive. Because of the strong connection and commitment between external adviser and internal facilitator we soon managed to establish the following:

- Two-thirds of the Partners became trained Facilitators.

- An assessment of the Business Strategy of the firm was undertaken using fairly complex business tools.

- Demonstrating a self-critical attitude of wanting to improve 'personal relations' with others, the Partners 'willingly' undertook psychometric assessment and discussed their personal strengths and weaknesses so as to improve their personal performance.

- Presentation skills were undertaken with the purpose of further advancing the presentation abilities of Partners, thus adding value to their clients and growing their business.

- Training Teams were formed, and cascaded several Training Workshops through staff of more than a hundred people.

- Quality Improvement Teams were formed, and Partners listened to suggestions from QIT's driven by staff and implemented change.

There are rare examples of a professional law practice developing their platform for quality improvement and this was certainly achieved among other things by the teamwork evident between internal and external facilitator.

STRONG COHESIVE TEAMWORK

Chemistry in an internal-external role when creating change is based upon chemistry and teamwork: ensuring that the best interests of the client are always established and at the same time being honest when required is critical in being able to monitor progress.

I can recall with pleasure working with many people and developing very positive relationships. Each time our relationship was based upon rapport and establishing joint objectives.

Working with Margaret Cuthbert, the Quality Manager of a major insurance company, we created a very innovative launch to the programme by ensuring that the one-day event for the top team was rigorous in content and the top team would be exposed to the best practitioners in the field. Through our efforts, we established the best speakers who had implemented change in very successful businesses and thus gained credibility for the programme from Step 1. We would not have been so successful if we had not worked as a team and at the same time challenged each other's thinking. When the programme was continued Ursula Green, Margaret's replacement, was equally skilled and committed towards developing a strong focus upon implementation, taking TQ still further down the road for the company.

There are many examples of working with others which can be cited which caused success in TQ for the relevant business. This was due to internal and external change agent working in unison. There are many instances we hear of where this is often not the case and where relationships are strained or imposed. This is critical to success in communicating the message to the constituents in the organisation.

It is equally highly unlikely that success would be evident within a business with just the efforts of a sole internal or external facilitator driving the programme. The teamwork is evident. A strong external facilitator is required to tell the client the truth and often to challenge the 'internal politics' of the business. The skills of a good 'internal facilitator' keep the external consultant's feet on the ground and open doors to key people in the business.

It is obvious that this relationship is the key to effective implementation and is often over-looked by too many businesses. This chemistry and energy between the internal and external is important and is central to sustaining the programme over the long term.

The remaining part of this chapter focuses upon the specific role of the TQ Manager or facilitator with a slight emphasis towards Production so that the more tangible aspects of this role in manufacturing culture can be explored. All comments remain applicable to both Service and Production and are equally valuable for people in a variety of business sectors and industries.

THE TQ MANAGER IS THE AMBASSADOR WHO CREATES CONFIDENCE IN STAFF, SUPPLIERS AND CUSTOMERS

In one particular organisation, which manufactures components for the automotive industry, the TQ Manager is active in promoting TQ with all the company's suppliers. After a comparatively short time, while managing training, development and other issues, he, in liaison with others, such as the Purchasing Manager, reduced the supplier base to a manageable number. They ran an external Supplier Development Programme, told their suppliers what was expected and started working more closely with them.

SUPPLIER DEVELOPMENT INITIATIVES

There were many instances when suppliers were providing material for manufacture based upon assumed specifications. This had created significant scrap, but had existed for such a long time that everybody had assumed that nothing could be done to resolve the problem. It transpired that the manufacturing company had little idea of the specification of the material – because they had never questioned whether things could be improved.

There were many instances when supplier and customer came closer together. Hard as it may seem, suppliers visited the company, went through the manufacturing process appraising the reliability of raw materials, and came up with alternative material which would be more appropriate for the use to which it was put.

Likewise, a QA Manager at a US-owned company manufacturing microwave antennae organised a Supplier Development Conference for two days. All suppliers were invited. Those who attended promised they would make all attempts they could to resolve manufacturing problems. This conference generated other similar events when the QA Manager would host sessions trying to reduce rework and build collaborative relationships with suppliers. This regular event has now become an established part of the culture.

PLACEMENT OF SUPPLIER PERSONNEL WITH THEIR CUSTOMERS

Suppliers now understand the quality of the service they provide. In some instances, suppliers are asked to locate a member of their staff with their customers so they can experience at first hand the quality of the material received. This short-term assignment gives instant feedback on what it is like to receive the 'product' and process complicated documentation.

ASKING SUPPLIERS TO DO THE IMPOSSIBLE – THEN CHANGING YOUR MIND!

This reversal of roles does much to enhance the service provided in all areas – it is not just product-related. It is also interesting to see what sort of reputation 'customers' have with their suppliers. In one instance, the customer, a producer of original equipment to the motor industry, had made an emergency phone call to their supplier to set up special facilities to produce a large number of components (sub-assemblies) – to be delivered yesterday! These were to be assembled over a weekend and shipped to a major car manufacturer. The supplier set all the wheels in motion. They rearranged production schedules, negotiated overtime and additional weekend and shift-working with their employees. They halted work in progress, stripped machines and set up new tooling and arranged for extra delivery of raw materials. There was to be a direct delivery, from the supplier, eighty miles away, to their customer. This would then be processed and delivered to the car company. This emergency required a great deal of planning and preparation, and called for the goodwill of companies and employees alike. At the last minute, priorities were changed and the supplier was no longer under 'pressure' for the sub-assemblies. The result was a supplier, further down the chain, who had expended a great deal in financial terms to please his customer. The radical reorganisation had created 'ill will' with the supplier's staff – all for nothing. This 'accelerator' effect reinforced the image of a firefighting customer.

HELPING SUPPLIERS DEVELOP THEIR OWN SYSTEMS

TQ Managers with whom I have worked have also provided a support system to those suppliers who find difficulty in developing their systems to meet the requirements of their customers. The outcome of this is the finalisation of a separate Supplier Development Programme and certification similar to the Ford Q101 system. Suppliers do find this of special value and discover that they in turn can reduce their costs of rework – thus freeing resources to provide a cheaper and better quality product to their customer.

In some companies the Supplier Development programme has generated an initiative to create a New Products Implementation Programme when suppliers are involved right from the start in the design of New Products. This reduces unnecessary rework at all levels.

There are also instances when the 'cascade' approach has worked in relation to SPC and Just In Time. Suppliers seeking ways of improving their service have sought help from their bigger customers, looked at their systems and become committed to Quality Improvement. These efforts sometimes culminate in a major Total Quality Drive.

ROBBIE THE CHAMPION

Robbie Taylor, MD of The Taylor Group involved in diecastings and plastic injection moulding, has taken a brave step. He identified his main larger customers of each of his four plants in Scotland and sought their views on his operations. A detailed questionnaire relating to service received was circulated to the top twenty customers in terms of revenue and it was interesting to examine the results. There are always ways of improving what you do! He is a champion of Quality and committed to improving Quality of product and service. Robbie has now extended his research base to the 80% of his customers who generate 20% of his revenue and he is sure that he may get a slightly different response. Now what is important about his approach is that he is looking for things which are wrong. He wants to know what it is that 'turns the customer off'. Is it the product, could it be documentation, delivery or consistent standards?

Robbie will find out how to improve because he canvasses his customers. How many other CEOs would risk the response from such an exercise?

CASCADING TQ TO SUPPLIERS

Many TQ initiatives started with these programmes described above and have created a TQ culture which has been cascaded down from customers to suppliers and so on. This is the chain reaction of TQ which is more prevalent in Japanese Industry – with the resultant benefits.

RICHARD: THE ENTHUSIASTIC TQ MANAGER

If we are not careful we can lose out on the impact of a TQ Manager who is 100% committed to TQ. Richard Tinkler, a TQ Manager for a very successful engineering company, was sold '100%' on TQ. He spent all his time talking to and converting people. Every time he talked with suppliers and customers alike, he sparked off enthusiasm. Every time he talked TQ, he added value to the reputation of his company. This enthusiasm is a desirable trait in any TQ Manager – but is it always present? I doubt it. I question whether this is the norm. I think it extremely important that the senior group think through the type of TQ Manager or Co-ordinator they need to do a good job (see inset on page 75). I am afraid that too much attention is focused upon technical expertise rather on the 'public relations' side of the exercise. There is little point in having a deeply analytical introvert as TQ Manager – when you have the choice of a self-confident, assertive, charismatic individual without the same analytical powers. After all, he can always be equipped with the 'technical expertise' by teaming him up with 'analysts' – but we do need an individual with influence and persuasion. Don't forget there is not a trade-off between analytical ability and ability to influence! So it is possible to gain the best of both worlds.

Job description: **TQ MANAGER**

Objective: To ensure the success of the TQ Drive

Responsibility: to Managing Director

KEY JOB FUNCTIONS (SPECIFIC)

1. To co-ordinate the collection of data relating to COQ measures in all functions/ locations. The TQ Manager should be the recipient of information driven by line/functional management.

2. Produce, collate and disseminate COQ information to the TQ Co-ordinator.

3. Collate, monitor and co-ordinate progress regarding action plans. Although, ostensibly, this is a line function – information must be collected at the centre to communicate progress.

4. Collate functional/departmental plans for TQ progress. This requires collecting information and concentrating upon milestones and methods for measuring progress.

5. Ensure that all functions have developed their own CATs and that each CAT has developed a short report/list of priorities from which to work.

6. Ensure that CATs are formed on an inter-functional basis.

7. Ensure that all staff/employees have attended TQ sessions.

8. Ensure that publicity of TQ progress is promoted through the necessary media.

9. TQ Manager to communicate with the Quality Improvement Team to assess progress.

10. To ensure that functional areas take ownership of TQ.

KEY FUNCTIONS (GENERAL)

1. To be actively involved in setting up Quality structures meetings and other forums for TQ improvement.

2. To promote the TQ concept and gain commitment from all employees.

3. To arrange, as and when necessary, the setting-up of training programmes for all employees in TQ concepts, processes and activities including Training Trainers, CAT problem-solving, etc.

4. To manage other trainers/facilitators as may be necessary. (It is anticipated that this would be a dotted line relationship – because responsibility must lie ultimately with the functional head.)

5. To maintain an effective marketing programme of TQ activities – this should include generating information for briefing meetings.

6. To report progress to the QIT on a regular basis. Reports to include measurements.

PERSON SPECIFICATION. An outline specification is included below:

1. Must be able to communicate effectively across the entire organisation. (He will need to be able to sell/reinforce the TQ concept at all levels.)

2. Must be persuasive and influential. (A key function is to sell the concept.)

3. Needs to be enthusiastic and persistent. (Someone will always need information/ training.)

4. Imagination is required – there is much scope for creativity, ie. publicity and internal marketing.

5. Organised. It is not envisaged that the post will carry a large staff back-up; requires a logical systematic approach with the ability to keep ordered records of progress.

6. It is not a prerequisite that the job-holder needs specific experience in QA or TQ/SPC. Personality and enthusiasm are the key factors.

THE PRESSURE OF TQ CAN CREATE INSULARITY

Too often when a TQ initiative begins, TQ Managers can be quite insular in their approach. They have so much to think about that they stay within the confines of their specific responsibilities. Imposed targets and time constraints tend to reinforce this behaviour. It is just at this time that the TQ Manager should stand back, avoid tunnel vision and ask himself whether similar companies have experienced similar problems. Finding out who is doing what and how with TQ will pay enormous dividends.

Spending time assessing who else is interested in TQ in the same industry, in different industries, making contact, visiting companies undergoing the same drive, will add breadth and avoid tunnel vision. There are many companies involved in TQ who would value others showing an interest. TQ Managers developing a 'support system' can help enormously and avoid pitfalls which others have encountered.

ICL BREAKFAST WORKSHOPS

ICL, which has been progressing Total Quality for a long time, arranged a series of free seminars and workshops demonstrating just what can be achieved. Managers attending its 'breakfast sessions' can learn a great deal. British industry in general has never been renowned for sharing its secrets, even with companies in other industries. What we need are more TQ consortia orientated towards avoiding the problems of implementation, composed of user organisations. TQ Managers committed to the TQ concept must make the first move and create the interest. Companies like BP, British Telecom, GE Plastics, Andrew Antenna, Dow Chemical, ICL, Digital and others are pleased to help their suppliers and others on the road to TQ. The TQ Manager should be have a powerful personality. He has to enthuse people to think and work differently. If you pick the right TQ Manager to champion the cause, you can move mountains. There is nothing that can't be achieved if you have committed and professional champions within the company.

LIVING IN THE REAL WORLD

Developing champions within the company is all very well, but organisations do not have unlimited resources from which to choose a co-ordinator to facilitate TQ. We can suggest that organisations should be sufficiently committed to select, develop or recruit the right person to do the job, but for many Management Teams, funding a TQ drive requires a shift in resources which should not be made unbearable on other demands. But neither can we solve all our problems by throwing money at them!

We are sure that, given time and money, we could develop the right profile of a Manager suited to promote TQ and match it exactly – but we all live in the real world and recognise that the reality is "we have to achieve more with less". But please do not take this comment out of context. All organisations require some injection of 'prevention', however you define it, to reduce rework or at least start the trend. There must be an initial investment in 'internal resources' in order to demonstrate commitment: deeds, not just words, are the order of the day.

RECRUITING A TQ MANAGER IS NOT THE ONLY ANSWER

We have to recognise that there is a limit to the resources we can allocate to TQ, but increasing head-count and recruiting outsiders does not always change the culture. Head-hunting a manager who has nurtured TQ in one company is no guarantee that he will be able to do it in others. The company has to be prepared for change. Some are not. Recruiting an outsider may appear to solve the immediate problem of finding someone to take responsibility – but the appointment of one person cannot by itself change the style and attitudes of the rest of the management team. Here is where the commitment and the responsibility for TQ must lie. The TQ Manager is the instrument of the Management Team. He implements policy – but he must not be seen as the only active adherent to TQ. He facilitates change, prepares the base and collects and disseminates data and information. The functional manager must be the Leader who brings Quality to his function. This is imperative because the Functional Head has the experience and wisdom to know the system, the way it operates, and is aware of the major leverage points for change.

WHO SHOULD MANAGE CHANGE?

There is a general debate on the key players, but who should hold the responsibility? It should not be an external consultant, although he should have the major responsibility when the drive is first underway. Gradually his role, impact and his influence should recede. The time taken for this to happen is determined by the speed at which others in the company take their role seriously and reflect words with actions.

In the case study on page 107 we can see that, over time, the responsibility for implementing TQ is shared between the internal TQ Manager, the Functional Heads and external consultants. This proportion of 'responsibility' for implementation, however, changes over time. In fig 11 we can see that everything is going to plan. There is a close relationship between the internals who are accountable and the external change agent. As the external gives up roles and responsibilities when the TQ drive progresses, we can see that these responsibilities are claimed by internal staff. As we proceed we can see that there are 'step jumps' – most usually related to critical activities which have been completed. These activities include the completion of: Senior Management Training; The Diagnostic Phase;

Completion of Cost of Quality Measures; Departmental Purpose Analysis; Training Trainers; Staff Training; Problem-Solving; Corrective Action Teams, etc. Over time responsibilities and roles change and these should be taken seriously to demonstrate commitment. At the end of the intervention the internal TQ Manager, his colleagues and associates take over full control and manage the process.

In the case study on page 107 there are serious problems. After some time the internal staff fail to take responsibility. At first this may not appear evident, but as time goes on we can see a definite gap or 'failure' to grasp the responsibility. As agreed responsibility and roles are taken from the external consultant we can see that there is a failure for the 'internals' to take the rein. This can happen for a variety of reasons.

The typical way of solving this problem is get the consultants back in to take over the programme or run more 'training workshops', hoping that enthusiasm and drive will be maintained by others. This is highly unlikely because if a structured plan and agreement for implementing Total Quality is not in existence – it won't arise just by accident. Fundamentally, there should be checks and balances at each stage of the drive which must be maintained before progress to the next stage. This ensures that a rift is never allowed to develop.

We may be aware of who should do what in terms of internal and external accountability, but who inside the company should drive it?

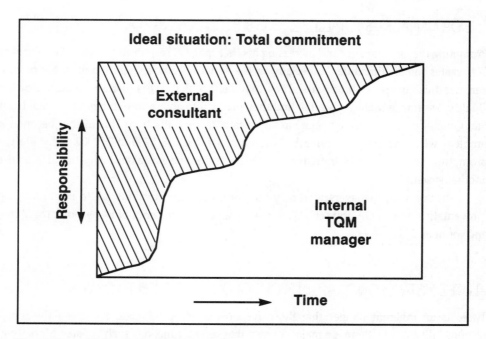

Fig. 11 Responsibility for implementing TQM

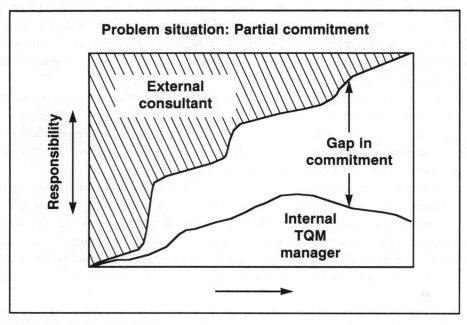

Fig. 12 Responsibility for implementing TQM

THE QA MANAGER IS TOTALLY RESPONSIBLE FOR DRIVING TQ!

Promoting the QA Manager and increasing his/her range of responsibilities to take control of TQ creates major difficulties, especially in the service sector. Others within the structure perceive this change as it appears. They may believe that TQ is just an expansion of the Quality Assurance Manager's remit and they may fail to accept fully the fundamental truth that Quality problems can originate in all areas of the organisation. This further becomes a problem when we hear the remark: "I thought we had BS 5750/ISO 9000. Why are we promoting another quality initiative?". This reinforces the mistaken belief that TQ is just another system.

In this way, managers who may administer service functions fail to appreciate the 'preventative' role of QA and see TQ as another sophisticated series of inspection procedures and routines.

ALL THE MISTAKES ORIGINATE IN PRODUCTION – GET THEM TO DRIVE IT!

There is an inherent danger that those responsible for production are given the initial responsibility. Again, there is a major concern that service functions such as Sales, Marketing, Finance, Personnel and others see the TQ drive relating to production facilities only.

Bear in mind that TQ is concerned not only with developing strategies, structures and systems, but also promoting behavioural change. This can only happen through providing staff with the skills, attitude and motivation to bring about change in their style of management. This requires an individual who is genuinely sensitive to the behavioural issues.

A no-nonsense, results-driven individual may not fully understand the transitions and changes which others have to undergo in order to activate TQ. This does not suggest that the converse, a sensitive, feeling, process-orientated person, is best for the job. A mixture of these two broad 'types' is important if the change is going to be effective.

HUMAN RESOURCE SPECIALIST AS TQ MANAGER

It has been debated whether the Personnel or Human Resource specialist is a natural choice for TQ Manager. There is some wisdom in this view, although this could be equally expressed for the Commercial or Sales Manager taking over the role.

TQ is about creating change through attitudes and for some organisations who wish to drive TQ utilising their own training resources, this is an interesting and productive choice. Obviously, the size and support of the training function is important as to whether this is a reality, but experience in a US chemical company, a US medical company and a UK brewery suggests that, given adequate resources, this can be extremely effective. This is so because the companies in question had a stronger than fairly high commitment to change through people, *prior* to embarking on the TQ Drive.

STATUS

Obviously, the higher the status of the TQ Manager the better. In all honesty, a member of the Board is a preferable choice, although there are circumstances when smaller companies have few Directors and it is not feasible. Perhaps, if this is not a possibility, it is wise that the person selected is sufficiently close to Board members that he/she has the authority to bring about necessary changes.

THE CHIEF EXECUTIVE SHOULD DRIVE QUALITY

It must be said that if the TQ Manager is not a Board Member with full responsibility to see TQ through to the end, there will always be doubts about commitment from other levels of Management.

In all honesty, the TQ Manager should be the MD of the Company. I have heard MDs shout in horror: "I don't have time, I don't think that you understand my responsibilities –

I'm very busy". It is for these reasons that the MD should take responsibility. Few will argue with him – unless there is a justified reason to halt TQ. He may not have time – but neither does anybody else. The MD leading the drive tells people how important it is and how they should allocate their time. Their time allocation should be no different from the MD's. If he has time to devote to preventative action, there is no reason why others cannot follow. This is probably the single biggest factor which slows down the success rate of any drive. Getting this right first will create a key change in the culture.

Because the MD has responsibility, this does not mean that he has to do everything himself. He can appoint or delegate duties to his people on the Board and ensure that they have full responsibility for TQ in their functional area. But on no account should TQ responsibility be cascaded down to someone who does not have an impact upon corporate strategy and action. This is a sure sign of window-dressing which fools no one.

ROTATING TQ MANAGERS

Again, this is another possibility when Board members subsume the role for a period of time and then hand responsibilities on to others. The advantages of this approach are that everyone has, at some time, to get involved and drive the programme, and that the results of the actions of Directors are observed and assessed. The big disadvantage of this strategy is that one Director or Manager, who may not be committed, or finds it hard to make the transition himself, may just 'breathe in and out' until others take over. Overall ownership of the operational side of the drive may be difficult to define – and time spent defining and, in some cases allocating, blame, is time when TQ may be decelerating and reinforcing the prejudices of those who believe it is only 'flavour of the month'.

TQ should be driven by the Board at a strategic level. The question and practicalities of operationalising the TQ Drive may be another question.

MANAGEMENT TEAM RESPONSIBILITY

Setting up a management team to oversee and take specific roles and responsibilities can be a real winner as long as the key co-ordinator ensures that particular responsibilities are defined in terms of specific outcomes. In other words, goals, milestones and objectives are defined in a realistic, achievable, measurable and tangible sense so that progress can be reviewed and action taken should ambiguity over ownership arise.

PART-TIME TQ MANAGERS

Responsibility may be given to an individual to promote TQ with a corresponding reduction in other duties. Whether this becomes a reality is dependent upon acknowledgement of the time which has to be expended to do the job properly. In one case, a manager had so many responsibilities and production targets that he spent more time on those things for which he was being paid, rather than his peripheral duties of TQ. Success and advancement within the organisation was equated with achieving results, and knowing this, the manager naturally allocated time and resources in direct proportion to perceived rewards.

The organisation could have helped the situation by reducing other 'commitments' and understanding that TQ was not so easy to implement. The manager may have benefited if he had been more assertive in his role. But, of course, he had to consider how far he could rock the boat.

This is a very real problem for some organisations. Managers are given projects to complete, but still realise they have a career path to return to once TQ is established.

COMPATIBILITY

Teamworking and building relationships are extremely important between internal and external consultants. The time gaps between meetings, between internal and external consultant, especially at a stage when external consultants withdraw from the organisation, for a short time, are breeding grounds for misunderstanding. Being involved in other projects, in other industries, with other companies, can lead to communication problems, but many consultancies recognise this problem and take preventative action.

THE TASK FORCE – SOMETIMES A WASTE OF TIME

Sometimes companies decide to pursue the TQ initiative by setting up a Task Force or TQ Policy Group or Committee. This can create a great deal of frustration for those on the team. For success there needs to be action. Having been introduced to groups assigned to examining the applicability of TQ to their own operation, I am not surprised that things don't seem to happen.

This is not always the case. The Task Force have a great deal of difficulty in defining their terms of reference. Without a very structured approach, this sort of group will be feeding back little in the short to the medium term. As in some areas in the public sector, the fastest way to kill an idea is to delegate it to a committee – this can be exactly the same strategy.

Delegating a Strategic issue to a committee made up of people from all areas smacks of the promotion of inertia. Unless there are some key players on the team, with the status and charisma to make things happen – nothing will happen. The committee may have good intentions and will perhaps work as individuals or sub-groups, visiting other companies who are practising TQ, attending conferences on the subject, having guest speakers, etc. But unless this information, impressions, ideas, etc. are fed back and acted upon, there will be no move forward.

Few of these groups will meet on a regular basis. Only one example have we encountered where members of the Task Force were allocated to their duties full time for a period of three months. Even with this commitment 40% of this particular group appeared to be passive and willing to 'watch' while others started the ball rolling. If you are considering developing a Task Team or Force to assess TQ and its applicability to your company, pick your team carefully. Make sure you have a Transformational Leader, who is committed to changing things. Ensure that he/she has plenty of support for admin work. Ensure that a member of the team is sufficiently analytical to guard against the Leader flying off at tangents.

MISSION OF THE TOTAL QUALITY TASK FORCE

1. Develop a company-wide strategy to implement TQ.

2. Provide direction and guidance to implement TQ at various locations.

3. Ensure consistency in the TQ initiative, but also ensure that TQ is tailored to location.

4. Assess the present state of Quality awareness within the company.

5. Adjust the process to meet varying business needs.

MAJOR ACTIVITIES

a. Establish commitment.

b. Publicity and communication.

c. Assess COQ and agree a model and/or a consistent method of assessment.

d. Ensure that TQ is consistent with other company-wide initiatives, ie. MRP, SPC, MRP, JIT, Customer Care.

e. Manage the process of change. Work on those factors which will hinder progress.

f. Provide checks, ie. communication, organisation structure, etc.

g. Recognition issues.

h. Ensure that a policy is created which is owned by all.

i. Provide a service, ie. pilots and feasibility studies.

OPERATIONAL ISSUES

1. Develop a company-wide strategy to implement TQ. (Before this can be achieved it is necessary to build a committed team.)

Issues to discuss:

   a. Composition of the team.

   b. Rationale to pursue TQ.

   c. Ensure that all Task Force members are aware of TQ. It may be necessary to develop an off-site awareness programme.

   d. Output of programme is remit of TQTF (Total Quality Task Force). Feedback to company and approval for the next step.

   e. Agree goals.

   f. Assess current checks on readiness for change in locations and cultures.

2. Provide direction and guidance to implement TQ at various locations.

   a. Ensure that culture of organisation and historical background determine the level of Quality created.

   b. Communicate to all locations in a meaningful way.

   c. Develop company strategy and relate to every other function to check for consistency. Research and feedback recommendations to Board of Directors. Ensure an Action Plan with time frames is completed.

3. Ensure consistency in the TQ initiative, but also ensure that TQ is tailored to location.

Carry out checks:

   a. Assess readiness for change. Attitude Survey.

   b. Organisational structure and reporting relationships.

   c. Communication audit.

4. Assess the present state of Quality awareness within the company.

5. Adjust the process to meet varying business needs. Decide priorities, ie. existing and future; Safety, Quality, Schedule, Quantity, Cost, JIT, etc.

ISSUES FOR DEBATE

Where does this leave us? These issues are real. Many organisations have experienced these problems and will continue to do so in the future.

We need to ensure that managers and consultants debate these points. We need to ensure that no false 'assumptions' about roles, responsibilities and expectations are made. We also need to recognise that there is no easy answer. This means in some cases that mistakes will be made and that remedial action will have to be taken.

Change is not easy. What I hope will be recognised is that mistakes can be made and that change is a 'learning process'. Standing back and examining the operational issues and learning from the experience of others, preventing problems arising, in this key area will enable us to make the transition to TQ a smoother one.

SUMMARY

Prepare the way for Total Quality. You can underestimate the amount of time needed to appraise the things that could go wrong. Remember the key to effective implementation is developing an internal capability for change and this first starts with a positive relationship forged with the external consultant. The synergy and the mix of these two people can strengthen the implementation plan

Success depends upon those whom you have chosen to take TQ forward internally – so don't give responsibility to the deadwood, however senior, thinking that their 'status' is enough to see it through. You need to use your best people.

Bullet Points

- Ownership is the key and it rests nowhere else but at the top.

- If the MD makes an excuse of not having enough time to devote to TQ as a major responsibility – how can he expect others to take it as a key responsibility?

- Choose Transformational Leaders who can change things quickly. We need people who will take calculated risks and challenge the old ways.

- Don't give all the responsibility to external consultants to create change. If you do this, when they leave, so will the concept.

- Ownership for implementation must be shared between internal people and outsiders. Draw up an agreement detailing expectations, roles, responsibilities and time frames for completion. If you don't have a firm route to achieve TQ, it won't happen by accident.

- The TQ Manager should be your best man – the guy who can establish rapport with your most bloody-minded suppliers, a man of charm – but who isn't afraid to say what he thinks.

- TQ can create other initiatives. Work with suppliers on the basis of developing 'preferred suppliers'. Jointly draw up criteria for evaluation. Keep records and ensure actions are taken by the Purchasing Manager after due consultation with suppliers.

- If suppliers won't change – change them.

- Appraise your external suppliers. You will be surprised at how well your internal suppliers match up against the criteria which you impose on outsiders.

- Organise events of recognition when suppliers attend and are publicly praised for the hard work they put in to Quality Improvement – a practice employed by Jaguar and others.

- If you have a problem with a supplier and he takes no notice, ask for a member of his staff to work with you. Processing the inaccurate documentation, experiencing the receipt of faulty or damaged goods, will soon get back to home base.

- Don't ask suppliers to do the impossible and then change your mind. They are supposed to be partners.

- Recognise that some of your suppliers are only as good as the guidance they are given by their customers. Help them to develop systems to make things easier for you and them, and costs will drop rapidly.

- Ask your customers what you are doing wrong. Encourage them to be critical. You can only improve things which you know are wrong. You can't improve when you have no feedback on performance. Encourage others to be self-critical.

- Enthusiasm in the key TQ movers is infectious. Choose TQ implementation people with caution. You need a combination of vision and persuasiveness followed by analysis.

- TQ is a major change and it can sometimes force or pressurise managers to think in tunnel vision and concentrate within the company. Improvement comes from looking outside, by talking with people who have done it before and made mistakes. You can learn from their experience.

- We live in the real world and have to work within resources – but if you don't want your drive to fail – ensure that you get more resources for the start-up.

- Don't feel that head-hunting TQ Managers from other companies is the answer. One man cannot take the place or the responsibility of the Management Team.

- Ensure that clear responsibilities exist between internal and external change agents.

- Do not make the QA Manager responsible for TQ. You will reinforce the belief that TQ is just another system and the responsibility of one discrete area.

- Don't give full responsibility to Manufacturing Managers. You will reinforce the belief that the Service Units have no part to play.

- Human Resource Director is the natural choice for TQ Manager – just ensure he has the right status and he is not just a personnel guy understanding terms and conditions just masquerading as Human Resource Development.

- The best choice for driving TQ resides with the Chief Executive.

- It is possible to rotate the responsibilities of the post among Senior Officers – but it can fail more often than succeed.

- Part-time TQ Managers don't work. When the pressure is on they tend to concentrate upon those things for which they are paid – probably productivity at any price.

- Total Quality Task Forces can be a waste of time – if they have little guidance and those to whom they report have little idea of what they want anyway! They can work – but it needs a good structure and a good Leader.

- These issues are real. Don't discount them. There are many companies who wish they had explored these areas prior to committing themselves.

- Challenge outmoded systems, procedures and ways of working, which stop your people taking the initiative.

- Speeding up delivery and accuracy of information, reducing blockages and cutting across bureaucracy within units is what Horizontal management is all about.

- Developing relationships, delegating, team-building and getting results through others is a strategy which succeeds.

- Cut out waste – rejecting the slow, bureaucratic process – and replace it with a strongly focused culture promoting Quality and Service Excellence.

- Cultures are created by the actions and deeds of Heroes and Anti-Heroes. The stories about these people, the incidents in which they played a part, reflect the culture and are told and retold to your suppliers, customers, competitors and your staff more than you realise.

- You'll never get rid of the grapevine – it can work for you if you control it.

- Believe the worst of the stories which relate to your company. Do everything you can to take actions which counter the negatives.

- Values are the Building Blocks of Culture. Reinforce them – practise them in your management behaviour and inculcate them in others.

- Culture is about People Management and caring for your people. If you don't value them – why should they value you?

- Assess the appropriateness of your culture. Consider what action you can take to reject any old fossilised culture and replace it with something dazzling and exciting.

- Recognise that change is not easy. We all go through Transitions. Try to make it comfortable to those who will follow you through the Curve.

- Do you remember where you are on the Curve? Where is everybody else? And what action have you taken today to help others move through the Transformation?

CHAPTER 8

Meeting Customer Requirements

ORIENTATION TOWARDS THE CUSTOMER

To achieve a meaningful and customer-focused culture in any organisation, whether in the public or private sector, we must focus upon meeting the requirements of customers in order to strengthen the competitive edge. This is the fundamental consideration behind any Quality drive. Our mission, if we want to be customer-facing, is to focus our attention on asking the customers how we can improve the service we provide to them. CEOs should go out of their way to find out just what it is about the culture of their business which fails to delight the customer. Once the internal barriers to providing 'Service Excellence' are acknowledged, then we should expend all resource to provide a service delivery mechanism which will guarantee high customer service resulting in even more business.

The foundation of superlative customer performance rests on being self-critical and asking others to comment upon our performance. This means listening to what we do not want to hear. We should go to extraordinary lengths to explore the level of 'dis-service' we provide. We should encourage criticism even if this is negative – because we should realise that the chance to succeed and provide superior service comes from our looking at all the occasions when we fail.

CAN YOU EVER FOCUS TOO MUCH ON THE EXTERNAL CUSTOMER?

This open approach often brings to reality the things we would rather not hear, but it is the opportunity really to do something about the service we provide – to do things better. Many

Gurus in Customer Service believe this to be one of the real keys to long-term competitiveness. However, there should be some balance in our approach. There can be a danger that we focus too much attention on the customer and direct our TQ Drive towards a Customer Service orientation, focusing too much on the perceptions of our external customer. If we are not careful we may focus too much on telling ourselves and advertising how good we are. This is where Customer Service becomes confused with promoting a public image founded upon clever public relations, which has little bearing on meeting a desired need. This is not improving Customer Service. It is manipulating and changing the perception of our customers which may not be based upon reality.

There can also be a danger because we fail to consider the implications of putting all our eggs into one basket, focusing upon external relations with our key constituents to the detriment of our internal customers.

Building a strong culture will continue to improve performance for the eventual buyer of the service or product which we provide – but we must be careful that we get the balance just right.

For instance, the following situation of a company committing to Customer care can create conflict within the infrastructure of the business. Imagine running a training workshop for all grades of employee and focusing entirely on the external user of the service – the external customer. There may be a danger that people attending will switch off, for the simple reason that 95% of employees within most companies never even meet the customer! They may be involved in the internal processes of providing and contributing to an overall service for the customer, but there is never any situation where they interface with the customer, whether through face-to-face contact, telephone or letter. Put yourself in their situation in the Workshop. They might think: "This is all very interesting, but I never meet the customer – so anything on continuous improvement is not applicable to me". We recognised many years ago that often those attending Workshops on Customer Care never relate this to their colleagues in other departments or functions within the organisation – hence our orientation towards 'fixing' problems with the internal customer first.

It is difficult for people working at the same function or workstation every day to understand the impact that their work has on the overall satisfaction of the external customer. What is important is that management has to communicate strongly that they all have an equal role to play in improving Service Delivery, but fail to recognise it because so many staff employed are never exposed to, or meet, the external customer.

This difficulty is particularly evident in the service sector. Staff employed in clerical, supervisory and managerial positions within the banking and finance sector, retailing, professional services, the Health Service, Local or Public Authorities, could interpret the customer only as someone who purchases the end product or service of their business. If staff perceive the end user as the 'customer', the initiative is not generating the responsiveness and improvements in performance which could be gleaned by examining the role of the internal supplier-customer chain. It is wise for any organisation to enlarge the definition of customer from those which only a small percentage of their staff actually meet.

INTERNAL CUSTOMER

We believe that everybody within an enterprise should consider the interaction between themselves and their 'internal customers', those who are next in line. Failing to grasp this notion can kill the most effective TQ Drive. It was for this very reason that British Airways introduced both a Customer Care and a Total Quality Drive. They recognised that you cannot have 'one without the other'.

Every day we are dependent upon the quality of information, decisions and resources supplied by others. To illustrate the point, the Quality of information which Personnel practitioners receive from Line Management will determine the success of Personnel Practice, ie., Recruitment, Selection, Appraisal, Redeployment, Manpower Planning and Training. Anyone responsible for providing a 'support service' to others should realise that they are an essential part of Quality which is provided to the external user. Even more important, we need to understand that the interaction between functions and departments is critical if we want to improve everything we do. So often we argue that we should first improve internal service delivery before venturing to go external with a Customer care drive.

WHO ARE MY CUSTOMERS?

Your customer is anyone who is dependent upon you for the supply of goods or a service. It is someone who can't complete a job to an agreed level or standard on time without your timely input. You provide the resources, information and decisions upon which others act. In other words, your customers are dependent upon you to provide a high quality service. If you fail to deliver, they in turn cannot provide a good quality service to their customers and so on.

WHO ARE MY SUPPLIERS?

As we have customers so also do we have suppliers. Try not to think of suppliers as the people external to your business who provide you with raw materials, stationery, power and fuel, etc. Think 'internal' suppliers, those within the company who supply you with all you need in order for you to do your job. We can see that any company no matter how small has a network of suppliers and customers. This network creates a mutually dependent relationship. If there is a breakdown between internal customers and suppliers, then Quality of Service within the company will be poor and those receiving it externally will get poor quality.

WORKING AGAINST EACH OTHER – THE SERVICE SECTOR

Sales staff working for a major insurance business would regularly organise seminars for self-employed business people. The purpose of these sessions was to advertise the tax benefits associated with Company and Personal Pensions. The Workshops worked really well and generated a great deal of interest from business-owners – so much so that sales staff had considerable demand during these sessions to purchase these 'services'. Because they were so busy, sales staff neglected to attend to the fine detail when completing all the documentation setting up the agreement. Because of the complexity of the transaction, information regarding the details of the formation of the company or partnership were required before the agreement became legal. Sales staff, being very motivated and wanting to create rapport with the customer, did not always attend to the fine detail required for this legal transaction to be completed accurately. Consequently, when these agreements were being processed at Head Office, details had to be reconfirmed in writing with original documents submitted. On one major occasion many agreements never reached their apparent fruition. Workshops had been held in mid-March encouraging business people to invest their money in order to avoid tax at the end of the financial year. Because of the confusion with the requirement for company details and documentation, these agreements would not be completed before the end of that tax year! You can imagine the response from those new customers when they heard the disappointing news that their transaction with the company was 'null and void'. All were extremely unhappy that they would have to pay to the Inland Revenue the amount of money they had hoped to invest in their future.

It is obvious in this and many other examples in the Service sector that all functions, customer-facing and those that support customer service, must work in unison. This was not the case and in this example there were clearly different objectives for the administrative processing centre and the Sales force. Only by Re-engineering the process and working closely as suppliers and customers was this organisation able to offer 'error-free' service to all customers.

We work with businesses delivering services and utilise Process Mapping, a tool for continuous improvement which can be used with internal service providers to do things right first time. Here we focus upon defining and agreeing requirements between everyone involved in the process so that error-free service is the result.

THE CUSTOMER-SUPPLIER CHAIN MANUFACTURING

Consider the mutual interplay between a Sales department, a Research and Development area where Engineering Drawings are completed, and Manufacturing locations. This example existed in a large engineering company.

Sales staff spent a great deal of time with customers. Most Sales people in this company had some level of engineering expertise, but this had been gained over many years. Because of some of the demands of their customers, Sales staff had to be pretty quick in responding to rush orders – otherwise this would mean lost business. Sales had to have a 'quotation' into their biggest customer almost immediately so that they stood a chance to secure business. They were under a great deal of pressure and had very little lead time. The major problems which contributed to a short lead delivery lay with the provision of new products which the company provided. Increasingly, more and more of new business was of this variety – because of the changing expectations which their customer was requiring. Consequently, lead times were reduced to the bare minimum.

Salesmen would return from the customer with a requirement to tender a quote for the business. Before the quote was assessed, a great deal of information had to be generated to support the internal costing of product delivery. If the information was incorrect, the quote may be too high, thus making the firm less competitive against others quoting for the business. If it were too low, because of a failure to incorporate all costs, it would mean that the business was unprofitable. Clearly there was balance to be sought in order to generate the right quote.

WORKING IN SPITE OF EACH OTHER! – PRODUCTION

Because salesmen were keen for the business, they would promise early delivery to the customer of 'sample parts' for testing. This date was firmly set. The Salesman would return and talk to the people in R&D, who would start generating plans for discussion. There are few R&D establishments which don't have a backlog of work, and this company was no different. Consequently, other work in progress would be put to one side, while the new priority work was slotted into its place. New drawings had to be generated. These would be the basis for manufacturing set-up and assembly as well the foundation required for the design for the toolmakers. There was a failure to assess and develop customer-supplier relationships.

One major problem was that few designer/draughtsmen had actually visited their own various manufacturing locations. There were six plants spread over a fairly wide area in the Midlands. Upon investigation, it became clear that some of the draughtsmen did not even know where the actual factories were located. They were unaware of location. How reliable was their understanding of manufacturing process within the plants? It soon transpired that there was little understanding. Assumptions were made about techniques of assembly and the 'cost estimators', those responsible for working out the total unit cost of possible manufacture, were widely out in their assessments. Consequently, some of the estimates provided little profit for the company.

In some cases this created further problems. Because priorities had not been agreed between departments everywhere, firefighting was evident in most weeks. For instance, Engineering Drawings arrived late for Toolmakers. Toolmakers had to work three shifts to complete the tools for the manufacturing process. This cost a great deal and was passed on to the customer – eventually! Because of the constraints on time, tools weren't tested, only to find in the manufacturing process that they did the wrong job, creating rework. Tools did not fit specific technology in some locations and soon broke in manufacture in other plants.

The Toolmakers were unreliable and could not provide a back-up service for repair. The reason for this was that the Purchasing Manager had been told to take 'toolmakers' from the cheaper end of the market. Toolmakers at the cheaper end existed because nobody else used their service and they did not have the up-to-date machinery on which to prove the tools. Consequently, their overheads were lower and they were able to provide a cheaper service – at least in the short term.

TQ is doing the right job and in this example everybody was extremely busy, but no one was really being effective. There was a radical need to develop closer relationships between customer and supplier. Here the emphasis was placed on meeting the requirements of the external customer – however crazy – whereas some attention should have been placed upon the 'internal customer' relationship. If we fail to get this relationship right, we will not meet the needs of the external customer.

GET IT RIGHT INSIDE THE COMPANY FIRST

Again, balance is important in providing a service or product. Being customer-focused does not mean becoming unprofitable because of amendments to the delivery of a service. In some cases, agreeing to bend over backwards for the external customer is a grave mistake if it creates a great deal of chaos and rework within the company. This is not to say that we should not attempt to meet the requirements of 'externals' – but we need to be realistic. We should not agree to the impossible if it creates more problems within the company

QUALITY DIALOGUE

In a major business a typical project meeting would go like this:

SALES MANAGER

"I don't care whether you can make the production date or not. You said you needed 17 weeks' lead time, but the customer wants it in 14 weeks. Is that so difficult? Listen, my guys spend a lot of time getting orders. We keep you in a job. It's difficult out there. Can you complete the order or do we lose the business?"

PRODUCTION MANAGER

"Well, that's all very well for you, but we have to make the product to specification. R&D tell us they have not got enough time to do the drawings. They don't want to send them outside to sub-contractors – but they'll have to, at great expense to us, to make your deadline."

SALES MANAGER

"No way. They have to be produced in-house. We don't want externals doing the drawings again. Last time the tools were wrong and it was all traced back to their drawings."

And so the story continues. We don't think this instance is a one-off occurrence, but is rather the norm for many companies. The secret to customer service is get things right inside the company before going outside.

In this example, the customer probably doesn't realise the chaos which is created by changing lead times even though the product is delivered on time.

Many would say the customer doesn't care as long as he receives the product right first time, on time. But this again has to be taken in context because this product will be artificially priced at manufactured unit costs plus reworked costs. In this instance, the customer may have to bear the costs of inefficiency of the supplier.

Essentially all costs incurred by suppliers and customers failing to work together, either internal or external, have to be passed on to the customer – otherwise companies would go out of business. Many customers don't realise they are paying artificially inflated prices!

MAJOR TRAINING INITIATIVE

There is a requirement for departments to work together instead of in spite of each other. There is a need to do things differently and change the culture of the business.

One approach when TQ training is underway is to create Supplier-Customer Workshops where a small number of people from different departments and functions are brought together to discuss problem areas, with Quality of service and product in mind. This approach helps share negative stereotypes of each other, reject these as negative, and discuss new ways of working to improve service.

LISTING YOUR CHIEF CUSTOMERS

When Managers attend these sessions they sometimes tend not to think of others around the table as being their customers. It is quite a transition getting people to appreciate that their customer has needs and requirements and these have to be met first, before we attempt to meet the requirements of external customers. Getting people to generate a list of customers and suppliers is useful because we use this information to enquire as to the frequency of interaction between internal customer and supplier.

Not surprisingly, we tend to find that often suppliers of information tend to talk fairly frequently and spend 80% of their available time with 20% of their customers – so what about the others? Can you imagine the impact of this behaviour on the supplier-customer network within the average business?

This means we tend to invest some time with some customers and little with others. Who determines the choice of which customers we should work with and how is this prioritised? Usually, the suppliers of a service determine, sometimes in isolation, who they will supply and who will wait or who can endure second class service. Suppliers often do determine the choice and priority of meeting requirements without recourse to discussion.

There are many instances, in Supplier-Customer Workshops, when internal customers feel that their suppliers spend too little time with them trying to solve problems. They feel short-changed. And this reinforces the belief that: "Those guys are not interested in improving things, so let's keep clear of them". This can be a rift which creates untold damage between and within departments, and leads to win-lose relations in teamworking.

PERSONALISE CUSTOMER-SUPPLIER INTERFACE

Asking customers what they need from you is a question many internal suppliers have never put. They may be surprised by the answer. Let's look at a simple example.

EXERCISE

Think now of a customer with whom you have a particular problem. (Remember the customer must be internal to the organisation.) Write down the problem. Why is there a problem? Presumably this has something to do with the service which you provide to him or her.

Now, write down your perception of the requirements of your customer. What are they? Please be specific. Now think from your customer's perspective. What are his requirements of you? Be detailed. Write down specific requirements. Now compare the two lists. Are they somewhat different and why?

This exercise is an extremely powerful tool when integrated as part of a Workshop session. Knowing where problems are within the company, finding a known area for improvement and collecting data prior to a training session is a prerequisite for improvement.

The information from the two perspectives is then used to generate lists from these different perspectives. Disclosing these lists to both parties, internal customer and supplier, creates disbelief. They are exposed to 'requirements' which they had never considered before. The misperception of 'requirements' then becomes the focus for discussing things and improving service.

Currently, in too many organisations, insufficient time is spent in this activity. It is critical that this is reversed in order to promote effective teamworking.

BUT WHAT ARE THE REQUIREMENTS?

The requirements are the standards by which the output of a person or unit can be measured. Requirements include time to do a job, a set standard of performance, the resources to complete work, including information, performance targets and best practice. They also include decisions which have to be taken and passed on to others. Requirements are not just related to 'tangible' items such as resources and decisions – but also to processes, ie. there is a requirement for draughtsmen to talk with manufacturing people to ensure that the methods identified for manufacture and quoted in technical drawings are feasible. This means the draughtsman/engineer may have to talk with the people who actually do the job. Those on the shopfloor are the customer of the draughtsmen, and, likewise, the designer is the supplier to those in manufacturing.

As part of a Cultural Change Drive, the personnel of a drawing office agreed to meet people who produce the product. This was a major step. Some designers and draughtsmen had been employed for over five years and had never been on the shopfloor. Clearly, their perception of how things were organised differed from reality. As part of an Action Plan for change, visits to the shopfloor were to be a regular occurrence with much interaction between the internal supplier-customer chain. As part of a 'best practice' Workshop it started with the designer/engineer introducing himself to the people who assembled the product.

This introduction created an instant rapport with assemblers, who asked designers why they designed things certain ways. They discussed scrap, manufacturing capability of equipment, Failure Mode Effect Analysis and so forth. (There was to be some staggering improvement in Design and Process FMEAs.) The designers learnt from their experience, changed the estimates for manufacturing assembly and discussed these with cost estimators. It was amazing the impact that this had on morale on the shopfloor. The designers and draughtsmen were no longer the guys with white shirts who lived in ivory towers but had started to appreciate the value of conversations with their customers.

People took requirements seriously – for the first time.

WHAT HAPPENS IF WE FAIL TO MEET THE REQUIREMENTS?

It's pretty obvious. We deviate from the expected performance or level or quality of service or output. Material, orders, information, does not arrive on time. Production is slowed. This becomes even more of a problem in a service area because the 'intangibility' of what is offered is not apparent as much as a failure of parts not being manufactured or shipped late. If a lorry was waiting for parts and they were not ready, there would be an uproar. But documentation, ie., reports, annual appraisals, working party findings, accounts figures, drawing and many other things, which may be even more important for the organisation, but do not turn up on time in the right place, does not appear to be of the same urgency.

There seem still to be dual standards between the product and the service side of business. Some may claim that this is a vast generalisation, but this is what happens in industry today. Figures and information can always be subject to guesstimates, but for product – it must be there, and it must be right. And yes, it just so happens that companies can go out of business with a product which is defect-free. Failing to provide a service, maintain internal controls, can lead to company failure probably quicker than poor product. Time is well invested if staff spend enough time and attention examining the perceived 'intangible' service between internal customers and suppliers and examine its consequences for their competitiveness.

IS FAILING TO MEET REQUIREMENTS SERIOUS?

Yes. It can be very serious, especially if the deviation or error is not spotted and is compounded by others. Consider what happens in a production process if an error creeps into the product and is not spotted. A great deal of manufacture can take place before the error or deviation is uncovered and, unfortunately, sometimes this does not happen until inspection after the final assembly stage. This can contribute to a huge cost in terms of Rework if left unchecked.

We argue that this is even more serious in the service side of the business. Information which supervisors believe is correct is passed to others who use this information for decision-making. Because supervisors are busy they don't question the figures, and assume others check. These errors are compounded.

WHAT CAN WE DO TO AVOID AMBIGUITY IN REQUIREMENTS?

Meet, discuss and agree 'requirements' with our customers and suppliers. This is the Preventative Action upon which TQ is based.

COMMON PROBLEMS OF NOT MEETING CUSTOMER REQUIREMENTS

Ill-defined and inaccurate Requirements. Our customers can make too many assumptions and develop unrealistic expectations of the service we can provide as suppliers. If customers and suppliers fail to discuss requirements there is going to be a surprise when delivery of service or product does or doesn't take place.

Unrealistic Requirements. We often agree to the impossible and wonder why we suffer from self-induced stress. On the spur of the moment we agree to achieving things which are beyond our control. This self-imposition of targets can act as a short-term motivator, but if it becomes part of day-to-day organisational life, sooner or later someone is going to be found out, hurt and disappointed.

Non-achievable, measurable or quantifiable Requirements. Two or more people or departmental representatives can get together to talk about things in fairly general terms, fail to summarise an agreement in precise terms, return to their departments and wait for others to deliver whatever has been agreed. There is too much 'flexibility' in requirements. There will be little likelihood in this instance of delivery of anything taking place.

As each person retreats to his respective department he develops his own general expectations of the overall effect. Failing to tie things down to specifics and measurable targets and sub-targets creates a great deal of room for error and assumption.

Requirements are not discussed, tested or agreed with customers and suppliers. There is no joint agreement on targets and priorities. Again, too much is left to chance. People do not seem to have a clear idea of what is expected of them. Somehow, by accident, it would appear the defect-free service or product is going to arrive. TQ helps us to work to eradicate misperception of requirements so that we are all working for a common goal.

Lack of commitment to your requirements from your customers and suppliers. Another classic problem. Customers and suppliers sometimes develop a departmental attitude which focuses upon their own needs. They fail to remember that other people have demands upon them and they tend to treat others rather badly. Others perceive your problems as yours alone and want to play no part in resolving them. This failure to develop team spirit kills TQ.

Requirements are not 'owned'. Managers fail to take responsibility and communicate them to their staff. If no one takes ownership for a problem – no one is going to solve it. Recognition of problems is something which is critical to success, working together to solve problems and fix them once and for all is the key to success.

MEETING WITH CUSTOMERS AND SUPPLIERS

Assume a meeting has been called to improve the provision of your services to your major customers. What issues would you debate? These are the crucial issues which help develop the required team spirit. There is no reason why, during a Project Planning meeting, all internal suppliers and customers present cannot generate a list of issues for clarification. These can then become the focus for Customer-Supplier Workshops. Once we have developed the commitment to work together, we can examine the major barriers to working together.

TWENTY FACTORS WHICH STOP OUR MEETING THE REQUIREMENTS OF OUR CUSTOMERS

What are major factors stopping your meeting the requirements of your customers? It is relatively easy to generate a list of at least a hundred items – but we think it is important to look at the top twenty items from experience and relate these to the majority of problems within companies. What is noticeable is that all these factors are behavioural. They are not strictly dependent upon resources. They can be challenged and beaten if people have the will to change their attitudes.

1   Ambiguous instructions. There is no clarity in what is wanted between customer and supplier.

2   Misinformation either by accident or guesstimates. Too many use SWAG as a method for calculation. Managers not wanting to be caught out by their internal customers or suppliers will use 'Swinging Wild Ass'd Guesstimates' as an alternative to accurate information. The consequences are predictable.

3   Agreeing to impossible deadlines because of fear or believing that imposing unrealistic demands upon themselves and others will create the will to achieve. This fear-driven strategy may work in the short term, but will fail quickly with TQ. Attendees at Workshops suddenly start using these examples of the 'counter-culture' to discredit the Drive. There can be another side to this example – that of the imposed requirements. This never works.

4   Little understanding of constraints and demands of our customers. This unwillingness to explore the problems of others runs against TQ to such a degree that a joint problem-solving approach would be anathema.

5 Lack of forward planning by ourselves and our customers. There is so much firefighting in industry and commerce today that customers and suppliers never have the time to get together, or so they say. People can only forward plan when they involve others. The future success of companies is infrequently determined solely by the success of one solitary department so it is important to spend more time working together, instead of against each other.

6 Being insufficiently selective when defining requirements. Again, lack of perceived available time plays a part here as an excuse but not a legitimate reason. Being selective and precise is imperative in order to filter out the major points for agreement.

7 Lack of training/inadequate training. We always find it amazing that staff can be spared to be trained in TQ for two or three days – but they have never really received good quality basic training, just to do their job. Many cannot use the technology available, are computer illiterate and have never attended the most basic of management training courses.

8 Lack of co-ordination. Failure to lead through teams and horizontal management will create a functional organisation where there is little interaction.

9 Tunnel vision. "Let me do my job and you stick to yours." It is too prevalent and negative. Senior management are to blame for not doing something about this in recent years.

10 Customers' inability to assess own requirements. The customer may be ignorant of the service which can be provided for him by the supplier. The supplier must then realise that he/she has an educational role to play in helping the customer to assess his requirements.

11 Suppliers' inability to help customer recognise and identify their requirements. Sometimes the supplier is ignorant of the help that he can provide to his customer – or, even worse, is unaware of the ignorance of the customer. This is particularly the case with Systems people when they talk with their customers – perhaps people in Line Management. Sometimes, Systems staff have to treat their customers as suppliers, getting them to think what they need in order to do their job. Systems people may have to tell them what they can do in order for Line Management to appraise what is available and possible.

12 Poor time-management and objective setting. Lack of time is a major excuse for failing to get together to discuss requirements. It is an excuse – because if managers valued clarifying requirements – they would make time for it! If they do not value it – they will find an excuse not to do it.

13 Lack of warning about urgent requirements. This reflects the short-term drive of many businesses. Everything is firefighting or a surprise. Perhaps this keeps the adrenalin pumping around the system, but it does not promote long-term effectiveness.

14 Assumptions. "I thought you wanted it the same as last time," or, "I thought you would not mind waiting." Assumptions exist because there is a failure to be precise and define standards of performance. Attention to detail is all it is!

15 Poor communication and listening. "I hear what you are saying" is an over-used and pointless phrase. Passive hearing characterises too many Managers who believe that they are the source of meaningful improvement. What is required is Managers opening up and actively listening to what others are expressing. Couple this with the certain knowledge that precise notes on agreements between customer and supplier are not a thing we see often in an organisation. There are too many verbal agreements which are open to whatever interpretation managers choose. There is no surprise that there are different perspectives on requirements, and no surprise when people do not live up to their promises.

16 Poor understanding of priorities. It is interesting to note that too few people within companies are really aware of where the company is going. There is some misunderstanding about priorities and the means to achieve objectives.

17 Unwillingness to bargain and agree is characteristic of areas where there is a great deal of rework generated between departments. Requirements tend to be imposed upon the suppliers of goods or a service. Imagine the working relationship created.

18 Passing the buck to other people and departments is a common feature. "If X only provided us with Z on time." Rejecting this failure to take and share ownership is the foundation to the solution of this problem.

19 Unaware of own responsibility. Often people can be ignorant of the role they can play with others. Imagine how strange the alternative would be to someone who has worked in a culture which has always operated on a strictly functionalised basis?

20 Inability and unwillingness to criticise personal performance is a common trait in many organisations and can be the single biggest threat to getting customers and suppliers working together.

CLARIFYING GOALS

It is important to note that functional groups or departments do need to clarify the reason for their existence. These goals and objectives need to be communicated to all staff within the function so that they have a real grasp of their 'mission'. Ideally, the DPA will be created from the existing culture and the comments and views developed from those in the function. But, overall, staff will gain a better grasp of meeting requirements when they have a better picture of what they should be offering to their customers. "If you don't know where you are going – any road will get you there" is an approach which we have to reject.

SUMMARY

Customer satisfaction is the fundamental motivation behind Total Quality – but too much attention should not be focused at first on the external customer to the detriment of the customer-supplier relationship within the company. It is critical that there is advance on both the external and internal aspect of customer service. Getting the balance is right and is best expressed as "first we need to row together to provide excellent customer service within the business before we move outside to the external user or consumer".

Bullet Points

- Superlative performance relies upon being constantly self-critical and knowing we can do things better with our internal and external customers.

- Seek out criticism: 95% of success comes from examining the 5% of failures.

- Don't get involved in Customer Care until you have satisfied yourself that you have an Internal Customer Care Programme.

- Don't ever equate Customer Care and Total Quality with a Public Relations approach to corporate change.

- Everyone has customers and suppliers and the sooner we can work together, the sooner improvements will be made.

- Total Quality Management is about challenging requirements, talking with our customers and agreeing new requirements. As business changes, so do requirements.

- Requirements include information, decisions, resources, materials, time, standards. These should never be imposed upon others. Much better to have joint ownership.

- Total Quality is reflected in the deviation from Meeting your Customer Requirements. Total Quality is about narrowing this deviation to zero – so that suppliers' and customers' requirements are the same.

- Total Quality attitude between customers and suppliers is NOT a matter of accident or luck. It has to be worked for.

- When there is disagreement with customers and suppliers, the emphasis should be on agreement, dialogue and joint problem-solving.

- Meeting Customer Requirements 100% of the time equates with competitive advantage.

- The relationship between customer and supplier should be strengthened by the interaction. Negative stereotyping of departments should be minimised and teamworking encouraged.

- Avoid ambiguity when agreeing Requirements. Ensure that Requirements are specific, realistic and measurable.

- Reject assumptions and question woolly thinking.

- The factors which inhibit Meeting Customer Requirements are behavioural in nature and are often self-imposed and self-perpetuating.

- Departmental Purpose Analysis, as a process, can be founded upon major discrepancies between internal customers and suppliers.

APPRAISAL OF CUSTOMER-SUPPLIER RELATIONSHIP

1. WHO IS MY CUSTOMER?
Your customer may be a person, department or unit who relies on you to provide goods, services, decisions, information or advice.

2. WHO IS MY SUPPLIER?
Your supplier is a person, a department or unit, who provides goods, services, decisions and advice to you.

3. PROCEDURE
Do you have a formal or an informal procedure between yourself and your customer(s) or the supplier(s) for stated goods and services? Do you have procedures which are not used or are out of date? Identify them now. Do something about them.

4. RATING YOUR CUSTOMERS
How would you honestly rate the service you provide to your customers? Score out of ten where 10 is excellent. (Pick five customers with whom you know you have problems. Rate them now.)

5. PRECISION – CUSTOMER

a. Does your customer clearly state what he/she wants? (Think again of five customers and the service you provide. Rate them now.)

Yes every time	score 3
Most times	score 2
Rarely	score 1
Never	score 0

b. Does he/she give you all the necessary information in order for you to meet the requirements? (Do this exercise thinking of five internal customers where you know you have a problem. Score for each customer.)

Yes – every time	score 3
Most times	score 2
Rarely	score 1
Never	score 0

c. Does your customer have an input to the request for the service? (Score for five customers.)

Yes	score 3
Quite a lot	score 2
Very little	score 1
No	score 0

6. PRECISION – SUPPLIER

a. Do you think you provide adequate instructions to your supplier? (Think of five suppliers – pick some whom you have problems with.)

Yes	score 3
Sometimes	score 2
Not sure	score 1
No	score 0

b. Do you give your suppliers enough time to supply to your request?

Yes	score 3
Sometimes	score 2
Not often	score 1
No	score 0

c. Do you regularly review the quality of service between you and your suppliers?

Yes	score 3
Sometimes	score 2
Not often	score 1
No	score 0

There is no profile to assess your scores against. The relative figures should be sufficient to set up meetings with your most important customers and suppliers.

WHO ARE MY CUSTOMERS?

1. List your chief customers.

2. What do they need from you? How can you ensure that you provide them with their REQUIREMENTS, on time, every time?

3. When did you last discuss REQUIREMENTS with your customers?

4. Assume a meeting has been called to improve the provision of your services to your MAJOR customers. What issues would you debate?

5. What THREE major factors stop your meeting the requirements of your customers on time, every time, without error, defect or omission?

WHO ARE MY MAJOR SUPPLIERS?

Think of your suppliers. How can you ensure that they provide you with the necessary information, decisions, standards, services or goods on time, every time, without defect, error or omission.

1. How can you ensure that your SUPPLIERS meet your REQUIREMENTS?

2. What actions can you take to reduce ambiguity in the services they provide for you?

3. To what extent do your REQUIREMENTS, and the suppliers' perception of your REQUIREMENTS, match?

4. Why is there a mismatch? What are the major causes of ambiguity?

5. Have you and your SUPPLIERS agreed objectives and information required jointly? If not, how were these agreed and when?

6. What specific action will you take to clear up any ambiguities between your requirements and the suppliers' perception of your requirements?

TRANSFORMATIONS UK LTD.
Meeting Customer Requirements: Memo Pad
To:
From:
Date:
Subject:

My Requirements are:
1.
2.
3.
4.
5.
6.

Can you meet these requirements? If not, could you note down alternatives for discussion?
1.
2.
3.
4.
5.
6.

CHAPTER 9

Right First Time

A common language usually accompanies the introduction of TQ as it progresses through a company. And this common language is often permeated with little phrases or terms designed initially to project an idea or new way of working to all staff. It is important that these terms and words become commonly understood and come to represent the way things should be conducted in the culture of the business. Rework, COQ and terms like Right First Time (RFT) are all phrases which are designed to help people understand the underlying process and the impetus of the drive. I like to think we have a novel approach to the concept of Right First Time as a behavioural standard of performance which should start in service support areas first. I highlight this during Workshop sessions when I explain what the requirements for attending are and which have been agreed prior to attending:

- Turn up on time and listen to the perspective of others.

- Digest and complete the necessary reading and preparation before arrival.

- Prepare to discuss three organisational practices which you consider are preventing the business from achieving quality.

- Be positive and enthusiastic in discussion and find ways to make good ideas work.

- Challenge any practice if this hinders effective implementation of change in the company.

If these requirements are met, then they have performed Right First Time. They have met the agreed requirements for the session and we have achieved Zero Defects or, in other words, we have not deviated from our agreement.

Participants are usually quite relieved that RFT is sold to them in this way as no more than common sense along the lines of 'doing what you say you will do'. They are relieved because we have avoided launching into statistical process control (SPC) and all the detail which people associate with RFT as a process to ensuring manufacturing accuracy.

I believe the biggest problem that we have as 'change-makers' when introducing TQ is selling this as a process which is equally applicable in service and production environments. So when I start with RFT as a concept I discuss the behavioural standards in service areas rather than focus on controlling manufacturing standards in a business. We will refer to that area later on in this chapter.

BEHAVIOURAL STANDARDS FIRST

A major motor vehicle leasing company was driving the concept of Service Excellence through its company. This company had a Head Office where all processing and support functions took place and a Branch Network of 38 offices.

We worked with each of the support functions first and were discussing the concept of RFT and performance standards in a training Workshop. I was highlighting that RFT was not perfection – a concept which was confused with the phrase 'Zero Defects'. To illustrate this point we discussed how responsive we were to answering external telephone calls. I had worked on a Drive for TQ with Bass Breweries and the performance standard for Reception staff was to respond to a call every seven seconds. Dow Chemical in its drive for Quality had perfected a zero ring response rate using advanced technology – that is the phone did not appear to ring at all to the external caller – but the Receptionist had advance notice of this on her calling-in switchboard. How was that for responsiveness? However, as the discussion progressed we talked about performance standards when receiving internal calls from customers and suppliers. Those attending the session came from the Marketing Department of this motor finance business. Most agreed that in the open plan office if someone was away from his work-station it was not always common practice to attend to his calls – even if passing the desk.

Right then we agreed through their manager, Gary Jennison, that the performance standard for responding to calls would be within three rings or less (for the whole department). They agreed to monitor performance and change the standard if it was too rigorous. At the same time they also agreed a common response when first talking with a caller. Believe it or not, this became the performance standard within that Marketing office virtually overnight with 99% of calls being answered in less than three rings. The appreciation of Right First Time and the setting of performance standards in a service environment had become apparent immediately when people became consciously aware of the importance of responsiveness to internal and external customers. This behaviour quickly spread to other departments throughout the business who were committed to Right First Time and became a key feature of their customer responsiveness throughout their Branch Network. Also working with other support staff we agreed the following behavioural standards which were now consciously applied:

- Business dress – so there was no ambiguity.

- Smart and casual dress for attending training Workshops.

- Standards for dealing with telephone enquiries.

- Standards for Meeting Management.

- Response rates to written enquiries.

- Agreement for solving disputes.

- Agreements for prioritising work.

- Standards agreed to maintaining tidiness in the office.

- Dealing with outside contractors and agreeing delivery of services.

These and many others standards became a constant when previously they were 'taken for granted'. Most organisations could benefit quite radically by agreeing and practising these behaviours and standards, and not just expecting their manufacturing colleagues to maintain them as their sole responsibility.

PERFORMANCE STANDARDS IN PROCESSING WORK

These 38 regional offices in the motor finance business would service a series of Auto Dealerships – and, basically, the product that the company sold was point-of-sale finance to the motor industry. Leases, Contract Hire and Hire Purchase were the main products, with Insurance products tagged on behind. What was interesting about working with this very successful business over a three-year period was that there appeared to be different performance standards employed within each of the regional branches. For instance, to process a Lease in Birmingham it could take four hours, whereas the Lease could be processed in two hours in Southampton. We were interested why different standards existed in different parts of the country and set a challenge to the 38 Branch Managers to establish what they considered the right performance standard should be for completing, processing and setting up a lease with a new customer.

By focusing our attention on this process, Managers started to measure work completion – not something they previously had been trained to do. It would seem that the 'assumption' was because the work was administrative and paper-driven it was not possible to measure performance. However, one manager in particular did a great job. Graham Ashley-Fenn was manager of the most southerly of the Branches and simply asked the women who completed the work what the standard could be. What were the parameters for completing Leases, Contract Hire, Hire Purchase and the various Insurance products they sold? He was pleasantly surprised to find that performance standards which were agreed as possible by those who operated the process were far higher than his own personal expectations.

When he fed this back in a training session to his other colleagues some were surprised that he had given up 'apparent' control to his staff to let them set standards. We made the point – that it should be staff who work and own the process who probably have the most accurate picture of what the standard should be. They are also the best people to talk with about ways for improving the process. The alternative is to 'over-control' the process and confuse the issue with managerial interference. Graham created the right impression that the role of manager was to act as a coach, provide support, drive and training to let his staff just get on with their job. The time of the manager to control things and people and check and inspect work demonstrates that the culture needs a healthy injection of empowerment to make things happen quickly. TQ is about relaxing 'over-control' to just let people get on and do their best for the company.

Looking at performance standards of those who provide support systems before looking at the manufacturing process is imperative if TQ is to take hold within a business.

GETTING THINGS RIGHT FIRST TIME

There is a real danger when we start using phrases like 'getting it Right the First Time' that they will be perceived by employees as no more than rhetoric and exhortation. Catchphrases publicising the cause soon become worn and meaningless. It can become even more pronounced when someone has a bright idea to have posters printed. Posters adorn the building with the RFT slogan well displayed. It soon becomes a meaningless TLA – three letter abbreviation. There is another danger, and that is that these phrases are used for the wrong purpose. Too often we have heard this phrase (RFT – Right First Time) used in a negative context, to allocate blame and catch people out! Right First Time is a state towards which a company is moving. It can be used in too literal a manner, when instead it should be used positively so that we can learn to do things better.

We have to be careful that phrases, which once had meaning, become clichéd, colourless with little vibrancy or life as their use becomes more common and as the drive progresses over time. We have to ensure that the Right First Time mentality really is that. It must become part of the managerial way of doing things by Managers and others in authority leading by example. Right First Time is after all the only acceptable standard of performance for the Total Quality company.

RFT IS A STANDARD OF PERFORMANCE

Right First Time is a performance standard. It is about performing and achieving work which is error-free. This is the foundation upon which the positive attitudes towards TQ are made. Many traditional QA Drives focus upon standardising procedures and agreeing specifications for inspection. The Right First Time approach is concerned with surpassing the present performance standard and replacing it with zero defects.

The RFT approach is a 'performance standard' which we want everybody to gradually acquire. Please note the word 'gradually'. We cannot expect people to change their behaviour overnight. Right First Time is about only passing those things on to your customer which meet his or her requirements.

ERROR-FREE WORK

This approach is concerned with getting all staff, whether internal suppliers or customers, to perform error-free work. This principle helps us forge the chain of quality between all functions, units and departments. Overall, the Right First Time philosophy helps us to reduce the requirement for expensive rework by preventing problems arising. Fundamentally, this is about developing a strong value in everybody so as not to pass something on which we know is wrong. This might sound easy, and it is.

RIGHT SECOND TIME THREATENING TQ PROGRESS

For instance, a major US-owned market leader in medical technology had been developing a TQ Drive for quite some time. A great majority of the staff had been through the educational process, and managers in plant locations were making some attempt to bring down the cost of Quality by taking preventative action. Several years into the programme, the R&D boys developed a new product which would revolutionalise a number of products in the industry.

Sales staff did not waste any time. They saw this as a great opportunity to consolidate market-share. A great deal of fuss and hype was generated about the new product and, of course, the sales force went out selling. Before long the Sales people had accrued $20 million worth of sales – although as yet the product was still undergoing tests.

Although the prototype and the tests suggested that the product would be reliable, when the plant eventually went into production, some time later, the QA people discovered that there had been a design error which could have lead to failure in 2-3% in the product. At first they were shocked, realising the impact that this would have on the TQ programme. No one seemed to question that the product would be released. There were many urgent meetings with senior staff from Head Office mulling over the possible consequences.

It was touch and go. Although this was a multi-billion dollar company with a reputation for Quality to protect, there was a school of thought that suggested that the product should be released into the marketplace! It was hypothesised that, in the few cases where there was breakdown – the company could service the product, rework it or substitute it with a reliable model when a new more compatible design was approved. Clearly this 'acceptable quality level' was showing. If 97% of the product was okay – then ship the lot and put up with the rework. After all it would not cost too much. The company would still gain $20 million in the short run and rework costs wouldn't be too expensive. This was the argument. The only problem was that the 100% Quality Zero Defect Goal was being compromised, and who says that it wouldn't happen again? This time the AQL (Acceptable Quality Level) may be 97%. Would it be 93% next time and 89% the time after? The argument was: Who cares? Rework costs aren't high anyway and look at the potential $20 million revenue stream. Clearly, if this 'behaviour' was accepted it would lead to the violation of a major principle of TQ which would kill the incentive behind the Drive.

TQ HEROES

The Senior Staff at the manufacturing plant stood for no shipping option until the product was Right First Time, much against the view from some in Corporate Headquarters. Some managers had their heads on the block and their careers on the line. They were total advocates of TQ. Those risking their jobs for a 'principle' also recognised that this event was critical for the successful take-up of TQ within their staff. For some time, the staff in some units had been looking for an excuse to confirm their prejudice that management was not serious about Quality – was this to be the first example? They almost had their wish come true. The CEO entered into the debate and made the only choice possible. They scrapped $20 million of equipment and started again.

The company lost face only with a very small percentage of their customers – and only in the short term. Apart from the odd customer, most accepted the reason for withdrawal from the market and were happy to wait the extra nine months for Error-Free Products. This display of commitment reinforced the belief in the company that the senior officers were serious about Quality Improvement.

Most important of all, it created among the staff a level of trust never before witnessed. The company was serious. People who had pushed TQ and put their jobs on the line were classed as heroes. Stories of how local managers convinced corporate officers of the wisdom of the TQ approach were told, with the resulting effect that morale and job satisfaction went through the roof. This incident also acted as a catalyst to those who were doubters. Resistance to TQ fell.

RIGHT FIRST TIME IS DEVELOPED BY EXAMPLE

What that story tells us is that cultures need time to change and critical incidents like the one described can act as the death knell or the success of TQ. Overall it reflects the phrase:

"We do what we value and we value what we do."

Actions reflect attitudes and values. Attitude change mirrored in actions and behaviour is the foundation upon which Quality grows and flourishes to become a way of life. This requires people at all levels who have strong values to lead by example. Those who possess a strong positive attitude are those who are committed to improving individual, departmental and organisational standards of performance. This attitude and the enthusiasm generated from it can take companies far above their competitors in terms of Quality of performance.

ERROR-FREE STANDARDS

Work which is error-free is a statement of our own personal standard of performance. More importantly, it means that people with this standard will positively stop errors creeping into their work. They are their own inspector. They do not require antiquated methods of control. They want to do things right. They have pride in their work. But although they are their own inspector, they want to do more than just check for errors. They want to prevent errors arising and this means looking for ways to stop errors taking place. Staff, if trained, also come out with lots of ideas to prevent problems arising. This is the approach behind 'fool-proofing' which the Japanese have turned into an art form. Those interested in 'fool-proofing' deliberately go out of their way to look at every possible combination of what can go wrong in manufacture and then take preventative action – just once, to eradicate the problem.

FOOL-PROOFING: THE JAPANESE APPROACH TO PREVENTION

When walking around Japanese companies, it is amazing to see the level of sophistication in fool-proofing. From simple examples at Toyota, where cars are covered with protective strips to avoid scratched paintwork during assembly, to Nippon Denso, where the achieved performance standard for manufacture and assembly of brake drums and other automotive components is zero defects – it is incredible. Simple devices, developed by operators, are located all along the assembly line. Jigs are designed to reject metallic items which do not conform to a standard. Nippon Denso have not had a major problem from any of the car manufacturers they have serviced for the past twenty years. British managers witnessing this experience were astounded, considered the behaviour of suppliers to the automotive industry in Europe, and wondered what the performance standard would be in this country.

QUALITY IMPROVEMENT STATISTICS

This devotion to duty is even more marked in Japanese manufacturing plants. There, we are told that employees constantly provide suggestions to improve everything they do. This does not include just manufacturing areas but clerical and administrative procedures. It is quite frightening when statistics are bandied about. On average, the Japanese suggest that they get something like 100-140 ideas from each employee. The really frightening statistic is that on average they tend to implement 80% of these suggestions.

Why does this approach work? It is quite simple. Employees see a wonderful opportunity for Quality improvement in the most general of senses. The idea may speed up production – but it does not have to – the improvement may be to do with cost reduction, quality improvement, health and safety, ergonomics, improvement in teamworking and other soft S's.

IMPLEMENT IMPROVEMENT – DON'T KILL THEM WITH TALKING

On a trip to Mitsubishi, a group of us stopped by the assembly line and talked through an interpreter to a shopfloor employee. We asked him about the suggestions he had recently given to his Manager and his Quality Circle. He talked about a suggestion of which he was most proud. This had to do with moving a button from the floor area of his workstation, just beneath the assembly line, to a place which was waist level. The suggestion had been approved by the Circle seven days prior to our visit. Five days after the proposals were approved, the button was moved. Movement of the button did not increase productivity or improve quality – it stopped the employee bending over every three minutes. He now felt more comfortable and was extremely grateful to the organisation for taking an interest in his welfare.

Can you imagine the effect that action would have on the morale of employees? It would encourage more suggestions – because the company cared about its staff. It demonstrates that the management of the company are really concerned about their people. They don't just implement those things which will lead to significant cost reduction or productivity or Quality Improvement – they are prepared to improve everything. They are committed to zero defects, not just in manufacture but equally in people management.

Bearing this last story in mind, think and honestly answer one simple question: *In the average UK plant – what would happen if an employee suggested the movement of a button to ease the operations he performed?*

Would management respond and move the button? Would they feed back and tell the employee it was a good idea – but could not be implemented because of a particular reason – or would they do nothing?

To be honest, in too many cases in some sectors nothing would happen or there could be a 'cynical' response which discouraged any further involvement for improvement! The reason for this is the great British disease – the 'us and them' attitude which is founded upon how 'control' is shared between those who manage and those who are managed. Attitudes in the UK have hindered rather than helped TQ initiatives in the past 20 years and will continue to do so until we create a needed change in culture!

In all truth, the average British company does not recognise the contribution staff can make to continuous improvement. Compare ourselves to our Japanese rivals. Just as an example, Toyota announced over eight years ago that its Japanese employees made 1,903,858 suggestions, of which 97% were adopted. How does this compare with figures for European industry?

And please let us not explain away this process of managing a preventative culture as a quirk of the Japanese culture. To compare Japanese-owned companies and Joint Ventures in Europe and the US, Quality Improvement is just as high. So let's be realistic. This is not a feature of the 'Japanese' but a feature of the approach they use – which can work in all European and US companies, given time, planning and patience.

SUGGESTIONS STRETCH FAR BEYOND MANUFACTURING TO SERVICE

Many suggestions affect performance in manufacturing areas, but careful examination by Toyota has ensured that the hands-on approach by employees can be improved and continued in all areas. The result of this is increased efficiency, cost control and a happy, motivated and satisfied staff. This approach is clearly desirable – so what action can we take in Europe and the US to promote the Right First Time attitude?

Companies such as Hewlett Packard, ICL, Corning, Digital, Rank Xerox and many others prove that these performance standards can easily be achieved after developing a strong performance-driven culture focused upon replacing Rework with a major investment in Prevention.

RFT MUST BECOME A PERSONAL STANDARD OF PERFORMANCE

It means that the individual prevents errors from intruding into his or her own personal work. The errors which creep into our work and are passed on to our internal customers are compounded and then on to the recipient of the service or goods, the external customer. The customer's dissatisfaction then becomes a significant Quality problem. How long is it before the customer becomes sufficiently upset with our lack of attention to detail that he decides to go elsewhere – to our competitors? In markets which are growing slowly, an increase in sales for one company usually means a reduction in sales, work and job security for others.

Only when RFT becomes the expected standard of performance for everybody can we ensure that errors are not compounded and passed on to the customer. We must understand that the result of failing to take preventative action is a loss of market share and a reduction in profit levels. There are some cases when the cost of putting things right can cost more than the revenue received for the product or service. This is not healthy and can lead to only one conclusion: "Customers learn quickly; and do business with organisations who are only committed to Total Quality".

PERSONAL VALUES AND STANDARDS

We would not expect airline pilots to adopt a less than 100% commitment to take off, flying and landing. Neither would we expect a dentist to adopt a sloppy attitude. Sometimes we can be very critical of others but not always sufficiently critical of ourselves. We know that the sloppy attitude is indicative of others as service providers, but the key to continuous improvement is to start with examining the quality of service which we supply – start with changing self first.

Often when we do things wrong we can rationalise and find a reason for the error – usually external or dissociated from our involvement. When others use the same tactics and explain this in the same way there may be a tendency for us to claim this as an 'excuse'. For instance, in many businesses managers state that they never have enough time to prevent errors arising – but I quickly state that we always seem to find the time to rework things to put them right. In similar vein, many complain that they are so busy firefighting, and extinguishing yesterday's problems, that they never have time, the resources or the support to work on preventing tomorrow's problems. This is an excuse not a reason, and becomes part of the agreed 'organisational list of excuses' created to avoid the pain of changing and improving performance.

The 'never enough time' syndrome can be a strange attitude in organisations. It is strange because eventually they will have to find the time to fix things for their customers – or their customers will go elsewhere. So why not aim now to get things right the first time, and prevent problems arising again? Ask yourself a simple question: if you were in charge of the company, would you waste corporate resources failing to do things right first time and then redeploy resources to fix things after the event – further adding unnecessary rework costs to the business? Of course not!

The implications of this common problem are dire. When a TQ Drive begins, the words RFT fill the lecture rooms. It is broadcast on posters – but still the dominant attitude is 'fix it after things go wrong'! In the long term how can we encourage others to take us seriously and adopt this 'performance standard' when we don't practise what we preach?

SHIP IT!

Some time ago, a company starting a Quality Drive had a significant problem. Corporate Headquarters were not happy – neither were the shareholders – because managers in the plant did not seem to be able to get the throughput through the plant and to the customer on time. Strict financial controls were imposed upon the plant. They had to generate consistent revenue for the business each and every month. This translated into the company physically shipping the equivalent of £1.8 million of orders per month.

During the first stages of the Quality Drive, there was a great deal of confusion between Right First Time Quality products and the amount which must be shipped each month to meet financial targets. The company managed to keep to the projected target for the first three weeks of each month and then all hell broke loose during the last week! The company would ship anything – just to maintain financial targets. In some cases this meant the company was shipping half-full crates to customers with an attached note – stating that the rest of the consignment would follow shortly. In one example, the company shipped a set of empty crates just to buy themselves time from the Financial people.

To Corporate Headquarters the invoices dispatched indicated that the company was on target, but the shopfloor knew different. There were areas allocated for Work In Progress and these were growing each month. How were the employees supposed to take the Right First Time mentality seriously – when there were clear cases of this principle being violated and compromised all in order to meet disjointed financial targets which were imposed and not agreed with production capability?

We cannot expect this company to move overnight to a TQ culture – but why weren't the Management Team honest enough to tell the staff the truth? It's far better to talk about moving targets of RFT than to pretend they can actually achieve them.

CULTURAL CHANGE – IT'S NOT A FAIRY STORY

In the previous example there are two issues which need to be clarified: the commitment issue and the time issue. It was clear that the HQ staff did not share the same regard for TQ as the managers of the plant. A major question has to be answered. Should one then stop the TQ Drive until everybody is on board or should one continue?

A purist would stop the drive and wait for conditions to be perfect. A realist would continue the Drive but tell the truth.

A TRUTHFUL STATEMENT WOULD YIELD POSITIVE RESULTS

"We are aiming for zero defects – but you know we have a long way to go. We will make progress steadily. But we will not lie to you. There are occasions when we are implementing TQ that we may have to slide back three steps for every step taken forward. But we will inform you when this will happen and why! We will also tell you immediately after that crisis is over. Overall, we expect in three months to be spending less than 30% of our time on rework. Preventative-type activities will replace this over the rest of the year. Current circumstances suggest that we will not be able to achieve the values we espouse immediately, but please note we aim to get better every day – even if this progress appears slow. We feel it is best to share our vision with you about the future and recognise that the changes we need to make us more competitive will not instantly appear. Thank you for your patience – we are committed to improving our performance, however slowly and painfully."

TIME

Time is another issue. We realise that time can pass very quickly and that we seem to achieve little in terms of adding value, although we can be extremely busy reworking problems. This often has its cause in a failure to determine priorities: spending more time on short- rather than long-term objectives, failing to plan ahead, and letting the urgent take over from the important. Sooner or later, the culture prevailing accepts this right second time attitude as the performance standard. This is testified to in policy documents, when companies proudly proclaim that they will rectify faults arising from their products within a set time period. This creates confidence in the warranty, but does not actually do too much for the reputation of the product and the company.

We reject the 'right second time' approach because it creates long-term problems for the company. New employees may witness the 'second time' mentality and consider it acceptable to work to this standard. This soon spreads to become right third, fourth and fifth time.

An interesting issue is what action should we take with a company which experiences a high turnover of staff? How can it ensure that the culture always remains tuned to TQ despite the influx of new employees? There is no response other than a detailed Training Programme for all new employees. This could easily be integrated into an Induction Programme.

WHAT IS THE RELATIONSHIP BETWEEN RIGHT FIRST TIME AND ZERO DEFECTS?

Right First Time is simple. It is no more and no less than Meeting Customer Requirements. Knowing what customers need, renegotiating if circumstances are not right and delivering to that standard is all it is and no more. After a TQ Drive has been in operation for some time Meeting Customer Requirements and Right First Time will mean the same thing – Zero Defects!

Many managers get too carried away at first with the meanings of the exhortations and start questioning the validity of achieving Zero Defects. Some claim to tell others that this performance standard, although desirable, is impossible and demotivating.

Tell people that Zero Defects and RFT as the Performance Standard is not demotivating – because we don't expect them to start tomorrow. It isn't easy – but it is attainable if we can inculcate the attitude and want to stop errors arising. If we don't aim for Zero Defects we will never achieve it.

WHAT INHIBITS RIGHT FIRST TIME?

A great deal can inhibit the movement towards wanting to get things right. Chapter 4 looks at some of the issues on managing resistance to change and Chapter 5 examines some of the factors inherent in promoting 'cultural change'. These comments will not be duplicated.

The really critical issues are related to Training and Managing on a day-to-day basis. Staff have to be trained in how to do their job – otherwise they have no standard to work to.

On one assignment it was noted that most of the supervisors had been recruited from the shopfloor. This may have been good for internal morale and motivation – but the cost to the company was that there was little attempt made to encourage others with experience and ideas from outside to come into the company. Consequently, the people who achieved supervisory status were new to the demands of a supervisory position – but not new to the business or their colleagues who instantly became their direct reports. Because of the nature of the company, very little basic training was given. Supervisors also had the use of computers, but during a stay of a few months I found no one who had been provided with comprehensive training in either Supervision or the use of IT. The use of the computer was solely geared to inventory control and was infrequently used by staff because of a failure to train them in its application. Consequently, supervisors never approached managers to explain their problem in their operating of IT, as they perceived it to be a personal weakness which would reflect on their ability and competence. Consequently, little honesty existed between Supervisors and Managers about being sufficiently equipped to deal with the demands of their work, resulting in a less than efficient operation.

This example illustrates that failing to train staff even in the basic skills necessary to do the job 'right first time' and failing to listen to real concerns are serious problems for companies attempting to introduce TQ. TQ can still be achieved despite these setbacks, but its effect will take much longer to materialise and the culture for continuous improvement and learning will never really be embedded.

ERROR PREVENTION

Some companies decide that they are not going to progress the TQ Drive quickly. They realise that there are many cultural factors within the company which are inhibiting its growth. To start the ball rolling, they begin the Error Prevention Process. Some companies use a variant of this to unearth major Quality issues for immediate improvement after the training event and develop supporting documentation (Fig 1). But this process does not have to be a major event. It can be regulated and used extremely effectively – and it must be controlled!

If a company were to distribute the Error Prevention Documentation to all staff and ask them to complete it, they would probably be inundated with responses. Unless they had the right structure in place it is unlikely that they could do much about improvement and live up to the expectations of their staff. Here lies the need for controlling the advance of change. This means containing and taking charge of the change process.

The selective and constrained use of this continuous improvement process, together with the formal structure to create change and respond to 'right the wrongs', is a good incremental approach to implementing TQ and promoting RFT.

SUMMARY

It is important for performance standards to evolve through TQ training. Often the best people to agree performance standards of Right First Time are the people who own and work the process rather than those who manage it. It is clear that every process, either administrative, behavioural or manufacturing based, must be explored and a self-critical attitude brought to bear on improving service delivery. When standards are agreed they must be measured and continually assessed for the scope to improve continuously.

Bullet Points

- Right First Time starts first with those who provide service as support functions.

- Ensure that Right First Time is more than just rhetoric.

- Reject posters displaying messages of Right First Time if they are going to be the most powerful medium you employ to create change. This probably means you substitute behaviour with exhortations.

- Don't try to catch each other out and prove that others failed to do things 'right first time'. This is negative and focuses upon the 3-5% of what people may have done wrong rather than on the 95% of what they did well.

- Right First Time is a Standard of Performance. It is about promoting error-free work. It is about surpassing old standards and preventing errors creeping into work.

- By looking for possible errors, taking corrective and preventative action – we are guarding against compounding errors and passing them on to our customers.

- The Right Second Time mentality threatens TQ progress.

- Demonstrate your commitment to TQ by doing something which reflects the RFT philosophy. Do all you can to create Heroes related to battling the old culture.

- Right First Time is leading by example. "We do what we value and we value what we do."

- Everyone is his own inspector.

- Look for all the ways a process can fail and then fix it so it can't.

- The people we employ know more about the operational side of the business than the Senior Officers. Develop strategies to release these energies. Don't argue with suggestions – just implement them. Ensure that you don't focus implementation on productivity and cost reduction to the detriment of other issues.

- The service side has many improvements it can make to improve procedures and documentation.

- RFT must become the standard of performance by which we are all assessed. It must become our personal standard.

- Implementing TQ overnight is impossible. Managers in companies will continue to do things the wrong way. Telling your people why and when the 'old ways' will stop, gains more credibility than lying.

- Zero defects is not perfectionism. Zero defects is doing things right the first time and is orientated towards Meeting Customer Requirements. ZD = MCR.

- A failure to train, communicate and manage TQ on a day-to-day basis can inhibit the RFT mentality from becoming standard operating procedure.

- Conduct controlled exercises identifying areas where errors are most prominent. Control the exercise, otherwise managerial inaction to put right what is wrong, because of the size of response, will fuel the negative rumours about TQ not working.

ERROR PREVENTION PROCESS

Name   Unit   Date

The problem below is stopping me from performing error-free work. Could we investigate this problem and get it right first time?

The problem is:

The symptoms are:

Probable causes:

Action by Unit Manager:

Date:

Referral to Quality Director Date:

CHAPTER 10

Taking Preventative Action

PREVENTATIVE ACTION

Preventative action is an alternative to fixing things after they have gone wrong. Preventative Action means solving a problem permanently. You may be surprised to find that most problems which organisations cope with prior to TQ are never really solved and fixed permanently. Rather, the small problems are worked through but the really big problems, which create a great deal of rework, confusion and firefighting, remain with the infrastructure and the culture to re-emerge again in the future.

We tend to react to events as they arise and fix them quickly, in many cases concentrating upon the effects rather than the causes. Consequently, the symptoms of the problems are dealt with, but the factor which created the incident is still there – ready to arise some time in the future when the organisation is under pressure. Unless we can create a seamless organisation, with the focus on horizontal management with customers and suppliers working as one, we will continue to experience problems time and time again.

LISTING KEY PROBLEMS

When running Workshops we always ask managers to generate and list the sort of problems which they will be confronting in the next three months. Following completion, we ask them to create other lists of likely problems they will need to overcome in six, twelve, eighteen and twenty-four months.

The same key 'problems' appear time and time again on different lists. We can establish from this evidence that most problems you are about to experience are predictable and, more importantly, many are recurring. If this is the case, many problems have never been solved in the first instance – if they had they would not arise again!

IF YOU HAVE CONTROL YOU CAN SOLVE PROBLEMS. IF YOU DON'T, YOU CAN'T

Asking managers to cast their mind back over the years, we usually find that some of the 'recurring' problems have not been properly tackled at all. Resources have been allocated, effort expended and things fixed temporarily. But they were not fixed permanently. Many problems which plague Managers never seem to go away and this is because nobody has really developed a long-term workable solution – we tend to deal just with the symptom rather than addressing the cause.

Not unusually, we find that it is not the small problems that cause the trouble. Consider an inventory control, accounting or personnel problem. These issues will all have been fixed, there and then, never to arise again. The reason for this is that the manager solving the problem and implementing a solution will have had control over most of the variables which impact on the problem. In many cases, the problem will not have been shared with other sections, departments or units, of if it has it will have been relatively easy to fix. The smaller the number of departments experiencing the problem, the easier to fix it. This isn't a matter of size – but of control. If a manager has authority and control in specific areas, he can influence performance there. It is unlikely that he will be able to control the actions and behaviour of other units.

INTERNAL CAPABILITY FOR CHANGE

We believe that TQ only really takes place when an organisation develops its own ability to master change. This only comes about when a company commits to developing its line managers to become internal trainers and facilitators. Often we work with the top team of a company and then put a selection of its staff through an extremely rigorous and testing training. During the first series of Workshops, I presented to the managers and asked them about the role of the training and the brief they had received from their managers. It transpired that little if any briefing took place. They were just told to arrive at the training session and take notes.

We spent a considerable period of time explaining the strategy to these people before starting the drive. A simple error in failing to communicate caused a great deal of confusion for these people. The effectiveness of the programme was also hindered. Investing in prevention and devoting time and communicating intentions is probably the most important role that a manager can play in promoting the concept in his business and the one least practised.

In comparison, let us consider the problems which lead to rework. These are the really big headaches – but they may be no bigger than the problems which many managers face in their specific areas on a day-to-day basis. So what makes one problem different from another? It is not size. The determining factor, in addition to control, which influences the extent to which problems can be solved once and for all, is simply the number and variety of units of departments affected by that problem.

OWNERSHIP AND PROBLEM-SOLVING

No one will really 'own' the problem and take it on board as his responsibility. Let's face it, the really big problems don't have owners. One department blames another. Sales blame R&D for failing to develop drawing, R&D blame the Purchasing Dept for failing to co-ordinate raw materials flow, manufacturing blame everybody! Everyone passes the buck to somebody else. Because the interaction of departments makes the problem appear 'complex', no one knows where to start – nor wants to get involved. The chance of a problem being solved by four or more individuals from different departments and different cultures is not high in many companies (although a matrix management/task culture can develop superb solutions – but these are rare).

How many Departmental Heads or Managers are going to volunteer to solve problems? Very few, because they recognise how difficult it is to change things in other departments – especially where they have no authority or control for creating changes. Problems may be discussed freely – but they have no real home. No one wants ownership.

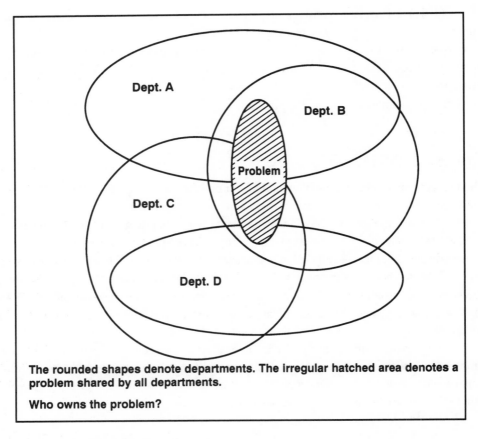

Fig. 13 *Ownership and preventative action*

THE RELIEF OF SHARED OWNERSHIP –
NO ONE CAN BE SINGLED OUT FOR BLAME

To complicate matters, when Departmental Managers experience a complex problem impacting upon all units at once – they can heave a sigh of relief! Why? They recognise that there are no clear lines between who is responsible for X, Y and Z problem in each department. Demarcation lines on 'ownership' are fuzzy – no one can allocate blame to just one person. Knowing this, they are aware that 'ownership' is shared and unclear – so there is little incentive to create change.

Sooner or later someone has to attempt to solve what is wrong, but it can be too late, and remedying the problem may cost the company a great deal.

The major problems, as already stated, frequently occur between departments. For example, in some companies there are conflicts between Sales and Contract Administration, between Manufacturing and Engineering, and Personnel and Line Management.

FIREFIGHTING CULTURES

Below are two cases which illustrate the failure to prevent problems arising.

We were working with a company producing heavy duty catering equipment for hotels, hospitals, schools, colleges and the marine market. The problems they encountered were such that they created a tremendous amount of rework. Scheduling was appalling. There was little overview of the major company problem.

The company was experiencing severe cash flow difficulties. A short-term, short-sighted decision was taken. In future all suppliers would be paid after the thirty-day agreed limit. Sometimes this was extended to sixty or ninety days. Customers were put under pressure to pay up. Because some of the customers were in the public sector, they were sometimes late with payment.

In the short term, some suppliers experiencing cash flow difficulties themselves put pressure upon the manufacturer to pay on time. When the response was negative, some suppliers stopped delivering and made it a condition that goods were paid for in advance. This created severe problems for the manufacturing areas who just did not have components to make the product. Consequently, delivery of product was late – which meant in many cases that the external customer imposed penalty clauses upon the manufacturer. This created even more cash flow problems.

This was serious. Work in Progress was increasing, goods couldn't be finished or delivered on time. Customers such as Local Authorities were outraged. The kitchens in schools and colleges were incomplete, creating problems for them in trying to provide a service for their pupils with no kitchen facilities! The results were catastrophic.

Likewise, a company producing engineering sub-assembly parts would agree to unrealistic delivery dates. Lead times for manufacturing items were reduced radically. The company had completed the sale with the customer and, whatever happened, the goods would be delivered on time – but at what cost?

Because of the rush, Technical Drawings were sub-contracted, and tooling rushed to manufacture without testing. Purchasing were pushed to reduce costs. Subsequently, the quality of raw material was poor, rework was high and production control was in a spin. Extra shifts had to be arranged and delivery to the customer by outside contractors was necessary, because of problems with scheduling delivery.

This incident became more regular and soon a common occurrence. Every Friday afternoon was characterised by managers dashing about all over the place trying to ensure that goods went out of dispatch to be delivered on time, did what was required and did a tremendous job, only to be deflated when the customer returned some of the items because of inconsistency/poor quality. This chaos and firefighting got worse.

CHANGING TO THE PREVENTATIVE CULTURE

Being critical of company organisation is easy – putting it right isn't! Changing from one culture to another is difficult. It takes time and a real devotion to company-wide problem-solving. All the managers in the two examples quoted above were diligent and conscientious. They thought they were doing the right job. After all, they were rewarded for working in this manner and this was reinforced by the weekly fiasco. What was needed in both examples was a company-wide initiative with everyone willing to contribute to resolve these problems for ever. Because the problems were so large no one had real responsibility for changing things, apart from the Chief Executive and, in both instances, he was cushioned by line managers who did not speak up. In these two examples, everyone was being defensive. The problem was 'somebody else's'.

Consider the consequences of not dealing with a problem like this in the proper manner. Time and resources are wasted, negative stereotypes are reinforced between departments, and the 'pass the buck' attitude is prevalent. It was hard to believe that all the managers worked for the same company. Taking ownership and working things out together is the key to preventative action.

WESTERN PROBLEM-SOLVING IS FIREFIGHTING

In the West, we have developed a reputation for putting things right after they have gone wrong. Organisations pride themselves on their "no quibble guarantee". We are proficient at setting up project teams to take corrective action, but we spend little time on preventing these errors arising. Employees are rewarded for quick thinking and resolving crises, but there appears to be little attention paid to those dedicated to prevention in the long term. We have the wrong approach to problem-solving.

Generally, too many of us spend so much time firefighting that we have little time left for prevention. How much time do people spend solving yesterday's problems rather than preventing tomorrow's? Could problems creating rework have been anticipated and preventative measures taken? More importantly, could others, either from your department or other functions, have taken some form of preventative action and thus saved your doing the job 'twice over'?

Think about how you can start preventing errors. Do you consider likely problems before you start a new manufacturing or administrative process or do you adopt the approach that a run-through will act as a useful pilot for further modification?

ONE HOUR OF PLANNING SAVES TEN HOURS OF CHAOS

The majority of problems can be controlled by understanding and developing clear objectives and requirements to cover all potential problems. Failure Mode Effect Analysis (FMEAs – both process and design) are useful tools to use to eliminate error. Requirements cover all the inputs, human, materials, decisions required, procedures and standards. A thorough analysis of Meeting Customer Requirements (Chapter 8) is essential and should enable most to solve problems before they arise.

Testing or using pilot studies is appropriate, provided that you can control the process. All variables must be regulated by you to ensure that test and pilots are a true reflection of reality. It is of no value to run a set of tests on a product if the environment generated for test purposes does not match the real work conditions. This is true for product testing, for DP systems, manual systems and procedures. Like must be tested against like and conditions documented accurately.

It is important that circumstances be taken into account when we are examining results/conclusions of tests.

It is clear from the examples generated that in order to Manage through PREVENTATIVE ACTION, it is necessary to adopt the right attitude and concern for owning the problem. Training in Problem-Solving skills is also an inherent aspect of PREVENTATIVE ACTION. Groups or teams of people may wish to get together to solve problems. They may have the necessary commitment but they do not automatically have the frameworks, the knowledge of problem-solving skills and statistical techniques which can help them.

KEY ISSUES IN PROBLEM-SOLVING

Talking about Preventative Action and putting it into effect are two different things. Most TQ initiatives have a formal structure where people come together to discuss the solutions to organisational problems. Prior to this they should have experienced the TQ 'educational process' and understood the philosophy, the key principles and the route the company is going to take to implement change.

At this stage, people become concerned about structures. Should our groups be voluntary, ie. Quality Circles, or should they be firmly structured around the nature of a problem and be called Corrective Action Teams, Quality Action Teams, etc.? The names and structures are unimportant at the moment (this is the subject of Chapter 13). However, the process of problem-solving is the key.

Too many managers spend too much time concentrating upon structure and neglect process. We will spend some time on process because it is critical to problem solution.

Everyone in the organisation needs to understand the techniques of problem-solving. They also need to be aware of statistical techniques. This is critical. Perhaps most important of all, people need to understand how they influence problem-solving by the way they work in groups, by understanding how they learn and reach conclusions.

TECHNIQUES ARE NOT ENOUGH: CLIMATE AND RULES FOR PROBLEM-SOLVING

Personality characteristics are important determinants of a 'problem-solving' style which people will utilise. Some people are quite 'process orientated' and are concerned that the sequence of stages in problem-solving are explored and that everyone attending has the opportunity to contribute, whereas others are extremely task-centred, and focus very little attention on people and the contribution they can make.

It is not surprising to find that the majority of people tend to be very structured (please note this does not mean logical), and orientated towards getting a right answer. It is necessary for people involved in problem-solving teams to understand fully the dynamics of problem-solving.

This does not mean that managers will be navel-gazing – but looking at the inherent features of problem-solving and generating a superior solution. Care and attention should be directed here, because the success achieved by problem-solving groups will soon be transmitted through the structure to others and will indicate whether or not their efforts have been successful.

To help this process it is advisable to develop 'rules' by which business will be conducted. Rules help enormously, provided that the group sees the wisdom in them and keeps to them. But more important than this is learning of problem-solving style.

SOME RULES FOR PROBLEM-SOLVING GROUPS

We all need some rules to guide us when we are working as group members. These rules help regulate the behaviour of those in the team and facilitate progress. Ideally, they should be displayed in a prominent position.

RULE 1.   Don't find ten ways to make a good idea fail. Find one reason to make it work!

RULE 2.   Don't be negative and say: "That won't work". Be positive and look for those things which unite CAT members.

RULE 3.   Don't do an 'over the wall', don't pass the buck.

RULE 4.   Listen to what others say and think through their proposals.

RULE 5.   Leave your role and status outside.

RULE 6. Draw up a short agenda for each meeting and stick to it. Don't deviate. Agree action and take brief minutes to reflect agreement reached.

RULE 7. Be aware of your own problem-solving style and ensure that you look at problems from different perspectives.

LEARNING HOW YOU LEARN AND SOLVE PROBLEMS

An excellent instrument for training problem-solving is the Kolb Learning Style approach. This suggests that we each have preferences in methods of learning and solving problems. These tend to be reinforced during our professional lives and, as we develop a preference, ie., being practical and fixing things as they go wrong, we develop a strength in this area. This gaining of strength in one or two ways of learning and problem-solving reinforces our belief that the style works best for us. We tend to become specialised, and increased use of one or more approaches means that we tend to neglect other relevant but less desired approaches.

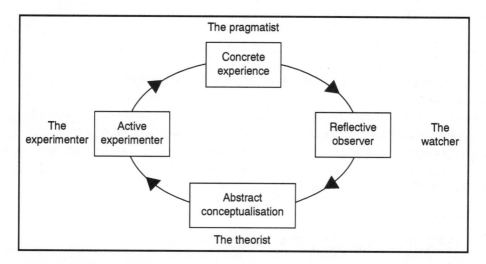

Fig. 14 *Learning and problem-solving styles (Source: **Organizational Psychology**, 1984)*

The Kolb instrument is extremely useful and one neglected by too many who believe that the answer to Quality Improvement is to get more people in a room talking around an agenda.

Problem-solving members spend a great deal of their time thinking through issues and obviously trying to solve problems. The ability to think clearly and solve problems in a systematic way is what differentiates the successful group from the unsuccessful. Those who cannot solve problems quickly are those who either lack the talent, skill, knowledge, motivation or the experience, to do so. We are not born with 'problem-solving ability' we have to practise it with others.

PROBLEM-SOLVING AND DECISION-MAKING

First of all, do not try to compartmentalise these two areas. They are not discrete. They overlap. You can attend a meeting and start applying the 'problem-solving' process to a particular issue, but if you are not careful, you will find others making decisions before the causes of the problem have been identified!

We can all jump to conclusions, make unreal assumptions and peddle our latest pet solution, in aid of saving time. This it may do in the short term, ie. dealing with an agenda quickly, but will we have solved the problem once and for all? It is unlikely. We may be so concerned with shortening the time allowed for the discussion with others that we do not solve the problem. In fact, we create further problems for ourselves, because we have not got it 'right first time'.

HOW CAN WE AVOID JUMPING TO THE WRONG CONCLUSION?

Sit down and think through the main issues. How do we normally solve problems? Do we debate at length and then vote? If that is the case, the decision is not based upon consensus, and it is likely that the decision reached will not have been gleaned from the whole range of alternatives.

Do we automatically think there is one right answer? This might well be the case when dealing with Accounts, Production and Distribution Schedules, etc., but most problems do not have one solution, they have many! What we have got to do is plan our resources to consider the best options.

CONVERGENT AND DIVERGENT THINKING

When we think of problem-solving, we tend to examine a logical approach to understanding the underlying causes of problems, but this is not the only approach. The logical approach is referred to as convergent thinking. The creative approach is known as 'divergent thinking'.

Convergent thinking resembles the rational, systematic approach adopted by many managers. There is nothing wrong with this approach, but sometimes a more creative, intuitive process of divergent thinking helps us look at possibilities and relationships.

The strength of convergent thinking relates to relying on 'what has happened', the information collected, and the sequence and process of enquiry. The divergent approach is based upon 'possibilities and relationships', and reflects the intuitive, creative element of problem-solving.

We can benefit from both approaches. Let us examine the rational convergent process first. Later we will explore the 'divergent' approach of Creative Thinking and Brainstorming.

The rational approach demands that we tackle problems in a number of sequential steps. This is the way we should think about the problem. But how often do we really think through the key stages and activities which we need to pursue, in order to find a right answer? Not as often as we would like to think. Sometimes we jump to the first answer which comes into our heads – or we pursue our latest interest or hobby-horse. In reality there are many cases where, because of time constraints or other pressures, the rational approach to problem-solving has been neglected and a quick solution chosen – which can have dire consequences for the individual and the company.

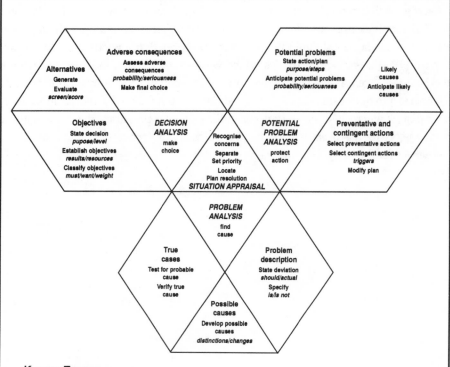

Kepner Tregoe

The Rational Manager

A large number of Fortune 500 companies have used this approach to great effect. Four basic processes comprise the KT model. Before we start we need to assess the present – the here and now. Situation appraisal is where we start every time. It helps us to make decisions about the routes we should follow – that is why it is central to the KT model.

Situation appraisal is a systematic approach to sorting out 'concerns' or those issues which need to be resolved in an organisation. This is separating the wood from the trees and trains people to prioritise their concerns and then choose which of the other three processes to follow.

Decision analysis – which is following a rigorous and systematic process for making a choice and reaching decisions.

Problem analysis – for finding the cause of a problem.

Potential problem analysis – for anticipating problems and preventing problems arising, or protecting existing plans or actions.

*Fig. 15 Resolving concerns through rational process (Source: **The New Rational Manager**)*

It is essential that all members use a logical sequential approach to problem-solving. Kepner and Tregoe in their book *The New Rational Manager* outline the framework for logical problem-solving. This structured approach to problem-solving helps highlight the key stages we ought to consider before jumping at the first solution which appears. Few managers really adopt a rational approach. This approach is an excellent way of introducing Problem-Solving and Decision-Making to members of Corrective Action Teams, etc. In past TQ interventions this has always been an extremely powerful tool for generating quality solutions. Time spent on these activities pays back dividends.

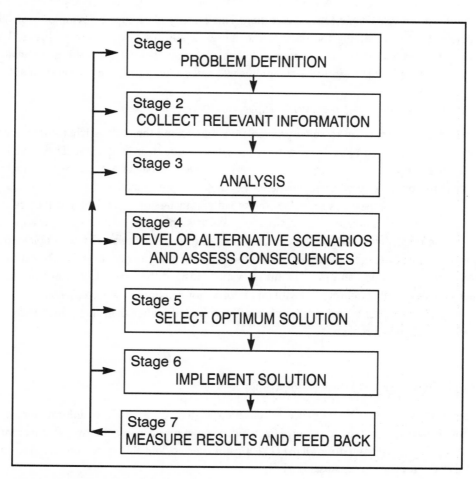

Fig. 16 Logical approach to problem-solving

THE RATIONAL APPROACH TO PROBLEM-SOLVING

STAGE 1: Problem Definition

A large number of problems are never really solved because group members do not spend sufficient time defining the nature of a problem. This means looking at the cause of the problem rather than the effect.

To illustrate this point, consider a visit to your doctor. You have found that you have a rash on your chest. The doctor gives you medication to relieve it. The rash eventually fades and the condition subsides. A week later, the condition recurs. You pay another visit to the GP and are prescribed the same medication. This remedy clears up the symptoms of the problem, but does nothing to eradicate the cause. Relate this to company problems. We should be certain, before we pursue a course of action, not take a wild guesstimate. Experience tells us that treating the symptoms will never solve a problem once and for all!

STAGE 2: Collecting Relevant Information

Some group members try to solve problems without asking themselves what information they need to do a good job. They let their prejudices guide their judgement. They let their preferences structure the solution. Even worse, they have a kit bag of solutions which are just ready to be applied to problems, whether or not they are appropriate!

The classic mistake is to look at the broad parameters of a problem and then relate these back to information or 'similar' situations which we have confronted in the past.

We are all aware that the more information we have, which relates to the problem, the more accurate our diagnosis will be. Some, unfortunately, make a grave mistake. They do not look at the information and say: "Is this relevant?". Instead they say: "How can I use it?". They equate available information with that information required to solve a problem!

How easy it is to use all the information collected, rather than that which is really needed to solve the problem!

COLLECTING TOO MUCH INFORMATION

A problem which many experience is collecting a great QUANTITY of information, but failing to have any regard for QUALITY. We can sometimes confuse the two, and feel that QUANTITY can be traded for QUALITY! It can never be, and this is demonstrated in the number of problems in organisational experience.

MEASURING EVERYTHING AND UNDERSTANDING NOTHING

Some people display a compulsion to measure everything which can be measured, and neglect other important variables, which may not be so easily measured. These factors may be equally important, but are neglected, which can lead to inaccuracies in problem resolution. Collecting vast quantities of data is somehow reassuring; whether the information will be of practical use does not seem quite so important a consideration.

MAKING TOO MANY ASSUMPTIONS

There is a tendency to make too many assumptions. Most are based upon our own many and varied experiences within a given situation. We can generalise, and this creates problems when we make assumptions between cause and effect.

STAGE 3: Analysis

When analysing cause/effect relationships, ensure that there are no significant intervening variables.

Be aware that all the facts will not 'jump out' at you at once. You may need to pursue other lines of enquiry to establish Intervening factors. Be careful and do not make too many assumptions.

STAGE: 4 Assess Consequences

While working through the Analysis phase and establishing cause and effect relationships, remember not to look for 'one right answer'. It is possible to develop a number of options which should help to achieve the goal.

Think through a number of alternative approaches and assess the consequences of each strategy. Think of the benefits in the short, and the long, term. Think through the disadvantages and the costs of the action. Then, progress to the next stage.

STAGE 5: The Optimum Solution

At this stage Problem-Solving and Decision-Making merge. Perhaps a formal group meeting may be required in order to achieve the optimum solution. Ensure that those most affected by changes are involved. If they have to live with the solution and put it into practice, surely they have a part to play in contributing to the overall approach and finer details?

STAGE 6: Implement Solution

This is one of the most difficult stages in Problem-Solving and requires more action than words. What looks promising on paper may not work in practice.

Most of these problems of implementation are human in origin, and require new ways of working. 'Change' can create resistance. It is worth considering the 'people problems' before implementing new ideas. Ask yourself: "In how many ways can this idea fail?". Address the doubts you raise, and be prepared to take corrective action. (See Chapter 4 on Managing Cultural Change.)

Managers achieve results through others. However good the idea generated by managerial staff and colleagues, if others will not put it into practice and accept the solution or innovation, it will remain a good idea and never become a reality!

STAGE 7: Measure Results and Gain Feedback

It is all very well creating change and moving on to the next problem. To ensure that you got it 'right first time', gain feedback on the practicality of the solution which has been implemented. Seek the views of those people who are most affected by your 'solution'. Their feedback is an important element in the problem-solving and decision-making process. Without their consent and input, how can you hope to win their support to implement your solution?

ALTERNATIVE PROBLEM-SOLVING TECHNIQUES

We have so far referred to the logical, sequential approach to the solution of problems, and paid little attention to the more creative approach. Creative Thinking and Brainstorming is an approach which has helped many companies solve complex problems. This alternative approach is particularly useful when there is no one right answer.

There may be a variety of answers 'close together', or one right answer to Production, Accounting or Engineering problems. Using the same approach for open-ended problems can be disastrous. You will spend a tremendous amount of time trying to find the one right way. It does not exist, so why look for it!

Let us look at more creative problem-solving techniques and examine their applicability within Problem-Solving Groups.

Brainstorming and Cause Effect Analysis has helped, particularly in Quality Improvement initiatives, where those who produce a component meet together and 'solve' a production or quality problem.

WHAT IS CREATIVE THINKING?

Creative thinking, an aspect of divergent thinking, is "relating those things which were previously unrelated". This means that the mind has to freewheel and overcome the self-imposed barriers which can stop our moving towards innovative solutions. Edward De

Bono, in particular, has spent many years teaching his variant of the creative approach to problem solution, called 'Lateral Thinking'.

Creative thinking is concerned with developing innovative solutions to traditional problems. It is also a set of techniques orientated towards extracting a large number of ideas from a group of people.

For instance, if you wished to use the BRAINSTORMING technique, the first thing you have to do is define the nature of the problem, and express it in one statement. For instance, let us assume that productivity within a department is falling. We may define the problem thus: *"In how many ways can we increase productivity within the department?"*.

RESTATEMENTS

Rather than seeking an instant solution we need to ensure we are really dealing with the overall problem. What we need to do is develop restatements of the problem, ie.:

" In how many ways can we increase group productivity?"

"In how many ways can we reduce unnecessary costs?"

"What action can we take to ensure we always provide a high quality service?"

"What manpower strategies can we use to ensure that both satisfaction and productivity remain high?"

Clearly, we can make as many restatements as we wish, but the overall purpose is to walk around the problem and look at it from different angles. This is most important. Otherwise, there is a tendency to pursue the old tried and tested techniques.

Having a group of employees restate the problem in 10-12 restatements is the first stage of a good Problem-Solving/Corrective Action Team Workshop. The next activity is to agree to work on one 'restatement'.

FREEWHEELING

Think through a trivial problem which faces the company and get the group to Brainstorm ideas quickly. This is not yet concerned with solving the problem, but with giving those attending the confidence to develop new ideas, however wild! Results from Brainstorming sessions indicate that some of the wild ideas, which appear outrageous at first, can generate some of the most innovative and effective solutions to problems.

RULES FOR BRAINSTORMING

The rules for BRAINSTORMING include:

1. Do not try to find one right answer. It does not exist. There are many answers which might be of value.

2. Build confidence among the team and stress that they should try to generate as many ideas as possible. These ideas must not be evaluated, but listed, to be discussed later. Do not evaluate, otherwise a lot of good ideas will never be expressed. They should be presented and documented quickly. Speed is of the essence. Brainstorming should not last longer than five minutes.

3. Avoid tunnel vision. Think through areas to take the group away from established practice. Do not let them dwell too much on old solutions.

4. Reduce the inclination of members to analyse suggestions too quickly. Evaluation is left for later. At the moment, the key activity is the generation of ideas.

5. Many attending Brainstorming sessions feel uncomfortable and fear appearing to seem foolish, and so do not contribute. We must break down barriers and encourage ideas, however outrageous they appear!

AGREEING CRITERIA FOR EVALUATION

Now that the session is over, the Group have to get together to agree criteria by which they will judge their ideas. Once these are agreed, eg. cost, administrative convenience, long-term impact, economical and technical feasibility etc., it is a comparatively easy process to evaluate your list of ideas.

LOGICAL THINKING

Here we move away from divergent to convergent thinking, where we evaluate the brainstormed proposals. This is the process we would normally go through if we always used the rational method of problem-solving, except that we now have the value of lots of creative ideas to evaluate.

This approach helps us develop new, innovative approaches to solving problems.

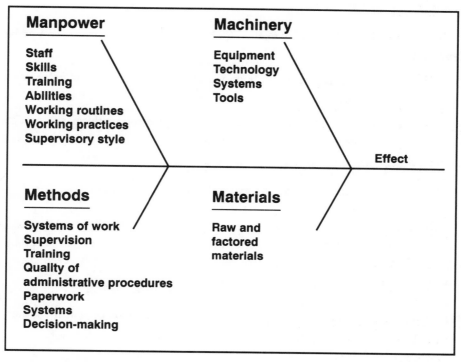

Manpower

Staff
Skills
Training
Abilities
Working routines
Working practices
Supervisory style

Machinery

Equipment
Technology
Systems
Tools

Effect

Methods

Systems of work
Supervision
Training
Quality of
administrative procedures
Paperwork
Systems
Decision-making

Materials

Raw and
factored
materials

Fig. 17 Cause/effect analysis

CAUSE EFFECT/ANALYSIS

This technique is used a great deal by teams of workers and staff involved in Quality Improvement initiatives. The technique has a logical structure and framework which is easily understood and it incorporates elements of creative thought.

Cause/Effect Analysis is a good, simple technique for examining the major factors which impact upon a particular problem. A 'fishbone diagram' illustrates the relationship between cause and effect.

Defining the symptoms of the problem is the first step to developing a 'fishbone'. Asking what is the impact of the 'effect' on employees, the department and the organisation? Describing the effect in detail is important. Listing the consequences, walking around the problem and considering it from different angles are all aspects of the creative approach.

A team of staff should get together to brainstorm the possible and probable causes of the problem as outlined below. Brainstorming and listing CAUSES should be related to the 4 M's.

WHAT ARE THE 4 M's?

The 4 M's is a simple and convenient method for isolating the probable causes of a problem under four headings:

Manpower – includes staff skills, training, abilities, attitudes, working routines and practices.

Methods – includes systems of work, processes, protocols, performance standards, best practice paperwork routines.

Machinery – includes equipment, technology, systems.

Materials – includes raw and factored materials, statistics, information.

The way to build up a Fishbone is to brainstorm and generate a list of all the possible factors, without evaluating, which could create the effect. After you have listed the probable causes, it is then possible to add them to the 'fishbone'. Now key areas have been identified for investigation, target-setting and review dates.

Using the 'fishbone' will not, by itself, solve the problem, but it will help examine the inter-relationships between the 4 M's and give sufficient information on which your action can be based.

TAKING ACTION

Problem-Solving techniques, by themselves, will not solve all the problems. They will, however, provide a basis on which it is possible to make a balanced decision. If a problem has existed for a long time, one cannot assume that action to solve the problem will succeed 'first time'. The short-term, intermediate and long-term steps must be considered.

The approach adopted will be determined by the urgency of putting right what is wrong, the resources at your disposal and the speed at which results are required.

ROUTINE AND COMPLEX DECISIONS

Although Problem-Solving and Decision-Making are inextricably linked, we may ask how should we organise our time to make the best quality decisions?

We must also look at the decisions, and ask ourselves whether they are complex or routine. Routine decisions can be delegated to others. Usually decisions are difficult to make because one lacks the necessary information to act in the best interests of everyone. As the decisions become more difficult, as the solutions to the problems become more complex, one will need the support of other people. They will give different perspectives and increased information.

This means that your 'people' skills will be brought into play. Think through the criteria by which others will judge your decisions and, if in doubt, remember that planning is the best way of ensuring that errors do not arise.

CHOOSING SOLUTIONS WITH A CHANCE

Although Problem-Solving Groups may have adhered to all the principles associated with problem-solving, one of the most difficult jobs is to put ideas into practice. Many Corrective Action Teams give feedback on their progress to the Senior Management Group. Before this can be achieved, it is worth considering the strategies used for selling ideas to others. It is at this stage that resistance to new solutions may be in evidence. Resistance exists because some may perceive the ideas, actions and recommendations of others as a sort of threat.

There are certain actions that can be taken to ensure that solutions, or preferred action, stand a good chance of being accepted by others.

Assessing the criteria by which others will judge your proposals is a good start. Looking at four areas should help: Is this idea administratively convenient? Is the recommendation technically feasible? Is the idea economically viable? And finally, is the idea politically acceptable to the organisation? If not, spend some time developing alternative strategies for change. Seek the opposing arguments from your colleagues and address their objections.

Objection-handling is the most important aspect of having ideas accepted. This requires a great deal of preparation, taking into account the personalities and roles of the people involved.

Now that you have assessed the criteria by which others will judge your proposals, it is time to assess the degree to which there is congruency or incongruence between proposals and the objections of others. Address these objections before presenting a case, order priorities and listen to what others say.

Build bridges and present your case in a non-threatening way. Look for win-win solutions. In other words, situations where all those involved benefit. This replaces the old idea of if one person or department succeeds, others must lose. We reject this approach and recognise the benefits and value of the team approach.

COMMUNICATION AND INFORMATION

This is perhaps the most important aspect of implementing TQ. Failing to communicate intentions, holding regular briefing sessions and informing on progress, will hinder success. What is sometimes surprising is the speed at which organisations undertake TQ Drives – yet who fail when introducing briefing groups. (The role of communication and briefing can't be underplayed and is part of the focus in Chapter 11 on Team Building and Participation.)

SUMMARY

Focusing upon Prevention instead of reworking things is critical to bringing about lasting change. At first, to gain momentum, you may need to invest a great deal in order to get rid of rework. The ratio can be as high as 10 units of Prevention to replace one unit of Rework – you will soon note that the old Firefighting culture starts to crumble to be replaced by new ideas, systems, procedures and ways of working. This is the only way to ensure that your efforts to reduce the cost or quality are not perceived as just a cost-reduction exercise.

Bullet Points

- Preventative action is the only alternative to constant reworking.

- We tend to react to events rather than manage them. We resolve short-term concerns, but never really solve long-term problems. We emphasise dealing with 'symptoms' rather than causes.

- Many of the problems we encounter are predictable. Managers can forecast and generate lists of things which they will have to resolve in the future – but still fail to fix them.

- If you have Control over problems you can fix them. If Control is shared with others – problem solution is more difficult.

- If problems are owned, they are solved. Too many problems are not owned and consequently no one does anything significant to put right what is wrong.

- If problems are shared, it is difficult to allocate responsibility.

- Firefighting is a natural state in many companies. Many enjoy firefighting, it is exciting. It has to be replaced by a calmer, more regulated pace and concern for planning.

- 'Sometimes one visits companies and wonders how departments function, in spite of themselves. It would be nice to see energy being expended in working together rather than wasted pursuing disparate goals.'

- Changing to the Preventative Culture requires a major change and promotion of problem-solving from being quick fixes to long-term company-wide affairs.

- Companies are pretty good at putting things right after they have gone wrong. Why is it so difficult to work on what we know will go wrong and fix it, rather than wasting resources to do things right second time?

- A genuine commitment to forecasting planning and sharing information must be desirable to replace the wild guesstimates approach.

- One hour of planning saves ten hours of chaos.

- If we genuinely value our people and want them to solve problems, they need to be trained in problem-solving techniques. Process is more important than structure.

- Providing techniques for problem-solving and decision-making is all very well – but generate the climate to want to do things. It will have a bigger payback.

- Develop and keep to rules of behaviour for groups involved in promoting new solutions to old problems.

- Learning about personal management style is a good first step and probably tells you more about how you make managerial decisions than attending courses on structured problem-solving.

- Managers like to think they are rational, logical, systematic and methodical. However, the evidence of managers using guesstimates, following their intuition and feelings, suggests that everybody could benefit from studying the rational process.

- Managers solve problems using a combination of logic and feelings. Is it not then wise to provide them with training so that they can become more logical and more creative at the same time?

- Spend plenty of time defining the nature of problems rather than jumping to quick solutions. Base decisions on accurate and reliable information. Analyse cause/effect relationships, assess consequences, select the optimum solution, implement ideas and seek feedback.

- Use creative thinking as a tool to generate a vast number of ideas from many people and make use of the fishbone diagram to isolate cause from effect.

- When taking action, ensure that all factors have been considered. Is the idea administratively convenient, technically feasible, financially sound and politically acceptable? If it is not, you will stand less of a chance of having it implemented.

- Don't give up on the difficult decisions . They take longer to implement and you have to have more of the culture with you to agree action.

- The accurate transmission and reception of information is critical to implementing TQ. Ineffective communication leads to inconsistent messages and conflict. Work on improving information and communication through the most powerful medium – management style.

CHAPTER 11

Teamworking and Participation

The previous chapter concentrated upon the actions necessary to move from a firefighting culture to a TQ Preventative culture. In particular, it was stated that having people trained in Problem-Solving techniques was important. However, just as important is examining the 'style' which each person uses when involved in the process of generating workable solutions. Personal style determines the route or pathways taken to solve problems.

Everyone can be trained in using Cause/Effect Analysis, but the effectiveness of those working on the solution can be inhibited if they fail to grasp the importance of personal problem-solving style. Each of us is driven by a preference to work, to confront and tackle problems in a certain way. This is usually determined by our experience and reflected in the way that we manage. Some can be locked into 'one best style' and fail to consider other ways of working. These personal preferences can sometimes be adopted, reinforced and rewarded by senior officers as the 'company style'. Having a number of people sitting around a table discussing problem areas all using the same approach will fail to generate the spark needed to create alternatives and change. Preferring and using one method of problem-solving suggests that other ways have been avoided. It is for this reason that we have to look at contributions of people working as a team.

DIFFICULTIES MOVING FROM THE TELLING TO THE LISTENING ROLE

There is little point talking about the joint approach to implementing Company-Wide Improvement through TQ if little effort is made to ensure that the drive is based on company-wide participation, where it is discouraged by strict demarcation between functions and departments.

There is a great deal of talk about team-building and team effort, but in many instances we don't give people a chance to contribute. For instance, some time ago working with a company we identified more than 100 people to be trained in Problem-Solving Style over a series of weeks. On one occasion the Sales Manager attended and took part in exercises. In every case he took over from those in his group and made the decisions for them. He adopted the same approach which he would use in the Sales offices. He talked. They listened. Here we had a major problem. Although the manager was committed in principle, he experienced great difficulty dropping his leading and directing role in order to listen to others and give their opinions a chance. There is a need for fundamental change in management style for this to work. If we fail to attempt to change style and examine the impact which managers have on others in groups, problem-orientated or not, then we are failing to change the culture. Employees find that no real change has taken place. If the 'Sales Manager' doesn't change and listen more to others, avoid making his mind up before others speak and asking others for genuine solutions before contributing, then employees will see no change at all. Some managers are frightened to change their 'style' because they think that means abdication or giving control to others. On the contrary, it is giving others a chance to contribute from their perspective.

ACHIEVING RESULTS THROUGH OTHERS

It is understandable that Managers and Supervisors do find it difficult to 'restrain' themselves from their normal role of giving direction, but it is essential that they examine their approach so that ideas from others can permeate the structure. Before examining the routes organisations can take to unleashing the potential of their people, it is wise to look at the key issues in the team concept.

We all recognise that managers are employed, not so much for what they can do individually, but what they get others to achieve. (Chapter 6 on Leadership looks at the role the manager can play in leading this process.) Enabling others to contribute is fundamental to TQ. This means we should be involving others in decisions and areas outside their comfort zone. Examples are given of clothes designers working for a large High Street retailing business not understanding the core technology employed to produce 80% of the designs they created. By exposing designers to the capability of the technology and the skills of the people, the clothes designed became so much more user-friendly to those having to produce to the design.

ARCHITECTS SERVING BEER

During a culture-change intervention to help a major brewery establish Total Quality in all areas of operations, we worked closely with a group of architects. In particular, Nigel, one of 68 appointed internal TQ trainers, was a new recruit and gave an example of TQ in action. Architects were employed to help not just in designing and building new pubs and restaurants, but also to design and co-ordinate the refurbishment of older public houses. Nigel talked of the induction process he experienced. At first he had found this of little value. He had to spend two weeks in a number of pubs. There he performed a wide variety of duties. He washed glasses, helped with deliveries to the cellar and aided in the general running of the pub. He found this experience to be invaluable later when he was involved in design work. The job had been made easier. He no longer saw the public house as a three-dimensional model but as a place of work. He understood more about the design of shelves for glasses, the design and location of the cellar (it was rumoured that some cellars in the past had been located in areas unsuitable for storing beer), and kitchen layout.

This is only a simple example of employee involvement as the precursor of TQ. Here the publicans helped the professional designer to understand the constraints in which they worked. He now understood the pub was not just a building but a 'social system' where design should be focused upon the movement and interaction of people, rather than imposing structures around which people must work.

EMPLOYEE INVOLVEMENT IN ACTION: UK PLASTICS

This approach was put into effect in the plant of a major manufacturer of plastics in the UK. As in most plants, Maintenance Engineers are continually busy fixing technology after it has failed. They recognised that many of the staff had a good working knowledge of the technology. After talking with the staff, the Engineers came to the conclusion that variation in performance of production technology could be predicted through the 'auditory senses' of the operatives – by the 'sound' coming from the machine. Instead of running the technology to 'breakdown', operatives were encouraged to shut down equipment temporarily and contact the Engineers when the pitch, vibration or sound of the machine changed. They could then begin to work on the equipment before significant damage occurred. This culminated in 'staff' suggesting periodic checks on equipment prior to breakdown and in the formation of a 'Preventative Maintenance Programme'. Now, instead of just relying on spotting inaccuracies, their visual and auditory experience was employed to predict failure.

In particular, this meant that downtime was decreased. When operatives using 'dicing machinery' (used to separate a continuous flow of hardened plastic into fine pellets direct from manufacture) were involved, it was possible to predict with some certainty the cause and time of potential failures. This was further analysed and, from this data, a Preventative

Maintenance Programme for 'the dicers' was established. This would have been impossible without the help from the operator. With this input it was possible for the machinery to run continuously 24 hours per day. This minimised downtime maintenance and made life a little more predictable for the Engineers. What is surprising is that the plant had been running for 25 years without this input or suggestion ever being put forward. TQ had helped unlock the potential of employees.

Similar ideas worked wonders for this plant. Groups of committed employees would meet as CATs (Corrective Action Teams) to prevent problems arising. Their experience was tapped and many disasters were averted. They, the staff, possessed the body of knowledge to make continuous improvement a way of life.

Following this and other successes, a Corrective Action Team or CAT was formed at the request of the staff to look at water utilisation within the plant. From initial investigations and analysis it was found that the company could reroute water, at no great cost, and thereby reduce operating costs by an amazing £80,000 per year. These successes do not come about by accident, but because staff feel that they have the opportunity to contribute and improve performance. This in turn is 'learned' from their managers.

ALAN HUGHES: RESULTS THROUGH PEOPLE

Although these examples were a direct result of TQ, the plant already had a fine reputation for 'improvement' in its most general sense prior to the Drive. In the past, staff at all levels had met to establish Employee Involvement and produced many suggestions to reduce costs, improve productivity and so forth. They had a major input into the design of machinery, its location and its use. Alan Hughes, the Plant Manager, had established the practice of involvement and TQ was an extension of this process. Alan had created the involvement culture over a period of eleven years. First he had established briefing groups. Then he ensured that his managers met every day to discuss the events occurring on other shifts and progress for the day ahead. The emphasis was not just on making better production targets. These 'ten o'clock' briefings and his weekly 'management' sessions were the keys to keeping a rein on what was happening within the company.

Alan was also promoting horizontal management through cross-functional training. He and his management team were committed to retraining the 19 key supervisors in skills in three discrete areas. At any time, these supervisors could assume duties in other areas. It created flexibility. But this was not the real purpose behind the training – it was to get supervisors to understand problems from a proper systems perspective. Previously, rigid job demarcation through technology had created a sub-system mentality where there was little understanding of things apart from on an area basis. What was required was a 'plant perspective'. Within this framework, supervisors and operatives did things differently. This illustrates that TQ is a continuous process which links in well with other employee involvement initiatives.

INVOLVEMENT IS NOT OBSTRUCTION!

There are scores of examples where employee involvement can help companies. But, there are also many instances when the views of employees are seen as no more than obstructive to business as usual. Douglas, now an Insurance Executive and Partner in a small business, looked back on his training in a large insurance company. There, he said, he came across many forms which were inefficient in design. The information required was routed around offices and agents with no apparent structure. Obviously, the Management Services people had never considered talking to the end user. When Douglas suggested improvements, his immediate supervisor told him to 'mind his own business'. Douglas did not want to give up, so he mentioned his ideas to others. He was greeted with indifference and did not make suggestions again!

It is clear that the secret of making TQ part of the organisational culture requires everybody's involvement. Given the opportunity, people will contribute, but only if they see something happen. Once people are involved or start contributing, the worst thing that management can do is to stop it! They can do this by ignoring ideas, telling people that ideas only come from management, failing to do what they say they will do, and negative reinforcement. Obtaining suggestions for improvement can be accelerated through positive reinforcement. Failing to recognise contributions will kill Quality Improvement.

FIND SOMEONE DOING SOMETHING RIGHT AND TELL HIM WHAT A GOOD JOB HE IS DOING!

Managers and supervisors spend too much time finding fault and telling people what they do wrong. The style of management which motivates people is orientated towards concentrating upon finding something good and telling people what a good job they did. This does not mean manufacturing a reason or generalising and telling everybody he is doing well. It means being specific in praise and ensuring that positive feedback is as close as possible to the desirable act which has taken place. This is the key to the motivation and the team-building required to promote the TQ culture.

Reinforcing positive contributions through managerial actions is the quickest way to ensuring that employees come up with ideas to make TQ work.

Communication is the foundation for real employee involvement. Few recognise the value of informing employees of progress or do not recognise how little their people are aware of company communications. Some companies value 'communication' and set up briefing sessions. These are usually organised to communicate top down.

BRIEFING GROUPS

In recent years, the briefing process has increased in the UK. Much of this is founded upon the work of the Industrial Society. Despite this push, many companies have not really benefited to the degree to which they were able to put briefing groups to work.

Briefing focuses upon the accurate transmission of information through the organisational structure and focuses upon the role that management can play. Many changes take place daily in an organisation and it is important that these are communicated effectively throughout the company. If a formal line of communication is ineffective, rumour and gossip will fill its place. Briefing rests on the 4 P's. Inform employees about **Policy, Purpose, People** and **Progress.** There are other variants of this approach, but generally this is a structure upon which to communicate.

FAILING TO LISTEN

The great danger when 'briefing' is to spend too much time telling people about changes and too little time listening. This is crucial, for failing to listen and act is the quickest way for things to fail. Obviously some communications are very formal and have to be passed on in a fairly structured manner to avoid inconsistencies in transmission. Such briefs must not be deviated from and are usually read to employees, but the majority of briefs should be interactive affairs where managers pass on a message, listen to the reaction and feed this back up through the management chain. Unfortunately, this is where too many briefing sessions break down.

Because of lack of time, managers transmit information one way, but fail to listen and feed back the reaction of their people. In some cases, the Briefing approach fails because the system falls into disrepute and 'briefs' are simply attached to notice boards. The communication ends there. Although it would appear that the activities associated with briefing have been accomplished to some degree, the true spirit is lacking. Clearly, a TQ intervention requires a sound briefing and communication system to be in existence. How can companies promote TQ with any hope of success when they cannot create a sound briefing system?

TEAM-BUILDING AND ORGANISATIONAL CULTURE

Creating a culture receptive to TQ is dependent upon creating the right management style, communicating and informing employees and developing team spirit. The team spirit must permeate functions and departments. There is little point having highly cohesive teams on strictly functional lines. That produces straight-line solutions. Teams must be based upon good horizontal principles with joint problem-solving in mind. Nowadays, there is a constant requirement in many organisations for functional experts to work together on a project basis. But after the project is over, the experts revert strictly to the interests of their department. We suggest that more time is spent developing cross-functional groups to appreciate the company-wide perspective. In the real business world, few problems have impact upon only one department – they have impact upon many – so it makes sense to develop this type of culture.

CHAIRMAN/CO-ORDINATOR

As a team role, specifies controlling the way in which a team moves towards the group objectives by making the best use of team resources; recognising where the team's strengths and weaknesses lie; and ensuring that the best use is made of each team member's potential.

COMPANY WORKER/IMPLEMENTER

As a team role, specifies turning concepts and plans into practical working procedures; and carrying out agreed plans systematically and efficiently.

COMPLETER/FINISHER

As a team role, specifies ensuring that the team is protected as far as possible from mistakes of both commission and omission; actively searching for aspects of work which need a more than usual degree of attention; and maintaining a sense of urgency within the team.

MONITOR/EVALUATOR

As a team role, specifies analysing problems; and evaluating ideas and suggestions so that the team is better placed to take balanced decisions.

PLANT

As a team role, specifies advancing new ideas and strategies with special attention to major issues; and looking for possible breaks in approach to the problems with which the group is confronted.

RESOURCE INVESTIGATOR

As a team role, specifies exploring and reporting on ideas, developments and resources outside the group; creating external contacts that may be useful to the team and conducting any subsequent negotiations.

SHAPER

As a team role, specifies shaping the way in which a team effort is applied; directing attention generally to the setting of objectives and priorities; and seeking to impose some shape or pattern on group discussion and on the outcome of activities.

TEAMWORKER

As a team role, specifies supporting members in their strengths (eg. building on suggestions); underpinning members in their shortcomings; improving communication between members and fostering team spirit generally.

SPECIALIST

Specialists are dedicated individuals who pride themselves on acquiring technical skills and specialised knowledge. They focus upon professional standards and show pride in their field and have an indispensable part to play in most teams.

REJECTING THE 'US AND THEM' APPROACH

There is a great deal of negative stereotyping between departments and within companies in general. There is too much of the 'us and them' or the 'win-lose' attitude in general, whether between Trade Union and Company, or shopfloor and management. If one department wins it is usually at the expense of others. What we should be trying to develop is the win-win attitude where people work together. The only real way to change is to improve Personnel Policy and Practice. This means changing the systems of remuneration, appraisal and staff development.

CAREER PROGRESSION CAN BE HORIZONTAL

People become slotted into a career structure which is functional in nature. We end up breeding specialists who are very good at their jobs, but who find it difficult to relate to those in other functions. Changing the career path – incorporating lateral development, valuing and rewarding cross-fertilisation – is the only way to promote horizontal management. What we have at present is the ridiculous situation where technical specialists have only one route to follow for promotion and an increase in salary, ie. upwards. Technical experts then hold the most senior positions within a company. Whether they can actually manage is not questioned.

Consequently, we end up with good 'technicians' becoming poor managers in charge of other technicians or experts. We lose our best experts. It is a fact of life that there are not enough places at the top for everybody. So not everybody is going to make it to the top. But what do we do with people who can go no further?

The traditional hierarchical structure will accommodate only a few, so what happens to everybody else? Is this the end of a person's career? It shouldn't be, but it usually is. Organisations should revise 'career structures' and build them on horizontal rather than vertical lines. Career progression should be based upon managers changing functions when possible. This is not to suggest that the Sales Manager should become the Engineering Manager, but there are many opportunities where horizons can be broadened.

Many companies already do this. A notable example is Ciba Corning Diagnostics, where the policy is to provide challenge for its people. They do a remarkable job and the managers benefit also. I first met Hugh Newman, a successful Sales Manager, some years ago. He was then being groomed for Personnel Manager. He was later responsible for UK

Acquisitions, then Regulatory Affairs, then the acquisition of Quality Standards – now that's proper progression horizontally to understand the business! Ciba Corning, a US Manufacturer of Medical Technology, recognises that the best way to obtain the best from people is to provide them with continuous challenge. This does not mean throwing people in at the deep end. It means considering Career and Succession Planning on a horizontal basis.

BREATHING IN AND OUT

After being in a senior position for some time, many managers lose their drive and enthusiasm. It is not unnatural for managers to slip into the 'fat and happy' state when they know they are going no further. They start to wind down. Yet the most successful people in the company, those who have risen to senior company status, still have a great deal of experience and enthusiasm to offer the organisation. In many cases this is not channelled, little action is taken and we are left with a manager whose experience can be measured in time rather than quality. Is it any surprise that some managers go through the motions each day, breathe in and out without making mistakes and then go home on the dot. They contribute little, fail to motivate others and create the 'non-achieving' environment for self and, even worse, instil this in their direct reports. The good, aspiring manager leaves the company – the future of the company left in the hands of managers 'dead from the neck up'.

Recently, a colleague and I gave a TQ presentation to a company. The Commercial Manager, Bob, was alive, alert and keen to promote change. He said: "We need to turn this company upside down – we need TQ, otherwise they will kill it." Who are they? The Managers. He couldn't have been more right. The Management Culture was one of longevity. Who could stay the longest? Bob had taken on the responsibility to make changes through TQ and inherited a senior team, 40% of whom had been in the same company in the same function, although at different status, for over 32 years! The rest of the team were equally divided between long-servers and new blood. We are promoting change, slowly, through the 'young blood'.

MOST MANAGERS ARE CREATIVE, COMMITTED AND ACHIEVING EXCEPT FOR THE EIGHT HOURS WHEN THEY WORK FOR YOU!

It is interesting to look at the lifestyle of these managers. If we take a sample out of ten of the managers who work in a business we will probably find that at least one is a keen and active member of his local church, another runs a Scout Group, another is a leading actor in a local repertory company, others are involved in running other businesses or contribute their skills to a voluntary organisation or lead and support the local youth football team. What we can deduct from this is that most managers and staff are enthusiastic, keen, creative, organised and achieving because they express these skills outside work. The key issue is: Are they allowed to express these same skills and motivations when they work for their employer eight hours each day?

There are still too many organisations where senior staff have occupied their unchanging and unchallenged role for too long. Their drive is blunted. A large percentage will be way past their peak. When this is allowed to continue what happens is that the best of the direct reports to these people see the writing on the wall and leave to go to an organisation where their talent and expertise will be valued.

This situation unfortunately still exists. The fault for this occurrence lies with senior officers who have wasted the talent and experience of their people. Is it not sensible to capitalise on the strengths of experienced and successful managers, share these with others in different functions who can benefit from their input and maintain a high level of overall company-wide motivation? The alternative is a culture founded on deadwood which is doomed to extinction.

Bearing in mind that the team-building and succession-planning issues are important – the real impetus can come only from a Management Team who are committed to change. They have to be able to acknowledge weaknesses within the company and do something about this. But first, the orientation must come from the top – which entails being self-critical.

TEAM-BUILDING – RIGHT AT THE TOP

Culture Change requires a complete turnabout in the way senior officers regard their company. They cannot expect all the change to come from below. They must provide the example for others to follow. Challenging assumptions and the role that the Senior Management Team plays in promoting success can come only from looking inwards first and then looking at how the Team works together.

It is not sufficient to look at performance at a superficial level, it requires some depth. Looking at personal strengths and weaknesses is a route which some Management Teams promote with pride. Some of the most successful interventions have taken place because the senior officers wanted to examine their impact on others. For these teams, the route chosen was Team-Building based upon psychometric profiles. This is an extremely powerful and under-utilised method for creating significant change.

Unfortunately, many still feel that the role of the behavioural specialist in management is solely to aid recruitment and selection. Analysis of strengths and weaknesses may lie in pursuing the same route – but with a different purpose to build a strong team.

PSYCHOMETRIC PROFILING AND TEAM-BUILDING

There are many common misconceptions of psychometric profiling. Some managers focus upon the use of 'psychometrics' as tests which can be passed or failed. This is a gross over-simplification and not true. A profile will give a good indication of 'what drives a manager or indicates his key preferences for interpreting the world or dealing with issues in his world'. When a manager understands his preferences and alternative course of action which, up to this time, he has not pursued, then he is at choice. It is then up to the manager to assess how the profile can be used to help the manager achieve even more in his area of interest. Profiles offer managers choice about how they want their future to evolve. Profiles can be an extremely valuable tool in a manager's personal development and what must be borne in mind is the validity of the profiles and their general credibility.

However, care must be taken. There are too many invalid profiles entering the market which don't measure what they say they do or they are unreliable and poorly researched – that is why it is important to work with experienced change agents qualified and experienced in generating 'best practice' from profiles.

Instances of the positive use of profiles follow. Although some instruments will be referred to, this is not an exhaustive list. Overall, the companies who have used this approach have believed there was a causal relationship between assessing management style and developing company values which are reflected in a new managerial approach, which influences the TQ culture of team-building and participation.

Characteristics frequently associated with each type

Introverts		Extroverts	
Intuitive Types			
INTJ Usually have original minds and great drive for their own ideas and purposes. In fields that appeal to them, they have a fine power to organise a job and carry it through with or without help. Sceptical, critical, independent, determined, sometimes stubborn. Must learn to yield less important points in order to win the most important.	**INTP** Quiet and reserved. Especially enjoy theoretical or scientific pursuits. Like solving problems with logic and analysis. Usually interested mainly in ideas, with little liking for parties or small talk. Tend to have sharply defined interests. Need careers where some strong interest can be used and useful.	**ENTP** Quick, ingenious, good at many things. Stimulating company, alert and outspoken. May argue for fun on either side of a question. Resourceful in solving new and challenging problems, but may neglect routine assignments. Apt to turn to one new interest after another. Skilful in finding logical reasons for what they want.	**ENTJ** Hearty, frank, decisive, leaders in activities. Usually good in anything that requires reasoning and intelligent talk, such as public speaking. Are usually well informed and enjoy adding to their fund of knowledge. May sometimes appear more positive and confident than their experience in an area warrants.
INFJ Succeed by perseverance, originality and desire to do whatever is needed or wanted. Put their best efforts into their work. Quietly forceful, conscientious, concerned for others. Respected for their firm principles. Likely to be honoured and followed for their clear convictions as to how best to serve the common good.	**INFP** Full of enthusiasms and loyalties, but seldom talk of these until they know you well. Care about learning, ideas, language, and independent projects of their own. Tend to undertake too much, then somehow get it done. Friendly, but often too absorbed in what they are doing to be sociable. Little concerned with possessions or physical surroundings.	**ENFP** Warmly enthusiastic, high-spirited, ingenious, imaginative. Able to do almost anything that interests them. Quick with a solution for any difficulty and ready to help anyone with a problem. Often rely on their ability to improvise instead of preparing in advance. Can usually find compelling reasons for whatever they want.	**ENFJ** Responsive and responsible. Generally feel real concern for what others think or want, and try to handle things with due regard for the other person's feelings. Can present a proposal or lead a group discussion with ease and tact. Sociable, popular, sympathetic. Responsive to praise and criticism.
Sensing types			
ISTJ Serious, quiet, earn success by concentration and thoroughness. Practical, orderly, matter-of-fact, logical, realistic, and dependable. See to it that everything is well organised. Take responsibility. Make up their own minds as to what should be accomplished and work toward it steadily, regardless of protests or distractions.	**ISFJ** Quiet, friendly, responsible, and conscientious. Work devotedly to meet their obligations. Lend stability to any project or group. Thorough, painstaking, accurate. Their interests are usually not technical. Can be patient with necessary details. Loyal, considerate, perceptive, concerned with how other people feel.	**ESFP** Outgoing, easygoing, accepting, friendly, enjoy everything and make things more fun for others by their enjoyment. Like sports and making things happen. Know what's going on and join in eagerly. Find remembering facts easier than mastering theories. Are best in situations that need sound common sense and practical ability with people as well as with things.	**ESFJ** Warm-hearted, talkative, popular, conscientious, born co-operators, active committee members. Need harmony and may be good at creating it. Always doing something nice for someone. Work best with encouragement and praise. Main interest is in things that directly and visibly affect people's lives.
ISTP Cool onlookers – quiet, reserved, observing and analysing life with detached curiosity and unexpected flashes of original humour. Usually interested in cause and effect, how and why mechanical things work, and in organising facts using logical principles.	**ISFP** Retiring, quiet, friendly, sensitive, kind, modest about their abilities. Shun disagreements, do not force their opinions or values on others. Usually do not care to lead but are often loyal followers. Often relaxed about getting things done, because they enjoy the present moment and do not want to spoil it by undue haste or exertion.	**ESTP** Good at on-the-spot problem-solving. Do not worry, enjoy whatever comes along. Tend to like mechanical things and sports, with friends on the side. Adaptable, tolerant, generally conservative in values. Dislike long explanations. Are best with real things that can be worked, handled, taken apart, or put together.	**ESTJ** Practical, realistic, matter-of-fact, with a natural head for business or mechanics. Not interested in subjects they see no use for, but can apply themselves when necessary. Like to organise and run activities. May make good administrators, especially if they remember to consider others' feelings and points of view.
Introverts		Extroverts	

Fig. 18 Myers Briggs type indicator (MBT) (Source: Consulting Psychologists Press Inc., 577 College Avenue, Palo Alto, California 94306)

DEVELOPING TRUST AT THE TOP

A number of companies have decided to promote this approach. Needless to say, many of the managers involved were concerned that the 'results' would be used for other purposes. A few general points should be considered. If managers are sufficiently trusting to undergo the 'rigours' of profiling, they should be fed back the results confidentially. Results should not be on general display. Sharing of results with others on the Management Team will be determined and paced by the managers themselves, not the consultant. How can one expect to achieve a change in culture and promote trust and concern for others if feedback is less than confidential? Finally, profiles should only be administered, interpreted and fed back by qualified specialists.

CHANGING STYLE THROUGH MYERS BRIGGS

One such profile is that of Myers Briggs. This is an extremely rigorous approach to looking at the differences which exist between personality types.

"All too often we come into contact with people who do not reason as we reason, or do not value the things we value, or are not interested in what interests us." The objective of using the Myers Briggs Type Indicator (MBTI) is to examine personality differences and deal with these differences in a constructive way. For instance, certain personality 'types' are attracted to specific professions. Their personality characteristics fit best with their role or post (although some claim the post develops and reinforces type). Others in different functions may find it hard to understand them.

Let's look at some examples. In order to do this we need to look at some stereotyped views of certain functional managers. It should be noted that these stereotyped images are for clarification of the MBTI principles only.

HYPOTHETICAL PROFILES

Let us look at a Marketing Manager and make some general assumptions. He/she may tend to be strongly innovative in outlook, will probably move quickly from one subject to another, will be good at looking at relationships between unrelated subjects and will probably have difficulty concentrating upon one subject for a long time, dislike activities requiring detailed and routine analysis, and make quick decisions.

Now let us consider a managerial position, this time an Actuary working in an insurance company. People employed in this work may be strongly sensing, trusting only their senses and what they can understand or analyse through logic. They tend to relate to all that is objective, concrete and tangible. It will be unlikely that they are strong extroverts and prefer to associate with a 'select' few. They may be good at analysis and systematic and rational, using methods and thinking to help them make decisions. They will not be quick to make decisions because they value their technical competence and will focus upon detail. They will be objective and will not be swayed by subjective opinion.

Putting these two individuals together in a close working environment may create difficulties if they are expected to work as a cohesive team. Although we are told that opposites attract, this is unlikely to happen in practice. People tend to be attracted to similar people, those who portray similar traits and viewpoints. People tend to gravitate towards people like themselves.

Each individual in this example may value the characteristic which he considers lacking in his colleague. Bringing together a number of people with strongly contrasting characteristics may create some friction and a failure to work together. Imagine the impact of this on temporary task or project groups when attempting to influence the pace of change in a culture? There would probably be more conflict than co-operation.

It is important to examine the differences between people and the actions we can take to promote teamwork. What we are aiming to do is to ensure that each manager will value the gifts which others portray. These gifts in others may not reflect the manager's preferences and for this reason they should not be rejected "because he is not like me"!

Understanding the 'gifts' which each member of the team has is a sure way of promoting a common team approach – but it is easier said than done and must be practised by an expert.

The Myers Briggs approach looks at four dimensions of Personality. The first being a measure of Introversion and Extraversion. The Introvert tends to be more interested in the 'inner world' of concepts and ideas and the extrovert the 'outer world' or relationships and possibilities. Clearly, a strong preference either way creates certain strong behaviours which have an impact on others. These also may be indicative of certain preferential managerial careers.

The second dimension is concerned with Perception. Perceiving means the way people become aware of things, people, occurrences and ideas, and how they absorb information from the environment, etc.

The third dimension is Judging and includes the processes of coming to conclusions about what we have perceived. Together, perception and judgement govern much of a person's outward behaviour. Perception determines what people see in a situation, and judgement determines what they do about it.

PERCEPTION

We can perceive the world in two ways, Sensing and Intuition. Sensing is becoming aware of things through our five senses. Intuition is indirect perception through our unconscious, incorporating ideas or associations. These may range from the masculine 'hunch' to the feminine 'intuition'.

Readers of this chapter who prefer sensing will concentrate on the words, readers who prefer intuition will read between the lines. Overall, we tend to favour one process over others. We neglect the other which we enjoy less. We probably neglect a 'process' because we are not too skilled in its use. If a certain process has been encouraged in our work life then it is natural for us to favour or prefer it. If we favour one method we avoid the use of other ways. Over time, and with experience, the preferred process grows more controlled and more trustworthy. This enjoyment of a 'process' extends into activities requiring that process, and we tend to develop the traits that come from looking at life in a particular way. We each develop along different lines.

JUDGING

Judging is the way we come to conclusions. One way is thinking, that is by a logical process, aimed at impersonal findings. The other is by feeling, that is by appreciation – bestowing on things a value based upon personal subjectivity. People tend to trust one process over the other.

A thinking reader will judge on the logical process of what is said; the feeling person on ideas which are pleasing or displeasing, supporting or threatening. The person who uses feeling is more alert to developing human relationships; the person who is more adept at thinking grows more skilled in the organisation of facts and logical analysis.

APPROACH TO LIFE

Finally, the the last dimension refers to your approach to life. If a person is 'Judging' in outlook he probably prefers an organised existence and plans well in advance. Others, with the alter native approach, are 'Perceptive' in nature and prefer to do things as they arise. They are probably more spontaneous and prefer to be flexible.

Consequently, people who share preferences for doing things find each other easy to understand and get along and work well together. Those who don't share preferences have difficulty understanding each other. This opposition can be a strain if these people are members of the same Management Team.

THERE IS NOT A GOOD OR BAD 'TYPE'

Understanding some of the differences between colleagues helps to understand how we and others organise our working lives and how we manage and work with others. We can also find out more about preferences for planning and decision-making.

Some managers, the analyst type, may be highly logical and systematic and find it difficult to get on with the visionary who trades on ideas and moves from one subject to another. Management development is all about understanding these differences and working through the conflicts.

PROFILES AND EXAMPLES

With the MBTI there are sixteen basic profiles. Understanding a personal profile and working to understand others with whom we interact ensures that a real team effort is achieved. For instance an ISTJ, who is quiet, thorough, practical, organised, dependable, who can work on projects independently, may have some difficulty understanding the views of an ENFP, who is high-spirited, friendly, ready to help and feels able to contribute to situations even if not an expert.

Knowing that certain occupational profiles attract certain 'types' may give some indication why there can be conflict between Sales Managers and Systems Analysts, Marketing Managers and Researchers, etc. Understanding the reasons for these differences is critical to effective teamworking. Types suggest certain leadership styles and leadership behaviours.

Saville and Holdsworth's OPQ Personality Profile can also indicate ways of working in groups and leading others. It is one of the most powerful instruments on the market and has been designed to generate information and relate to other 'managerial' profiles. Belbin's Team Types, for instance, is just one area which complements this approach.

There are a great deal of benefits which accrue to an organisation using profiles, but I will concentrate here on their value to the Management Team. The profiles help us to understand why we and others behave as we do. Failing to understand and deal with personal differences suggestions a rigidity in management style – which is not conducive to TQ.

In a successful software business, this approach helped the Senior Team to understand the conflict behind planning the roll-out of TQ. Some of the managers wanted a planned, detailed approach, others wanted to try a few 'flexible' pilots, while others wanted to think about it!

The senior officers in a major finance house concentrated upon their managerial style and the impact their style had on others. The majority tried to vary their natural style in certain circumstances. This was all in aid of gaining balance in managing the process of cultural change.

Many critics of this approach feel that this is too 'touching and feeling'. Some managers prefer the rigours of **strategy, systems** and **structure.** The Team-Building approach rests with **staff** at all levels, providing them with the **skills,** to change **symbols** and management **style** leading by example in order to create **shared values, synergy** and a new culture founded upon TQ.

This approach is pursued to better understand behaviour and actions. This understanding is the cornerstone for creating long-term cultural change. The use of profiles is gaining ground in most companies. It is only a matter of time before this is the central focus behind many major change strategies.

SUMMARY

Team-building focuses upon the soft side of change and is central to cross-functional working. Knowing personal strengths and limitations helps us all appreciate the value of our role and also the weakness we display when working in a team. Working upon becoming more self-critical, examining processes from team-building, personality-profiling or team-working will equip us with the skills to work more effectively with people from different functions and with different views of the world. We should focus more on adding value to managerial and staff skills by providing staff with opportunities to enhance their personal development. They will then learn to operate and seek ambiguity and stretch and grow rather than staying within their comfort zones. Personal development is required before effective teamwork takes place. You cannot force and control teams to get the best from themselves – you can only equip them with the skills and then let them grow the team.

Bullet Points

- Senior officers can only move from the firefighting to the preventative culture through changing the 'style' of their managers towards one which is cross-functional and team-focused.

- Don't under-estimate the changes necessary. Getting people to move from a rigid 'telling' culture to a 'listening' culture does take time and extraordinary effort by senior people.

- Moving to a 'listening' culture does not equate with abdicating managerial responsibility.

- When we identify poor service, we should call in the person who may have the best solutions – the person directly and physically responsible for the delivery of that service. We employ people from the neck up, not down!

- We only get results through others. Give staff and service people the responsibility and the scope to create changes. Leave them to it and get out of their way.

- Create opportunities all the time to Involve people. If things go wrong, don't blame them, ask them for suggestions for improvement. If you are developing a new product or service, ask for their viewpoint. It's free and effective.

- If you find there are managers who obstruct new ideas and improvements, give them the chance to change. If they don't change – change them!

- Try to motivate your people. Research tells us that positive reinforcement which is specific and delivered as soon as the desirable behaviour has taken place promotes motivation.

- Spend less time telling people what they did 3% wrong and congratulate them for what they did 97% right. Ask them for detailed plans on getting the lot 100% right next time.

- The effective transmission of information through Briefing Groups creates a climate of trust and co-operation. Fail to communicate and people think you don't trust them.

- If you do not cause Briefing Groups to work, you'll never achieve the full benefits of TQ.

- The organisational culture reflects teamworking. A frightened, fear-driven culture will be reinforced by win-lose team tactics both in and between departments. A TQ culture is founded upon win-win relationships.

- Reject the 'Us and Them' attitude. The more you recognise it, the more you reinforce it.

- Senior Management Teams deserve the managers who work for them. Career development is a strategic issue and should be taken seriously. The people who work for you now are the products of your Human Resource Policies of previous years. If you don't value your people – they won't value working for you.

- Don't believe that all career progression is vertical. Move to a philosophy which promotes, values and rewards managers working across boundaries.

- Most people are creative, committed and achieving – do they display these tendencies when they work for you? Develop Human Resource Strategies to promote the use of talent at work.

- Start Team-Building right at the top. Explore differences and learn to adopt styles.

- Accept Profiling and Psychometrics as valuable tools for promoting personal and organisational change. Learn how to improve how you interact, influence and lead others.

- Understand that change begins with self.

CHAPTER 12

Development, Learning and Training

The role of training, development and education is probably the most critical aspect of any TQ Drive. Training workshops should be designed to stimulate, challenge and provide attendees with all the knowledge they need to make TQ happen. If this experience is a failure, then those attending the sessions will gain little and you have reduced your chance of success.

Too many Management Teams think that their enthusiasm for TQ will be shared automatically by other employees. They believe that fantastic changes will come about when the training takes off! We know this will not always be the case. Many people will look upon the change as a threat to the security of their position and will avoid creating the necessary changes – especially Managers and Supervisors. This attitude is difficult to hide in training sessions – when case studies and action plans are explored.

Too often, Management Teams think that a spell of training will work wonders. Yes – if it is planned properly, and is tested and owned by more than the guy who stands at the front and trains!

Let us examine the ways in which Training can fail and the action we can take to avoid failure. Each of these points will be explained and tentative solutions preferred. But first let us start with the most basic of problems – examining the role of training in organisation development.

MISUNDERSTANDING THE PURPOSE OF TRAINING AND DEVELOPMENT

To be realistic, the role of training is one which is not always valued by all companies. Perhaps the reason for this is that we may find it so difficult to relate specific training events to particular organisational success. Too many managers see training as a luxury, undertaken only by larger companies who can afford to spread the costs over many functions and locations. This is nonsense.

Many managers discount the role of training because they find it difficult to relate training exercises to the bottom line. A fundamental point needs clarification. A great deal of investment in training may not be gleaned in the short term for a variety of reasons – but this should not be an excuse for not doing it.

Relating training initiatives to specific outcomes has to be the way to win commitment to change. If the training provider fails to offer tangible and positive outcomes from any training event then he is not sufficiently focused. Spending time and energy in planning can enable us to relate specific outcomes to training inputs.

I believe that an excuse used by many trainers is the intangibility of training and relating this to business results. I claim that if we know why we are training we should be able to monitor progress. "If we can't measure success, then little thought has gone into training design."

Training managers who have specified their objectives, designed drives to meet them and have carefully monitored progress are those who have gained most. A 'hit and miss' training affair does not create the required cultural change. Training as a method of change can be extremely successful if managed properly. But we must reject the generalised training event characterised by inappropriate material, irrelevant case studies and video presentations, delivered by trainers who are more committed to their own interests than to the wellbeing of the company.

Not all responsibility falls on the trainer, though. Some managers, when asked about their commitment to training, suggest defensively that the selection process is geared towards bringing the best calibre people into the structure, so there is little need to devote resources to training.

There is an implication that new recruits have received all the training they require. This may be true on a professional basis for today – but what about tomorrow? The really interesting question, which is never answered, relates to existing employees. Do they magically acquire the skills and abilities to cope with changes in the organisation? Are they able through a process of mental osmosis to acquire skills so they can fulfil a senior role in the organisation? No, of course not – managers have to be developed within the company to meet the challenge of the future. Companies that fail to do this had better start investing in the future – otherwise they won't have one.

TRAINING IN PROFESSIONAL AND TECHNICAL SKILLS ONLY!

Unfortunately, in too many cases in the UK, Training refers directly to professional and technical training only. As long as employees are trained in the latest state-of-the-art or techniques of their specialism or function, the 'management process' can take care of itself! The only problem is that the 'management process' is critical to the success of TQ, and if not properly planned and implemented, can create havoc and destroy a perfectly good initiative.

Too few organisations value training: look what has happened to the training function when there is a downturn in economic activity. Those activities which fail to bring in tangible results are sacrificed in the short term. The long term, in many cases, is made up of short-term fixes or decisions which are geared totally towards reducing costs and maintaining profit on the bottom line. It is not surprising that, in the long term, training issues are never fully addressed.

Consider the value of Trainers in organisations. Do they possess high status or is their position basically a job share with other responsibilities? For instance, I have worked with internal trainers who were also communications managers, and with trainers who also had responsibility for mostly technical training in the production area. This is so in too many cases, and too few companies fail to understand the role of Human Resource Development. Consequently, few managers have the same level of commitment towards training as the 'excellent' companies. Training is something which can be left to another day. I am glad to say not all companies portray this image.

For instance, IBM is renowned for its commitment towards development and training. Each manager receives at least five managerial training days per year. Other companies committed to the TQ culture do likewise, but they are few and far between. Mortgage Express, based in London, also commits to at least the five-day rule, as does AT&T. I usually find that in interventions, development activity increases both from internal and external providers and this directly correlates for progress in continuous improvements. Without doubt, the companies which value management development tend to be the more enlightened UK companies, most US based multi-nationals, East-West joint venture companies and the Japanese. Without doubt, the quality rather than volume of training is usually associated with the examples above.

Of course, many may dispute this view, but the reality is that too many companies fail to provide even the most basic training.

DEMOGRAPHIC TRENDS

Estimates suggest that as we move through into the early years of the 21st Century, the numbers seeking employment in industry and commerce on a professional basis will fall. This is primarily related to the falling birth rate in the 1980s and 1990s. We understand that at least 50% of the staff will be made up of women returning to work and, of the remainder, 50% will be young females. Many will be employed in a part-time capacity, clearly changing the employee profile, with some staff having several employers.

Alarm bells have been ringing since the early 1990s. Traditionally, most European and US companies drew, rightly or wrongly, upon the male population for employment. The reality is that young men will be in short supply.

To attract this scarce resource, companies will need to prove that they walk with the giants. Companies will have to take serious note of this challenge. Good quality young graduates are in demand. They will choose to go to the companies with the 'excellent' image. They will not be interested in those which have little commitment to training, development, career development and succession-planning. Given a choice, who would you focus upon as an employer – the company that has a strong performance-driven culture where quality people can progress, or the traditional bureaucracy where there is little scope for improvement and the control culture is strongly evident?

My contention is that too few companies have considered the severity of this problem. If we have not prepared ourselves for the immediate future, including equal opportunity, what preparation have we made for TQ?

This is bad news as we move through to the early years of the new century – little movement is taking place on the generalised training front preparing for TQ.

Companies committed to Training as a catalyst of change, both organisationally and individually, will find the transition to TQ relatively easy – does your company project this image?

TRAINING – WE ARE THE BEST... WE THINK!

While working with a company in the finance sector, the opinion of many managers was "We are the best at providing training in the business". This was hard to believe, because many supervisors and managers had not attended a training workshop for years! The statement 'The best in the business' had come about because of a specific comment made about a particular 'objection-handling workshop' run for a select group of salesmen. This one success was translated into a general belief that they provided the best training in the industry!

QUALITY OF PEOPLE

Training and development is one of the three most important investments any company can make, the other two being technological innovation, and research and development. Organisations fail to realise that the quality of their people is determined by the experiences to which they are exposed within the company. If these experiences are all short-term outcomes and technically orientated with little opportunity for development, then we cannot expect our people to come up with innovative ways of solving old problems.

An old culture geared to technical skills acquisition with no time devoted to critical review and development will create employees who are solely geared to improving their expertise in a narrow field.

Comparing UK company commitment to training to that of our foreign competitors is an embarrassment. While many companies renowned for the way they do things invest as much as 3-5% of sales turnover on training, many spend considerably less. Talking with managers from a company in the whisky industry, I was surprised to learn that they did not base their financial commitment to training on a percentage of sales turnover, but on the wage bill. Apparently, resources devoted to training exceeded 1% of wage bill the previous year. Most of the money had been spent on a training facility – which had never been used for training, but for meetings!

GREAT TQ TRAINING – PITY ABOUT THEIR INABILITY TO MANAGE!

To demonstrate the attitude of some companies to training, let me cite the following instance. While I was working with a large business, a senior manager took me to one side and said how pleased he had been with the training that they had received. However, he had some reservations. After discussing the good points of the course, he said that his supervisors were still deficient in leadership and team-building. He explained that: "They know what they should do, but they still don't know how to delegate, plan activities, hold meetings and motivate".

I was taken aback. What I learnt most from this encounter was that a two-day course on TQ does not even start to redress the failure of management over many years to provide employees with even the basic management education.

> *Companies need to realise that Training is the key to an improved culture. The prescription is simple. Become committed today to spending double, triple and quadruple on training. If not, you get what you deserve.*

> *First learn how people learn, then develop the Training initiatives.*

There are some similarities between training in athletics and management. The more successful athletics coaches tend to be those who have been through similar experiences to those whom they train. This is also true for managers. The coaches understand how skills and abilities are acquired and recognise that the major obstacles to training have to be overcome – these are usually self-imposed and related to attitude. The same is true for management. A coach would never design a training programme which would take an athlete to Olympic competition without making some appraisal of past performance. Coaches need to understand what turns their athletes 'on and off' and design programmes with this in mind. This is also true in management circles. The past performance of managers, identified in appraisals or reviews of training courses, will give some indication of strengths, weaknesses and potential. Failing to review the past performance of managers and supervisors before designing a training event is tantamount to disaster.

Clearly, we can benefit from looking at past actions to help us predict future behaviour.

DEAL WITH THE TENSION OR STRESS ISSUE FIRST!

Many people attending training workshops on any subject experience some level of tension or stress. If that stress is perceived as being a positive motivator, ie. they are looking forward to the challenge, the stimulation, the excitement, the debate, then it can be productive. But what happens when the negative elements of stress take over and the training event is perceived as being negative and punitive? This is evident when training has been used as a weapon, a device to make you do something rather than instil the spirit to want to learn.

PEOPLE DON'T LEARN IF THEY ARE AFRAID

In some cases, people believe their reason for being on a course is because of their poor performance. They are doing things wrong. It is not unheard of for managers to say that by attending a one- or two-day course, this will instantly eradicate undesirable managerial or supervisory performance.

Training in the negative sense and in the Dickensian culture is something you do to people! What are the consequences? Many trainers find that some people on the course are extremely tense and anxious. It is not surprising that the first half-hour or so of a programme can be a lonesome affair for the trainers with the trainees sitting rigid, afraid to speak up.

In one or two instances, fortunately too rare to suggest that this is the industry average, we find managers and supervisors on a course who have not been briefed on its purpose or their expected contribution. Clearly, lack of organisation and commitment to the event are holding back TQ.

Trainees need to be relaxed to take on board new ideas. Learning cannot take place in a climate of fear.

I have the belief, not shared by all, that training should be an enjoyable experience. It should challenge the previous experience of the participant and build upon a commitment to do better in the future. This is critical in any Quality Improvement initiative.

In order to learn, considerable unfreezing of attitudes has to take place prior to the training experience. Any 'Fear' associated with training has to be dispelled.

Who should take responsibility for this unfreezing? Most tends to fall upon the shoulders of the trainer, but I believe strongly that the line manager should be coaching the potential course delegate on the purpose and objectives of the course and expected contributions. Of course, this can only be achieved if the training course has been discussed at all management levels.

LET STRATEGY LEAD TRAINING

One of the most common failures in Training for Culture Change is that too much emphasis is given to the role of training as the activity which will create the TQ culture by itself. Experiencing a meaningful course on TQ will not necessarily generate TQ behaviour. It is the foundation upon which to work. There is a natural tendency to roll out training before the Management Team are really aware of what they want to achieve in specific functions and departments.

Training as part of TQ seems to be an activity which is encouraged because it is tangible – something is happening. The question I ask is "Is it happening at the right time?".

We all know that training has costs. People will be away from their work. Others should fill in for them. Those attending sessions should not be penalised by finding mountains of work on their desks when they return. Yet this is the norm.

We all know that in order to reduce waste and rework, we need to prevent problems arising, and this includes putting time aside for planning and training. Trying to make the transition without some commitment to additional resources puts stress and pressure on the staff and reinforces the belief that the company is not really serious.

The solution to this dilemma rests with Senior Management. The Training of staff in TQ and related techniques has to be thought through at a strategic level and training designed specifically for the future of the company. That is why it is critical that companies plan the implementation of TQ and spend some time considering exactly where they would like to be in the next few years and the resources they will commit to the transition. It is a waste of time committing resources to external consultants only. The major investment should be inside the company. This means the company has to know where it is going and how each department fits in to the picture.

TRAINING SHOULD ADDRESS CHANGING ATTITUDES

To reap the full benefit from the experience, trainers should spend some time talking about attitudes and change. There is little point giving out a great deal of interesting and highly entertaining information if you want people to concentrate upon 'doing' rather than 'knowing' things. Trainers often have a conflict of interest between using training material with which they are fully conversant, and that with which they are not – but which meets the real needs of the company.

If in doubt, ask a Trainer for specific objectives which will be achieved at the end of the session! What will people be able to do? What can they define? What methodologies will they use for solving problems? What are the likely outcomes? Where will the major problems arise? What action will they take to promote TQ over the next three months?

ESTABLISHING RAPPORT: INTERESTED PEOPLE LISTEN AND ACT

Establishing rapport is not easy, particularly with a new audience, but the rift between the trainer and trainee can be considerably reduced if material is strongly participative in nature. The Quality of the Change Agent is critical to success.

Formal inputs tend to be the order of the day. 'Mass baptism' can take place in large halls. Information is projected one way with little opportunity for meaningful discussion. In some cases, participative material can be discouraged – with the phrase "They are committed. They will fly with it. Just tell them".

Material which is presented in a lecture-type environment, which does not require feedback or questioning from the audience, will achieve little, except for those who make detailed notes or the few who have a long attention span.

Recognising that the average span of attention is not long – perhaps ten to twenty minutes – suggests that the medium whereby we instil the message has to be changed frequently, to take account of those who have 'fallen off' the learning curve. Lecturing for hours on end will not create a great deal of learning. Although we all learn and absorb knowledge and information at different speeds, we can maximise learning by changing, fairly frequently, our means of delivery.

Although this is not a book on 'learning' it is useful to know that most of us retain information in our short- rather than our long-term memory. Bearing this in mind, it is not surprising that we have a great deal of difficulty in recalling information we have absorbed some time ago.

If we can all look back at examinations we have taken years ago and remember the cramming techniques we used, we may have managed to remember sufficient to get through the paper but, come a week after the exam, we would probably have difficulty recalling 10% of what we could the previous week.

We know that simply exposing people to information is not learning. Recall is low. The reason for this is that we tend to take information into a temporary buffer, our short-term memory. If this information is not continually analysed, questioned and assessed in the immediate future, then we lose it for ever. It is never transferred to the long-term memory.

Failing to consolidate information effectively destroys it, so it is hardly surprising that a week or so after attending a course, we have little recall of the events which have taken place. Does this have any direct relevance to Training for TQ? Of course it does. A solitary training event, poorly designed and delivered, will have minimal effect. The effect can even be negative, confirming the worst fears and prejudices of those present.

Even the best trainer, the most interesting material, and riveting case studies, will fail if the event has not been planned properly and there is no follow-up or encouragement from Line Management.

LEARNING TECHNIQUES

Techniques which have been developed by Tony Buzan and others have helped many to assemble information and retain it in the long-term memory.

We must give serious consideration to the training issue and not take trainers at face value. We need to be critical of performance. We are willing to put our people in the training arena and, sometimes, fail to maximise the experience either because of failure to plan, or insufficient enthusiasm to make things happen quickly. Is it asking too much to put that extra 20% effort in planning and preparation to make the experience the best it can be?

Those who failed to plan should ask themselves this question: "How can we expect those attending training workshops to put into practice those things we value as important, when we have put little effort into the training experience itself?".

MANAGE THE LEARNING ENVIRONMENT

It is worth remembering that some psychologists tell us that we forget more than 95% of information we take in over the relatively short period of 48 hours. What impact does this information have on training design of TQ Workshops?

We need to manage the learning environment. What we should be doing is spending equal time on two key areas:

- Learning how others learn, prior to embarking on developing training materials, and

- Ensuring that the design of the learning experience is focused upon the 'customer' – the learner.

MAINTAINING INTEREST

Understanding learning difficulties, addressing obstacles to learners, is a priority before absorbing ourselves in the choice of learning materials.

We should address ourselves to maintaining interest, inviting participation, and giving concrete and visual illustrations. Tom Peters, guru of Quality and Customer Service, understands this well. On all his training audio and video tapes he presents a measurable picture. His enthusiasm and clever choice of anecdotes, examples and quotes reminds us all that the training experience can be considerably enlightened through presentation skills and understanding what turns the audience on. Expert trainers put equal emphasis upon the content and the process of delivery.

RELYING ON A PACKAGE

Training packages are an excellent vehicle for projecting a coherent message. A large number of people can be trained to use the material. It would seem to ensure consistency. Whoever uses the package should project roughly the same impression, but this is not always the case. So many companies are moving towards a more tailored approach to TQ. Packaged approaches do provide consistency in message, because the package may have worked well in other companies. But beware, there is no guarantee that it will work in every context. Material which goes down well in one environment may well not in others. Using the same material within different companies can be 'fatal'.

Another consideration is that using the same package for different Staff, Production Personnel and R&D departments can have its shortcomings. If the training is designed for a mix of individuals from different functions, then the material must be excellent to involve all, and relate to all functions present. It is unusual nowadays to segment training to specific functions, but this can be a real danger if companies have several locations separated by many miles. Clearly, the more cross-training the better. The quicker the walls between functional specialisations tumble, the sooner internal customer and supplier start working together.

AVOID LCD

Material which is sufficiently general in nature as to be applicable to all, smacks of the LCD approach – Lowest Common Denominator – which has its drawbacks. Reprinting a Quality Manual with the exception of a few pages is not the best way of demonstrating that management is serious in its intent on the design of training materials.

TRAINING OFTEN FAILS TO CHALLENGE ATTITUDES

Training has been defined as providing "The attitudes, skills and knowledge in order to perform and achieve a task". If this is the case, why do so many training programmes focus entirely upon information and knowledge? Few courses are 'doing' in nature. Even fewer really get to grips with the attitude-changing issue.

Addressing the attitude of trainees and having them DO things is critical. It is pointless having someone leaving a course knowing a great deal, but unaware of how to put it into practice. This opposes all TQ principles.

What we say and do is paramount in making people feel differently about their role in promoting quality. We need to attack the very fabric of 'resistance' to create a real movement in doing new things – getting rid of the old culture.

The Training experience should be focused upon changing the feelings and attitudes of those attending. The role of the trainer is to challenge old views and replace them with new tangible and concrete behaviours.

We want to send people away from sessions with the hope, enthusiasm and commitment to doing things right. . . first time.

LINE MANAGEMENT SHOULD REINFORCE TQ BEHAVIOUR

Focusing too much on information, quoting facts and figures, to the detriment of action, will never promote change. The right approach is to get people to do things differently in one small area of their work, so they can feed back at some later stage, preferably at a follow-up workshop. This action should be reinforced constantly so that it becomes a way of life. The trainer cannot always be around to reinforce the TQ beliefs, so Line Management has to take the message and ensure that consistent behaviour is promoted within the staff. This is not as easy as it sounds. The supervisory grades often will not fully understand the changes required to develop a TQ culture. They, themselves, could be fighting the cultural change, which in turn requires a significant change in their supervisory behaviour.

Employees may also doubt that TQ will change the culture of the organisation. Comments reflecting this are common.

"We have heard all this before. They said things would change when briefing groups were introduced – what happened? Nothing. They said exactly the same five years ago with Quality Circles. What happened? Nothing! Why should TQ be any different?"

Morale is not improved when supervisory staff fuel the mistrust by telling shopfloor employees: "Don't concern yourself about TQ – you'll be back firefighting tomorrow."

Having employees leave a workshop session committed to TQ is extremely satisfying, but the degree to which this can be maintained on their return to their workstations is ultimately determined by the behaviour of those with whom they come into contact most frequently – the managers or supervisors. Get commitment from them, and success will follow.

Success in TQ is related to the requirement to Lead, Communicate and Train – in that order.

CASCADING TQ DOWN THROUGH THE STRUCTURE

TQ slogans, expressed on posters, will never create the needed changes which will promote TQ. What is required is a major change or shift in how people think about what they do. This can only come about through systematic training and reinforcement of behaviour through supervisory and managerial staff.

Some have described this change in thinking as a 'Paradigm Shift' implying that we have to adopt a different way of perceiving and understanding what we do each day.

A classic example of a 'Paradigm Shift' is Copernicus's rejection of the notion of the Earth being flat. This revelation forced people to think differently. Many resisted this new knowledge as heresy. This change in perception changed our view of time and space, a viewpoint requiring a re-evaluation of our science, philosophy and theology. Perhaps a current 'Paradigm Shift' for some managers is that "control can be replaced with trust which would breed empowerment."

In a similar fashion, TQ changes the way we see things and how we perceive the way organisations should function. The TQ initiative should fundamentally change the way we structure and pursue activities within the organisation. That is why, when designing Training and Development workshops, we concentrate upon changing attitudes.

We have to change attitudes towards flexibility. We want there to be more cross-fertilisation between departments, functions and individual skills. We need more horizontal management, with managers spending a great deal of their time co-ordinating work – rather than building thicker walls between functions and responsibilities.

We have to reject the belief that there is an acceptable level of non-quality. Zero defects should be our purpose in everything we do.

We have to promote teamwork and encourage people to discuss their differences. Conflict is endemic within any organisation. Using conflict to build a positive bridge between units and functions is critical – if we hope to develop the climate of trust reflective of a TQ culture.

We need to change attitudes towards the resolution of conflict. In too many organisations, the purpose behind finding out what is wrong is allocating blame and kicking people! This has to change to a culture where things are identified as being defective, and they are put right straight away.

Avoiding blame can be a way of life for some people. Analysing internal memos generated by some managers suggests that too many are written with the sole purpose of covering themselves. TQ is about improving something every day and this cannot be achieved without taking a few risks. TQ has to challenge the risk-averse culture.

DOING WHAT YOU VALUE AND VALUING WHAT YOU DO

What we find difficult to understand is that most people have developed a value system of Right First Time in their personal lives. We witness it in most daily activities. For instance, we all expect that car drivers will maintain their good driving behaviour and keep clear from driving on the pavement and knocking people over. Thankfully it is a commonly shared value.

Equally, we expect most people to be disciplined when drinking and driving. Our value system demands it because of the harm and damage which could result from failing to do so.

When visiting the doctor, we expect that he or she will be committed to prescribing drugs which will help relieve the symptoms of illness and help us to recover. We do not expect to have to check the prescription with a pharmacist. We demand and expect a 100% commitment to Quality.

Likewise, when we travel by plane, we expect the pilot to be 100% committed to take-off, flying and landing. A commitment to less than 100% is unthinkable.

It is clear that we have common expectations which are reflected in social attitudes, but often we fail to apply these to work situations.

The Training experience must bridge the gulf between social behaviour and values, and work behaviour and values. Training which fails to get people to think about their value system, the effect this has on their attitudes, their work behaviour, beliefs and actions, is clearly too wide of the mark of what TQ is all about.

TQ WORKSHOPS AND ACTION LEARNING

To overcome many of the criticisms associated with the poor provision of TQ training, a number of steps can be taken. Overall, the training should be relevant, and based upon the real needs of those attending. The material should be specifically designed for the participants and plenty of attention should be given to the 'medium' or the method of imparting learning. Case studies designed around the problems experienced by the company should form the focus of attention.

I have found one of the single most important factors is the structure behind the training. Participants have to be aware that the ideas to which they are being exposed, the concepts they will explore, the structures they will investigate, all have one thing in common – these are the features of TQ which are to be placed and planted within the organisation. It must be emphasised that everything learned during the workshop will add value to Quality. Everything is geared to application.

Participants are aware, from discussing the objectives right at the beginning of the Workshop, that they will be expected to formulate an Action Plan for change before they leave the session. Even on a one-day course, lasting just seven hours, we always allocate two hours for Action-Planning. Before the session ends, everybody will have spoken and explained precisely what he is going to change when he gets back to work.

The Action Plan is composed of three or four pages and typical questions ask participants to identify their key result areas, to identify activities where a great deal of rework takes place, and areas where waste is evident. If they have difficulty working through this aspect of the plan they have to identify the 'service' they provide to their internal customers. Requirements are defined in many cases and this is an attempt to bring customers and suppliers much closer together.

Those attending are aware that they have to come back for future workshops having worked on action plans and, when they do return, to report on progress. Because the workshops are restricted to ten people at a time, there is a need to talk in some depth about possibilities. Action-Planning must be flexible. Those attending must have the opportunity to talk with their colleagues and their manager in order to ensure that their plan is achievable, measurable (or how can we assess progress?), realistic in the time frame and compatible with the aims and objectives of the department. Clearly, the Action Plan must be negotiable, otherwise people may be working counter to each other.

Participants have a commitment to make things happen as do those who supervise them. You can imagine the embarrassment for those attending a follow-up session where people taking part say they have been too busy or they have been blocked in their progress by others. One can see instantly where the blockages to TQ are within the structure.

The follow-up sessions should be held between 6 and 12 weeks after the initial session. So the first session puts TQ in perspective as a strategic imperative, the second series of workshops concentrates wholly on action and the experienced problems with implementation. It is no surprise to find that the focus of this session is on 'managing change'.

Prior to any formal input, it is best to structure feedback of the group on progress. This can take up to three or four hours, but the focus is upon recognition and recounting success. There are many benefits from taking this approach. Overall, the major feature is that people from all aspects of the organisation can assess the progress made in different areas, locations and functions. This feedback is a powerful motivator. It is also found that there is a great deal more recall of what happened in session one, because people have been engaged in putting theory into practice for some time.

Finally, at the end of this session, further emphasis is given to action planning for the final workshop taking place in 6-12 weeks' time. The focus of this session is problem-solving, especially in groups. Here, participants are given the structures and some techniques to work as members of teams.

What happens next? Well, managers at all levels should now be well acquainted with the process of action-planning and there should be no need to formalise sessions in quite the same way. This 'process' should become part of the culture. Managers and staff should meet frequently to discuss action plans for quality improvement. This should become part of the everyday way of doing things. To aid this process, it may be advisable to formalise the action-planning into a two-yearly Appraisal exercise – but great care should be taken here. Organisations may be moving ahead in some areas, but may carry with them some old habits/techniques. One of these may be an appraisal system which was designed for other times. Ensure that the Appraisal system really does complement the TQ initiative.

This Action-centred Learning approach is extremely powerful.

FEEDBACK AND CULTURAL CHANGE

We are all aware that creating a TQ structure takes time, and the problem here is that results will take some time to show. Tangible feedback has always been a problem when creating real strategic change, but this approach helps to focus attention on Quality Improvements which will have some impact in the short term. It acts as a tool to reinforce the drive for Total Quality and stimulates enthusiasm. Maintaining enthusiasm is probably the most difficult aspect of TQ to control when promoting changes orientated towards stimulating long-term cultural change.

Many of the Action Plans have a ripple effect. People recognise those things between functions which inhibit effectiveness. They also stimulate interest in new areas ripe for Quality Improvement.

This approach to Quality Improvement also encourages members of departments to work together to solve joint problems. Breaking down functional and departmental barriers is one of the objectives of this approach.

Many of the ideas and action plans achieved can be transferred to other parts of the organisation. For instance, when working with a large company distributing beer and lagers nationwide – we found that many ideas derived from manufacturing or distribution areas could be used in other locations on other sites. For the recipients, Quality Improvement was free.

The importance of sharing success should not be minimised in action plans. But this all comes down to thinking about the training of TQ using the Planning methodology at the beginning of the book. Looking at training failures helps us examine the action we can take to train the hell out of people and improve performance by leaps and bounds. From the 10% of failure comes 90% of success.

SUMMARY

Commitment to change is not enough: staff have to be provided with the necessary attitudes, skills and knowledge in order to create the culture for the business. Training should focus upon 'doing' as opposed to just knowing things. Development should be focused upon improving the competence of those attending; and special reference should be directed toward mastering change and improving the ability of managers to persuade others. Training is not a one-off affair, it has be consolidated into development plans and frequent feedback sessions organised around the critical skills to be acquired. Most effective is Action learning, when managers learn by doing and exposing themselves to situations where they may have to take a little more of a risk.

Bullet Points

- Learn to value and love training. Training is not a luxury. It is a necessity.

- Training is the second most important vehicle in creating cultural change. Leadership comes first.

- Training should not be the sole responsibility of external trainers – but the real responsibility of the Line Manager.

- People don't go forward on their own power. They need to be energised by others and be provided with the opportunities to develop.

- You get the people you deserve. If you don't help people go forward and develop – they slip backward.

- Training is certainly not only about Professional and Technical issues. Real change takes place when people feel competent to manage the process of getting people to do everything better.

- Don't debate the issue – double, triple and quadruple the size of the training budget. There are no known cases of over-training forcing business failure than under-training.

- Find out what other companies are really doing in your industry. Emulate their best practices. When you have achieved this, move on to emulate the best companies in other industries.

- Only compare your training with the best. It's easy to be the best at training when you compare yourself with turkeys.

- Recognise that if training is new to the company, then those attending may be anxious. Dispel their fears through preparation.

- Ensure that there is no excuse for non-attendance at training courses. Always put prevention before production. Arrange for others to do the work of trainees. If all else fails, do it yourself.

- Don't penalise people for attending courses by failing to reallocate their work.

- Line Managers should play their part in training. The more they attend training events, the more trust is generated by their staff.

- Design Training Workshops to change attitudes.

- Remember: people who are interested and involved, listen and act.

- Employ everything you can to hold participants' attention during training workshops. Keep the audience motivated and they will learn.

- Don't put too many eggs in one basket. Just because someone has attended a training event, don't expect that you don't have to reinforce behaviour on the job.

- We forget things quickly. Come up with bullet points reflecting TQ. Tell your people about them, communicate and canvas them. Most importantly, live by them.

- Encourage note-taking. Have posters designed with bullet points in mind.

- Understand the learning difficulties of others.

- Design your own programme and ensure it meets your needs.

- Ensure that Line Management reinforce the 'beliefs' in day-to-day behaviour.

ACTION-PLANNING: THE RIPPLE EFFECT

Mary Smith, an accountant, decided that she would work on reducing the amount of rework in the administration and processing of managers' expense claims. She defined the problem she experienced as due to many managers putting in individual claims for lunch and travelling expenses, even though these were incurred in a group, but only one receipt being handed in for processing. This caused considerable rework in tracing back through the claims, often months apart, to extract VAT/Sales invoice numbers.

Mary talked to her boss, George, about her action plan. George thought it too big a problem to tackle, so suggested that she contact Custom and Excise for information.

While the 'Custom and Excise' officials were on site, they helped her look though other issues and came across a real anomaly. The company purchased raw material from a sister company in Spain and paid duty on the purchase. The company machined the product and sold it back to Spain – neglecting to claim back the duty. The company had forgone this expense for fifteen years, losing £2,500 per month!

In this example, Mary made progress on her original objective, but exploring in her area also uncovered other problems which had been overlooked for years.

ACTION-PLANNING: REVERSING A PHILOSOPHY

Gerry Wilson is a Maintenance engineer who was continually harassed and spent most of his time fixing things as they broke down. The company had a clear policy. If it breaks – fix it!

Gerry had had enough of the Production Manager who never gave him enough time to do even the barest of preventative maintenance. So he concentrated upon one machine and recorded the true cost of breakdown. On average it broke down once every two weeks and it was always the same component. This cost the company an incredible £12,000 per year.

Gerry reset the machine to run at its correct speed. Production was rescheduled. Result: the machine has not broken down since then. Gerry is a hero. The Production Manager wants Gerry to look at other machines to develop a preventative maintenance programme. It looks like Gerry has changed the culture!

CHAPTER 13

Readiness for Change

It is critical that an in-depth analysis of the company is pursued prior to the start of a TQ Drive. Responsibility for the analysis must be allocated between internal and external agents of change, and suggestions made as to how TQ can be installed over time.

COMMITMENT DETERMINES THE SPEED OF SUCCESS

Obviously, every company will want to see results from its TQ initiative fairly quickly. Over the years, traditional thinking on implementation has suggested that the larger the company, the longer the time span needed for TQ to take hold. The reason behind this 'self-limiting belief' was the difficulty associated with promoting cultural change and creating the intense changes which need to be undertaken to shape the business.

It is of note that TQ can be rooted within the culture of smaller companies quite quickly. In a medium-size company employing in the region of 100-200 employees with a turnover approximately around £10-20 million, TQ should be firmly assimilated within a maximum of two years. What is important is commitment to change – not the size of the business.

When working with a 1,200-employee 'service' company, the Chief Executive considered that the 'cultural change' programme would take anywhere between five and seven years to take hold. When he said this, he was not relating to the running of training workshops, but to the change required to permeate through the management layers and influencing Leadership style. This is not an unusual belief that change takes so long. But change can be radically accelerated through focusing all attention on those who lead and manage others – the top 30% of managers who control the organisation.

Years ago, companies were quoting that change would take six to seven years to take hold – it only takes this time if you want it to. If you are committed to wanting it to influence the business quickly, this can be achieved – it just requires a change in strategy.

Consider the following proposition. Nowadays, can companies really afford to wait for six or seven years until the customer-focused culture kicks in and starts delivering results? In that time, the market could be completely dead or new start-up companies could have grown organically to eclipse the old players. However, when a company relies on a fairly standard and traditional approach to Quality and does not instigate a true Cultural change, then change will take this length of time. When organisations focus upon change through Leadership, there is every reason to create the compelling future in a short period of time – given the intensity, commitment and focus.

GE'S COMMITMENT TO SPEED

I have been working for at least eight years with General Electric (US) Plastics Division, its Motor Finance groups and its European Global Financial Services team. GE is a vast company, number 1 or 2 according to Fortune in terms of size; 200,000 staff; return on investment extremely high with a $70 billion turnover and high shareholder value. Its approach to change is simple. In order to constantly get better in your marketplace – you must change and improve. The goal of GE is to be Number 1 or 2 in every market in which it operates in the world, and the way it will achieve this is through its culture.

Jack Welch, its CEO, believes that one factor will separate GE from its competitors, and that is speed of response in every context. Delivering faster to customers and making and implementing decisions are the important characteristics of successful businesses in the 21st Century. GE has taken for granted that it will be providing error-free service and goods because it invested in the quality methodology in the 1980s and has now relaunched a drive for quality.

I am a firm believer that if someone wants change to happen, it takes as long as he wants it to take. In business, the 'self-limiting' beliefs which a manager possesses will determine the speed of implementation of the change. Now quality is not just good enough as the key differentiator in the marketplace. Time is the competitive advantage and this does not relate just to Service delivery. It is also 100% applicable in managing and implementing corporate change. So what action will we take to prepare ourselves for speedy implementation?

TAILORED DRIVES

TQ is not a package that can be taken from the 'shelf 'of one company and dropped quickly and neatly into another, and have the same impact. A package which is suitable for one organisation might lead to failure for another. TQ cannot be uprooted from one culture and grafted quickly on to another. It must be tailored to fit an organisation's special demands and circumstances. Organisations differ on a number of dimensions. Every company has a special history, values, culture and management system which makes it different from others. These are the factors which will determine the speed of implementation.

CULTURAL SURVEYS AND MANAGEMENT AUDITS

Cultural Surveys and Management Audits are critical to the effectiveness of TQ. Time needs to be invested in assessing where the company is now in terms of culture. Planning how to bridge the gap between now and the desirable future shape of the business is then undertaken. Senior staff who adopt this approach front-load their implementation plans. They discuss at length and work out in precise detail what they want the shape and form of the organisation to be. They define the characteristics of the business they desire. In particular, they define the role model of the people who will drive the organisation. They then cause this to happen through innovative Human Resource strategies.

The matter is not whether Cultural Change is good or not – but rather how can we ensure we do it right. Because if you do it wrong, and 90% of companies do, then it becomes even more difficult to resurrect the programme and start again. Many companies do repeat the exercise and get the same poor results.

Using Cultural Surveys and Managerial Audits will ensure that implementation is speedy and successful. A Cultural Survey will highlight the key problems in the business and suggest specific actions. As you may gather, problems reside with people and it is usual that their personal value systems may not quite gel with the values needed for the business to flourish and prosper in the future. Most businesses will have to replace a proportion of their management group if they really do require to change. No business can allow staff at senior level to block progress.

The Cultural Survey should highlight the major Hard and Soft S's that need to be addressed for change to be effective.

No one would genuinely wish to leap head-first into a TQ Drive without a thorough analysis and diagnosis of the special problems which impact upon the organisation; and for this reason an Audit must be conducted quickly. This is usually with the help of an objective individual or group. Focusing upon an external individual will provide the company with an objective view. Putting the total responsibility with a group of internals will create problems because of internal politics. These people are also dependent upon the organisation for their continued employment, which may affect their expressions of concern. The best approach is a mix of externals and internals, totally focused upon the best interests of the company. It may be desirable at this stage to form a small team of internal practitioners and external TQ experts who will adopt a no-nonsense approach and who are committed to feed back honest data to the company. Without stating the obvious, the focus of attention should be on how well people are led and the ability of the company and its key personnel to change.

IMPLEMENTATION PLANS

Selling the benefits of change to a company is easy when you can demonstrate that specific actions will yield specific results and outcomes. Now, if you want change to be speedy it can be – it all depends on the action the client is prepared to take. Once asked if Culture Change could work in a Bank in a two-year period, I answered the CEO honestly. Yes, if you support it and your team live the values. They did.

In the old days, people would say that TQ philosophy is not possible in the short term. They were wrong. The drive can be so structured that there is continuous feedback as milestones are reached and targets are achieved. This means that wanting to change culture is not enough, we need to structure a systematic framework that we can keep to. This framework should be communicated to all and is generated from stage 1 of the drive when we concentrate upon the Cultural Survey.

Some people refer to the Cultural Survey as an appraisal of where the company is in terms of Quality. Some prefer the Audit approach, but this is vastly different in nature and scope. Audits are all very well, but they smack of checklist management with a focus on the Hard S's, Strategy, Structure and Systems to the detriment of Symbols, Staff, Skills, Style, Shared Values and Synergy In other words, the 'audit' approach has an ideal of what Quality should look like within a company. The auditor than assesses the deficiencies of a system.

Once a Cultural Survey is complete, then comes the time for harnessing the more technical aspects of the business. Let's face it, they can be put right very quickly – the culture of the business is far more important.

What about the place of Quality Audits? These usually refer to Vendor Appraisal, Product Liability Assurance, Product Certification, Process Certification, Quality System Audits, Product Quality Audit, etc., whereas a Cultural Survey focuses upon the 'total organisation and the integration between the parts'. This approach examines the dynamics of organisational life, concentrating upon specific interactions between functions, symptoms of conflict between departments, management style, communication and briefing system, rework in product and service areas.

PURPOSE OF CULTURAL SURVEYS

The output of the Cultural Survey is an outline of the major problems experienced in TQ terms, the assessment of the predominant management style and its impact upon human resource management, communication and information systems within the company. Within the Report there is a plan or critical path which provides Senior Staff with a sequential step-by-step approach to implementing TQ. The senior officers then have a period to review the plan, before they meet to agree action to be taken. The 'Cultural Survey and Implementation Plan' then becomes the vehicle for change.

The Cultural Survey will be fed back to the Middle Managers by the Top Team on their operation. Then discussion must take place to win the approval of those who will probably be mostly responsible for implementation – Middle Managers.

Some may have difficulty with the proposals or feel that Quality is not their responsibility and reject them. Assuming the facts are accurate, the major problem here is dealing with resistance to reality and to change. Perhaps the manager cannot or will not perceive the culture of his function or perhaps he does not want to appear to lose control over his function. Whatever the reason, the Implementation Plan is the forum and the opportunity for real debate. Roles and responsibilities must be agreed.

THE IMPLEMENTATION PLAN

The purpose of this phase is to win commitment to change from all areas. Each Manager should agree with the plan or come up with an alternative approach which will convince every other manager present about his commitment to implementing TQ in his discrete work area. If there are dissenters in the Management Team, then this is the time to discuss alternatives or reject TQ as an inappropriate strategy for the company. From this stage on, Departmental Managers will be held accountable for progress within their own areas. Part of the responsibility will be geared towards promoting COQ measures, communicating the purpose and progress of TQ throughout the company, the pace of TQ and how and when it will filter down through and between departments. These are some of the many aspects of planning for TQ which have to be agreed. We can only assess progress when we have developed a flexible plan to implement TQ.

During the Diagnostic Phase, the formation of Departmental or Function Groups is organised throughout the company to appraise the purpose of their individual departmental objectives and how these meet 'synergistically' with the overall aims of the organisations. These are then assessed in terms of how they best fit with the objectives and purposes of other functions. This is basically an approach to examining the efficacy of internal customer-supplier relationships with a focus upon clarifying requirements.

Isolating the contribution of Departments to the larger gestalt or whole is critical in exploring how to cause more effective working between customer and suppliers cross-functionally.

To do this well, internal customers have to be identified, questioned, and results assessed to develop a realistic picture of service as a customer-focused process.

As progress is made, Managers should be working upon COQ measures. This information should come together and give Managers a better appreciation of problems which they have to overcome. This exercise, together with 360 degree communication sessions, will go some way to communicating the message to staff. TQ should not be a surprise but a compelling future for those committed to improvement!

TRAINING WORKSHOPS

Training workshops should be designed specifically around the needs of employees (see Chapter 11) and based upon sound action-learning techniques. Training should be provided for all staff.

Some managers ask whether all staff have to attend sessions. Recently, an accountant with a large company questioned the sense of having twenty staff from the secretarial area attend training sessions. He said: "The job is boring and they only work for the money". His perception of these staff and the contribution they could make was wrong and inaccurate. They had a major role to play in helping identify COQ measures and non-value added activities. They regularly came across a large number of inaccuracies in their work and were a rich source of information. We were surprised to find that the manager had such a negative attitude about his staff. Changing this attitude would help to release his staff's potential and liberate them from the role he had assigned them as thoughtless automatons.

All staff should be trained in where the company is going and how they can help forge the transition or fill the gap quickly. Gone are the days when managers would ask if a one- or two-hour session was too much. It would not even cover the basics – after all we want people to do things better, not just know what to do. Emphasis must be on repetition of skills until ability is acquired. Repetition is the mother of skill and is not acquired through watching a video or listening in a hall with 250 staff to a consultant perched up on a stage.

This carefully designed training initiative will be the most important event which anyone has ever attended, because it is geared towards harnessing the potential of the people and driving them all in one direction.

During training, emphasis should be on customer-supplier relationships within the company. Everyone should develop a personal action plan for implementing Quality within his immediate area of work.

All managers and supervisors should attend their workshops. At every Workshop I run I insist that a Senior Manager introduces the session. Other members of the Senior Management Group regularly visit to demonstrate commitment. They often attend formal sessions and their presence is required for lunch breaks. Here they talk honestly with participants about changes in organisational culture. This version of (MBWA) 'managing by wandering about' is critical if TQ is to be taken seriously.

Participants will have questions which only Senior Staff can address. Their attendance gives credibility to the message.

WHY TRAIN SERVICE AND SHOPFLOOR PEOPLE DIFFERENTLY?

It is critical that shopfloor employees have the same training, but there is a danger that some managers feel that these people should have more training than their clerical counterparts.

This is founded upon the belief that all the errors originate in 'manufacturing'. This attitude must be changed, as otherwise it would reinforce the old stereotype that shopfloor workers create all the problems.

COMPOSITION OF WORKSHOP GROUPS

Composition of workshop participants is also critical. We have found that the best results come from a genuine mix of all functions. Although this can create headaches in administration when working on many sites – it is the right thing to do. It is probably the first time that many people from different functions will meet. It gives them an opportunity to work together on exercises and case material and discuss the problems they have on a day-to-day basis. The effect of talking openly breaks down some of the negative stereotypes which have existed in some companies. Through one workshop, two people who had been working for the company for seven and five years respectively met for the first time, although they were on a shared site.

There are always instances where staff have worked in one location for a long period of time and have little idea of what other people do. I find it hard to believe that people who have worked for a company in excess of ten years still do not know others on a 250-person site. This says much about management commitment to communication, joint problem-solving and running the company.

MEETING FOR THE FIRST TIME IN FIFTEEN YEARS

At the end of one cross-functional Workshop session, the production people present agreed to arrange a plant tour for the accountants and purchasing people. Some of the 'white collar' staff had been with the company in excess of fifteen years, worked twenty yards away from the manufacturing plant, but had little understanding of what happened in there! This is not unusual. We have worked in breweries, insurance companies, chemical plants and so forth, where there had been little attempt to intermingle, interact and generally get to know other people. There exists a strict demarcation line structured on functional and geographical terms. Some of the clerical and supervisory staff had in some cases little apparent loyalty to the company. They could have been working anywhere, as a DP operator, a systems analyst, a secretary, a typist.

It is quite an interesting experience to ask some of the admin people what their company produces and in which market it operates, then listen to their response. Many have a very poor idea of the range of their company's operations. We cannot blame the employee for this. We know that it has not been a deliberate policy from Senior Staff, but it is the outcome of failing to communicate and involve others in the future of the business. In too many organisations this is the norm!

IMPLEMENTATION

Words and workshops can influence behaviour in the short term, but their impact on individual performance is dependent upon the pressure and intensity in the organisations to put the ideas into effect. For TQ really to work, companies must set up structures to put the principles into practice. Passion has its place in any change, but systems and structures are also needed to demonstrate a framework for making things happen.

STEERING GROUPS

It is necessary from the design phase of a drive to form a Senior Management Steering Group or Quality Improvement Team (QIT). This is the group of senior people who meet frequently to discuss progress. They oversee and take necessary actions to promote TQ. If the company has an internal consultant or Manager facilitating the initiative, he will report directly to this group.

There are problems with titles of such groups. Some companies create 'Quality Improvement Teams' to solve problems based upon representation from different layers and functions. This is all very well in theory, but they can be no more than talk shops focused upon employee involvement. They do not have executive authority and therefore their role is limited only to making recommendations.

Many different titles and Group names are used for these groups. Terminology isn't important as long as we concentrate on specific roles and responsibilities. The output from a Group is more important than its name, but it would appear many companies prefer the term QIT (Quality Improvement Team) to give focus to the team and its important role in implementing culture change.

INTERNAL AND EXTERNAL CHANGE AGENTS

The senior team of managers driving the company – the Quality Improvement Team – co-ordinates events. The TQ Manager is the catalyst who will probably work with an external consultant.

For external support you need someone who is well acquainted with TQ practice and who understands the process of managing organisational and cultural change. It is a distinct advantage if this person has a 'behavioural' background. The whole concept of TQ is based upon changing peoples' attitudes – it is unlikely that a systems person will have the same degree of understanding and, more important, empathy with the difficulties of managing change. The external need not be a TQ expert, but obviously it is desirable. Whatever the characteristics of the external resource he must have good grounding in Organisational Development and understand or have worked with companies managing change.

It is obvious that there should be a high level of integration between the QIT and the internal and external consultant. Meetings should be held frequently. They should not be too lengthy and should be designed around sharing information about COQ measurements, supervisory training, etc.

MAINTAINING ENTHUSIASM AND MORALE

Enthusiasm is something which should constantly increase during a TQ drive. It should be sustained. The role of the Management Team is to ensure that people are constantly given feedback on performance and the implementation of improvements. Obviously, positive rather than negative reinforcement is more powerful in motivating people. Keeping enthusiasm for TQ high is not always easy and this has to be the central role of the QIT or team driving the programme. There can be a danger that the QIT think that sufficient messages and examples have been set by them throughout the business. But communication should always be judged from the receiver's viewpoint rather than the sender's. There are few occasions when a company can over-communicate. This is one of those times when we do strive to over-communicate.

SCEPTICISM AT MIDDLE MANAGEMENT LEVEL

When TQ first arrives on the scene, the Management Team may be 'turned on' by the whole approach. Although there will be sceptics at first, generally TQ sounds, looks and feels like a good idea. Enthusiasm increases and, with it, the perception that things will change for the better! The dawning reality that change will take time and can be painful can reduce enthusiasm. Sooner or later, management makes the change and starts moving along the Transition Curve. Meanwhile, Middle Managers may have been kept in the dark and are wary of the concept. Attending training workshops may encourage them. They witness the success of others and start to create change, their enthusiasm for TQ rises until something gets in the way – such as Senior Management standing in the way of change.

Middle Managers may come up with brilliant ideas for preventing problems arising. Resources may not be available or action is not quick enough. Whatever happens, it has an effect on the enthusiasm and morale of the Middle Managers. So to avoid this problem right from the outset we should focus energy on winning the support of the Middle Management group to implementation. It will work with their support – it won't without it.

We must make all efforts to motivate others to support the programme. In the real world, many different personalities run large and small organisations. Rationality does not always guide their behaviour. There are times when managers pursue interests other than those of the company. The problems to which I have referred do arise. Knowing this may be the case that they might, and the impact they can have on others should be sufficient to want to do something about them. We should win their support and involve their suggestions.

Plans should be made to inject enthusiasm into the Drive every six weeks. Many people baulk at this being too frequent, but if you aim for every six weeks, there is a chance that you might get around to doing something within every three months!

QUALITY IMPROVEMENT PROCESS AND PUBLISHING RESULTS

Running workshops and setting action plans are only the start of the drive. Putting the philosophy into practice takes some effort. Depending upon the size of the company, there is a need to start the implementation phase after all have been through the training process. Implementation can take a number of routes, but let us stick to a formula that seems to work well.

Bearing in mind that all functions are generating information on progress through COQ measures, it is reasonable to assume that some of the major problems which the company faces have surfaced. Work can begin straight away to resolve these problems. Let us look at an example. Consider the example used previously. We have a manufacturing company producing hi-tech products. There are problems between Sales, Research and Development, Production, and Purchasing. Salesmen can sell all they can, pleasing the customer by adapting to his specific requirements. There is nothing wrong with this approach, I wish more companies recognised they had to be customer- rather than product-led. But the specifications of the customer are not fed back to Materials Management, R&D or Production. The Sales team promises delivery dates which are incongruent with the lead time for production, reinforcing the viewpoint that service staff create the majority of Quality problems within companies. The scenario is obvious. Similar problems are experienced by many within manufacturing. What is needed is bringing together those who are sympathetic to a TQ solution to work towards resolution.

FAILURE: PROBLEMS WHICH ARE TOO BIG ARE TACKLED FIRST!

The solution will impact upon everyone, so everybody needs to change. The interesting point about this example is that the 'problem' probably has not just arisen, but has been with the company for many years. Bringing representatives together from different functions may help to solve it. But there should be desirable conditions created for genuine solution. One mistake which is frequently made is the assumption that the organisational culture has changed! It may not. Those solving problems should try to win small successes, not go for the biggest problem which creates the most hassle, conflict and rework for the company. Trying to change the big things takes time.

The conditions for solving problems effectively are probably not in tune with the present culture. The preconditions for success follow. Everybody working on the problem should leave his role and status outside the problem-solving forum. They must be committed to coming up with a workable and realistic solution. The politics, which kill companies and destroy the morale of too many company people, should be left outside the session. Senior officers within companies should recognise that 'solutions' will only develop from an atmosphere of trust. Working under political constraints will produce a win-lose solution, where someone gains at the expense of others. Those attending problem-solving sessions need to be 'self-critical' about their performance and that of their section or function. Failing to meet these conditions is enough to send too many companies on to a 'quick fix'.

Already the conditions set for effective problem-solving appear to be more than what happens in the real world. What is important is that this approach should at least be given a try, or initiatives may fail, because the assumptions which are made about the style and attitude which people bring to the problem-solving session are far from realistic. People really do attend sessions to protect the interests of their departments, they do say things they do not not mean, they do not live up to promises, etc. This pessimistic belief is grounded upon experience. Doubtless there will be critics who suggest this viewpoint is negative, but at least it is realistic. Experience and comments in this book which reflect the pessimistic view come from a viewpoint shared with a large number of people who have had difficulty implementing change. I challenge anybody to prove that this perspective is distorted. An attitude survey conducted in any company after the introduction of TQ usually highlights major factors, as those outlined above, which should be addressed straight away. Nevertheless, let us look at a way out of this problem. The first major issue is that people are tackling the biggest problem the company faces. This is not wise.

PICK THE LITTLE ISSUES FIRST

The first major objective of using problem-solving and Corrective Action Teams (CATs) is not the solution of long-term problems, but rather to prove that problem-solving works. It is also a test of management commitment to implement the solution. It is to prove that people live up to their promises and that the expectations of all company people regarding the implementation of TQ are met. The alternative is to jump at the first problem and hastily develop a solution which is poorly implemented. Plan some wins. Ensure that the small successes are implemented. This reinforces the belief of all staff that TQ is here to stay.

We should pick upon small problems, bring together small groups of committed people to work through the solutions and implement them quickly. We should *initially* spend 80% of our time implementing changes which have 20% impact upon the bottom line. This may appear to go against all the teaching of the Quality Gurus – but in fact it does not. They talk of dealing with the **vital few**, rather than the **trivial many**.

Starting off dealing with the minor problems and putting things right has a profound effect on the organisation. For a start, people see things happening. They might not create such significant savings in money, but they do at least reinforce the idea that change is taking place. If implementation of solutions is speedy, and it must be so, people start believing that TQ is having some impact. If this is reinforced by senior officers proclaiming that overnight success, the morale of the workplace could go through the roof. For instance, dealing with a niggling paperwork problem or sorting out business expenses claims and increasing the speed of payment will have most impact on those most affected. It gives people confidence and belief in TQ. Working initially on those problems which are small in nature is incredibly important. Management should capitalise on solutions and publicise their success. If they fail to do so then they might as well forget all the effort they have expended. Newsletters should be written and published at regular intervals. After working on smaller problems, those committed to TQ have concrete examples of changes which have taken place. This creates the momentum to continue the drive. Generating enthusiasm and momentum is critical for success at the beginning of a TQ Drive.

STARTING OFF THE QUALITY IMPROVEMENT PROCESS

Very few companies will need to generate problems to solve, but for some strange reason they find it difficult to get started. The problems faced by any company must be identified, but by the people who do the work. This is important because if TQ has been developed to solve the problems of a small number of people at the top, then there may be little support for it from the bottom. People below the managerial grades must feel that the company is dealing with their problems. I maintain that if you can make life easier for an hourly paid employee or for a clerk working in purchasing or accounts, a more positive attitude will soon spread. Working on operational problems is where companies should start. Strategic issues should wait.

Japanese companies have maintained their success through implementing the ideas which come from the shopfloor. They seek continuous innovation and work on the mass principle. The more ideas accepted and implemented, the easier the job gets. Work becomes safer, more interesting and less routine. People feel that they can actually influence events. Job satisfaction increases and people take more interest. It is a fairly simple motivational formula. Ask someone to take the hassle, rework or problems out of his job and he willingly participates. The suggestions forthcoming probably have an impact on the 'bottom line'. People who feel that their managers listen to them are going to be more interested, and contribute more to their work. Having suggestions implemented is tantamount to telling the guy with the suggestion that his idea was valid, so much so that the Management Team took note and fixed things. This is not the usual practice of European companies.

Toyota **implements** 5,000 ideas per day. These ideas come from its 68,000 workforce. Each day they become better at everything they do. Can we say that? It does not need to be said that people are the most important resource available to every company. This is often stated in company reports, but the real truth is that we don't really value our people. We tend to hire them from the neck down! Listening to people, implementing their ideas and structuring things for them makes the job efficient and enjoyable.

One approach which is used to start off the scheme on promoting Company-Wide Improvement works incredibly well. The process is similar to a suggestion scheme, it cannot run counter to one if there is one in existence, but it can be integrated with it in time.

SUGGESTION SCHEMES CAN RUN COUNTER TO QUALITY IMPROVEMENT

Suggestion schemes rely on people generating ideas to improve the way they do things. The criteria for suggestions are quite general. Often schemes are not well received and there is an understanding that employees will receive a reward for coming up with ideas which save the company money. In the UK, the Industrial Society has publicised its use to great effect and with success. But the problem with such schemes is that they create a psychological bargaining situation, implying that if ideas do, for instance, reduce costs, then the employee will share in the saving. This is all very well, but I have known of an employee keeping an idea to himself until he was guaranteed a substantial figure in remuneration in return for the idea. I am not against sharing the gains, but the idea of individual competition is against all ideas on TQ. We are pitting the wits of each employee against each other rather than generating a 'collective' responsibility. Consider when employees draw the line between suggesting ideas for continuous improvement and those from which they can gain financially. This may reinforce individual competition and kills team spirit, unless the scheme is based upon group sharing.

PAYING EMPLOYEES TWICE!

I believe that employees are paid not just to do a job, but to think of better ways of doing it, although Human Resource Practice in too many companies treats people as no more than a necessary evil, a resource which has to be paid for in order to achieve results. On the other hand, many managers and supervisors believe that when they come up with improvements, these are incorporated in what they receive in their salary. We often tend to treat shopfloor employees differently. We can pay them twice! First we pay them to do a job. Secondly we pay them an additional amount for improving that job!

CORRECTIVE ACTION TEAMS

Corrective Action Teams are groups of committed individuals who are keen to improve Quality. Members are selected from different functions and departments to work together. CATs differ quite markedly from Quality Circles. Circles are formed from a natural work unit and usually work through a facilitator who may also be their direct supervisor. The facilitator will have been trained in problem-solving techniques and in the more enlightened companies this will include advanced statistical techniques, such as SPC as well as Fishbone diagrams. Quality Circles are composed of committed volunteers who meet either in their own time or the time of the company. It is common to pay for QC members' time when they meet outside working hours.

Corrective Action Team members are selected from a number of departments to solve a common problem. The selection of CAT members is determined by the nature of the problem. Enthusiastic volunteers are encouraged, but selectivity has to come into play. There is a need to choose from the group available and an important criterion is 'knowledge' of the problem under scrutiny. CAT members can work in different ways, but the orthodox method is to explain the nature of the problem with a facilitator available. He ensures that the group have rejected all departmental and personal preferences prior to starting on problem-solving.

CAT members are encouraged to adopt the logical approach to problem solution, spending sufficient time defining the problem and deciding on methods of data collection. This approach guards against jumping to a preferred solution. The group may then allocate responsibilities to individuals and agree to collect relevant information which may help them seek a solution. They then decide to meet again within a fairly short period of time to discuss the data collected. At the second meeting they may get involved in the 'creative' aspects of problem-solving and look for alternative ways of solving the problem. In a fairly short period of time the group should be able to come up with a list of probable options. They will need supervision and the help of a facilitator. They should not at first be left to their own devices. Their solutions should be tested for practicality. Addressing the questions about the technical feasibility, administrative convenience, political acceptability and financial viability of their conclusions must be discussed. If their work is at the beginning of a TQ drive, they should be set problems which have a solution. Scoring successes early on is important, the more difficult problems can wait to later.

One major flaw of the use of CATs is setting too difficult a problem to be solved. If problems have plagued a company for some time, they should not be considered by CAT members. When the CAT has developed a workable solution, its thoughts should be condensed into a simple report of no longer than two or three pages and a presentation arranged to Senior Management. For those who have never given a presentation before, it is important that the facilitator gives guidance. The success of recommendations will be determined by the manner in which the report is delivered and the reception by the Senior Group (QIT). It cannot be over-emphasised that the QIT look favourably upon the recommendations and reward effort by implementing ideas quickly. A failure to take note, recognise a contribution and act immediately cannot be over-emphasised as leading to failure.

NEWS TRAVELS FAST

News travels fast. If a CAT recommendation is taken in the spirit in which it has been given and implemented quickly, instant reinforcement to the rest of the company is acknowledged. A failure to implement ideas and workable solutions will justify the scepticism felt by some employees. This reinforces the belief that problems chosen for solution should be carefully vetted. When starting the process of problem-solving, the initial problems should be chosen carefully before work begins. Successful implementation and the progress of CATs is determined by management, who should be patient and not expect instant results to the major problems creating rework for them and others.

CATs should be carefully managed. The enthusiasm of QIT and CAT members can set an unbearable demand and pressure for results. Senior officers should be careful to manage the progress of no more than two or three CAT groups at first so as not to create an unrealistic demand on resources. The 'quick fix' should be rejected and careful, patient progress should be monitored. It is better to win 100% success early on by working with two small groups than fail with six or seven groups because of lack of resources.

QUALITY AND IMPROVEMENT PROPOSAL PROCESS

The generation of ideas to be solved by CATs should not be too difficult, but bearing in mind that TQ is based upon employee involvement, it is wise to get the workforce to generate the problems to be solved. Encouraging the workforce to participate in a short programme of identifying 'Improvement Proposals' is important. Forms can be designed to facilitate this process. This process, although resembling Suggestion Schemes, should be quite different. The Suggestion Scheme approach relies upon setting up a separate structure for improvement. This implies that suggestions can be submitted without consultation with others, especially line managers. Some justification for this may exist in companies where employees feel the solution to problems may be blocked by their direct supervisor, but rejecting this practice is the price paid for genuine company-wide improvement.

Improvement Proposals should use the existing structure. It is an admission of defeat to have to develop a new communication network especially designed for creating Quality Improvement. Employees who come up with proposals should first talk with their direct supervisor to discuss the feasibility of their ideas. Supervisors will have attended courses promoting Quality Improvement prior to the start of this process – so there should be some level of mutual understanding. The supervisor should take 'ownership' of the problem and take what action he can. This process is equally applicable in service and manufacturing environments. If the supervisor can solve the problem, he should inform the QIT or TQ Manager of the progress made. If he cannot find a solution, he should refer the problem to the TQ Manager and the QIT. These processes are easily maintained through a procedure. It is quick and responsive. The individual receiving the problems can then categorise these and refer them to the Senior Management Team (QIT) and seek their commitment to solving the problems. Once this is given, members of CATs can be formed to start work. The QIT members must give wholehearted support to any initiative, otherwise it is pointless in giving their approval to solving the problems.

This process works remarkably well. It is unlikely there will be a 'block' to implementation if QIT members have given their approval. Any resistance to analysis and implementation will demonstrate the failure to commit on the part of individual QIT members.

This process should be fairly easy to administer, but caution should be exercised when the number of proposals exceeds the capacity of organisational members to seek and implement solutions. When the limit is reached, everyone should be told that CATs have sufficient to tackle. For instance, if 550 ideas for improvement are received, the TQ Manager can use this valuable data to develop a Pareto Chart identifying the 20% of problem areas which create the 80% of rework problems for solution in the long term. After the success and implementation of CATs, work on two or three projects, then the larger projects can be tackled. It is imperative that managers manage the process. Calling a time for a natural break in 'improvements' is important because too many problems being identified can create major problems for the TQ drive. We should not take too much on at once. Each of the problems identified should be discussed and assessed. Progress should be immediately fed back to employees. If an employee gives ideas for improvement and has no response, it confirms his major concerns on the credibility of such a drive. However, if an employee receives feedback, even negative, on the unfeasibility of the project, he will at least have been informed. Failure to communicate success or otherwise can be a major stumbling block to company-wide initiatives.

TQ NEWSLETTERS

The TQ Newsletter should address these points, but is no substitute for 'personal feedback'. Personal feedback should be formal, not a comment voiced in passing. Newsletters succeed or fail by the commitment mirrored in the leading articles. If the same person writes articles every week, employees soon are aware that the TQ drive is taken seriously by enthusiasts only. Newsletters should reflect progress and praise the work of employees in any role they have taken.

TQ INTEGRATED INTO EVERY PROCESS

Starting a TQ initiative through Quality or Improvement Proposals is good in the short run, but what about progress in the long term? Although the process explained should become part of organisational life, there must be a major attempt to inculcate TQ into the fabric and culture of the organisation. Action Planning and the Improvement Proposal Process are two ways, insufficient to carry the drive through forever.

Attempts should be made to integrate these processes into the Appraisal, Recruitment and Training policies. This is not a difficult task and will ensure that people perceive TQ in general organisational terms. It will be necessary to develop an Induction package for new recruits and ensure that Succession plans are based upon the principles of TQ. This task should be encouraged only after success in the previous processes.

Every meeting, whether it is departmental or project planning in progress, should have 'Quality Improvement' on the agenda. There should be nowhere to turn where people can escape from the commitment to improve everything which is done. Requests for Capital Investment should be based upon TQ initiatives. Resources allocated on this premise will do more for TQ than will hundreds of posters and Newsletters exhorting Total Quality.

PARTNERSHIPS

This should extend beyond the company to include suppliers and customers. Adversarial relationships should be turned into partnerships. There is no reason why relationships cannot be developed with competitors to discuss mutual interests, except when this is morally or legally inappropriate. Companies can set up Supplier Development programmes and work with preferred suppliers trying to develop JIT relationships. Companies should encourage involvement in New Product Development where the input of suppliers can be valued and profitable. The limitations are created only by tunnel vision. Working together creating win-win relationships has payoffs for all and further promotes the vision of TQ being the binding philosophy which enhances the competitive edge of all.

SUMMARY

Several themes have been presented in the chapter. Initially, it is important to understand not just where the organisation wants to go but what its 'status' is now. Cultural Surveys and Management Audits give an honest and accurate picture of the culture at a given moment in time. These are of a strategic nature and help companies focus their energies on how they will bridge the gap between the situation now and the future desired state for the company. Also important are those who facilitate the programme – the partnership between internal and external consultant is critical in moving things forward through the Senior Team or Quality Improvement Team.

When discussing strategy it is also important to talk of the more practical 'tactics' which are possible to implement and these include whom we should train and the explanation we give of the key issues which need to be addressed.

Bullet Points

- Success in TQ is not determined by the size of the enterprise but by the level of commitment demonstrated by the Top Team.

- TQ has to be tailored to the special needs of the individual company. It cannot be taken from one company and dropped neatly into another.

- The Cultural Survey and Management Audit should concentrate upon Company-Wide Improvement and examine values, management-style communication and the resolution of conflict.

- Quality Audits differ from Cultural Surveys quite markedly. Audits tend to be organised around a checklist of what should be and tend to relate to Quality Systems rather than the management of company-wide cultural improvement.

- The Diagnostic phase should be jointly owned by the Top Team and the external consultant. At this stage it is important that all agree to an action plan which is realistic and achievable. It must be company wide.

- The Cultural Survey and Report may examine interaction within and between functions. This may be a good time for them to question their objectives and assess the service they provide to others — their internal customers, and the service they receive from others — their internal suppliers.

- Managers should go to as many Training Workshops as possible so as to reflect commitment to those attending.

- Devotion to the training of Service and Manufacturing personnel should be equally spread.

- Training workshops may be the first time that some people have met. This should be capitalised upon by structuring sessions so people can learn not just from the training material, but also develop relationships with others from different units.

- A TQ manager should have a good understanding of people. It is important that he or she understands how people work in organisations. He should also have a good knowledge of organisational dynamics and the management of change.

- When starting problem-solving with CAT members, ensure they work on establishing small wins. Do not pick the biggest problem you have encountered.

- Success from CAT members should be speedily communicated to all, otherwise the effort may have been in vain.

- The major characteristic of a CAT member should be that of being 'self-critical'. Politics and other negative pastimes should be left outside the problem-solving forum.

- Suggestion Schemes rely on setting up a separate structure for Improvement. Quality Improvement should not reject the formal structure but should reinforce it.

- Newsletters should have a large number of contributors. Readers soon pick up the 'hidden message' when some functions fail to feature in the Improvement Process.

- TQ cannot exist solely on the Improvement Process and the work of CAT members. Real success comes from integrating TQ into Selection, Recruitment, Training, Manpower Planning, Capital Investment Proposals, Appraisals, etc.

CHAPTER 14

Implementation and Review

MONITORING PROGRESS

Implementing TQ takes time and needs managers to monitor progress. Undoubtedly, a Manager within the company will have major responsibility and this will be shared, at least in the short term, with external advisers. There comes a time, however, when progress has to be reported. It can be quite a simple affair, relating back to the action plan or critical path developed in the Cultural Survey and Management Audit together with the Implementation Plan. For instance, the criteria used for assessing progress could be quite simple and focus upon COQ Measures, Quality Improvement, Quality Structures and the supporting infrastructure of Communication and Leadership by the Top Team or Quality Improvement Team. But first we must start with the core issues to do with the strategic element of changing the culture, and only when this has been completed go on to the tactical issues to do with forming Problem-Solving Groups and COQ measures.

ASSESSING THE CULTURE

Later on in this chapter, we will be discussing the importance of following the flow of discrete activities of tangible implementation – but that is measurement on a different level. But before we do this we need to assess how well the culture of the business is adapting to change. The depth of analysis required will be determined by the extent to which the Top Team want change to occur.

For instance, I am currently working with a very successful Genetics business which has set itself some very rigorous standards. Fundamentally, it went back to basics and agreed to conducting an in-depth Cultural survey. We established from the results that the organisation, although very successful, was very analytical, clinical in nature, cold and risk-averse and needed a step-jump in order to create the future which is possible to achieve. To meet its potential growth rate in the future, this company needed to grow managers beyond the technical 'comfort zones' and turn these people into real change-makers. The CEO was very focused upon the drive and is a firm believer in active Leadership and change. His vision is that the direct reports to the top team will display these qualities in addition to their technical skills.

To help form a foundation for this drive, he and his Top Team colleagues explored their Mission Statement, its meaning and how it was communicated throughout the company. They established that they needed to portray strong values to drive desirable managerial behaviour. A Values Clarification exercise was conducted and we worked on eight core values, involving staff at every level in the enterprise to work with us and agree the behaviours which should reflect the Values. So from this example, we started to measure the visibility of the Corporate Values to others in the business. We also started to monitor the degree to which managers displayed these Values in their behaviour and have created an innovative 360 degree appraisal exercise so that any manager can establish how well others assess whether or not he demonstrates set behaviours. There is feedback on performance and managers commit to taking personal responsibility for change.

MORTGAGE EXPRESS: MEASURING THE INTANGIBLE

Mortgage Express is a very successful business owned by TSB Bank. It has committed to assessing its culture on a regular basis as part of a major drive for Total Quality. Originally, its HR and Quality Director, Peter Taylor, organised the first Cultural Survey and then we worked together jointly on Cultural Reviews to assess and gain a reality test on what the culture was really like. From this initial work, the staff of Mortgage Express have now taken over responsibility for this process and it is completely owned by them. Interestingly, Departments within the larger organisation have taken responsibility for measuring and monitoring culture within their function. They use a questionnaire to measure 15 components of organisational culture and they display this visually as a histogram. This has become a very useful tool for managers to use to improve morale within their team. Managers can now commit to creating specific improvements in their discrete work area.

More than this, the Mortgage Express Top Team committed to reviewing their own Leadership behaviour and this became part of a rigorous 360 degree assessment where each Director was given individual feedback on his performance. They have now used this data as part of a Personal Improvement plan to further develop their already existing skills to manage and encourage change among all staff. The Top Team have turned their business around overnight using Total Quality and narrowly missed the 1996 British Quality Award, coming runner-up to ICL out of more than 200 applications for the award. They would never have achieved so much if they had not examined the cultural issues before pursuing the features of a TQ drive.

This illustrates the importance of dealing with Hard and Soft issues of the culture before working upon the mechanics of implementing quality on a different level.

DEALING WITH SPECIFIC IMPLEMENTATION MATTERS

Periodically, the internal TQ Manager should review action on COQ measures. In many cases these may appear to be going well in production areas, but there will probably be problems in the service areas. Knowing the likely blockages in advance, the TQ Manager should have spent sufficient preventative time with Purchasing, Personnel, R&D, Data Processing, Sales and other functions to ensure that measures are in place. Information should have been collected and displayed openly and be available to all people passing through the work area. For instance, some companies encourage all employees to develop their own COQ measure/s which relate to their personal performance. This may be as simple as looking at numbers of times late for meetings over a period of a month, creating unnecessary rework for others, monitoring occasions when instructions to staff have to be given more than once, etc. Although these measures may be difficult to quantify and relate to a financial COQ measure, they are a reflection of a desire to improve personal performance. This commitment should be encouraged.

COQ MEASURES DISPLAYED

The TQ Manager may wish to visit known locations of COQ measures and check for fairly simple clues. Are the measures visible? Are they accurate and up to date? Do they have meaning to the people who work on them and work in the immediate area? Is the area where they are located clean and tidy? If not, this may show a lack of concern and commitment to the overall goals of TQ. Are COQ measures displayed in corridors in service areas or are they hidden behind filing cabinets? Monitoring COQ measures does not finish here, but there will be sufficient visible information to indicate whether these are being taken seriously.

Moving from the physical location of COQ measures to understanding and meaning: how did the measures arise? Were they selected exclusively by the Manager concerned without reference to the work group, or did the group have a part to play in generating measures?

ATTITUDES AND COSTS OF QUALITY

Visiting people randomly and asking them the following questions may be helpful:

- Do you know what COQ measures there are in your location?
- Can you tell me why we are using COQ measures?
- What do the measures mean to you?
- Do you know where the measures are located?
- How often are they updated?

This is all useful data and if used diplomatically can bring a department which may have slipped backwards, perhaps due to work pressures, back on stream.

TQ SHOULD BECOME A COMMON LANGUAGE

On a day-to-day basis it is important to introduce TQ into, and for it to become, the common language of the business. If the only time that TQ is discussed between supervisors and employees is when they are trying to arrange attendance for future TQ training programmes, it is clear that TQ will not have too much credibility. TQ must become the common language. Supervisors and managers should attempt to talk TQ as often as possible.

IF WE CANNOT COMMUNICATE, FORGET TQ

No one should miss an opportunity to discuss progress on Total Quality. Developing a common language, reflected in the culture, takes time and is the responsibility of all managers. Readers may recall the example given earlier in Chapter 5 when a Management Team agreed to meet with their supervisors and chargehands individually. Their task was to speak with any two supervisors each day and note comments in a diary. The focus of the ten-minute conversation was to be non-operational issues, in other words issues related to the future growth of the company. Only a small percentage of the team managed to complete the task in the allotted time. I find it disturbing and of real concern if people find it so difficult to 'talk' with each other for no more than twenty minutes per day and report back. Even the embarrassment of having little to say in front of their peers was not enough to generate even a half dishonest answer. They said they did not have enough time!

The Management Team had all agreed these actions were necessary and would be of value. But despite their best intentions, less than half of the group achieved their objective. I genuinely worry about the capacity of companies in Europe to grasp the ideals of TQ when we have intentions which evaporate as soon as they leave a room. If we cannot perform a simple task and structure, a talk with our people and feed back, what chance is there that real cultural change can be managed through communication?

Communication is Simple: Taguchi Methodology, JIT and SPC really do require Commitment in Actions to make them work.

There has to be a genuine drive to communicate, communicate, communicate. If we fail in the simple things, how can we hope to succeed with the TQ-related initiatives like JIT, Taguchi Methodology, SPC, etc., which require more thoroughness and supervision to manage successfully?

Directing questions to operators, clerical staff, supervisors and managers gives a good indication of how well the TQ drive is going. The response gives scope for remedial action to be taken. There may be a further requirement than asking people about the 'frequency' of communication when we focus upon 'specifics' which have been relayed. For instance, it is hoped that the managerial and supervisory group will have given a great deal of thought to the role that their people can play in TQ. If they have not done so, how can they measure progress?

KNOWING WHAT TO DO

It is essential that everybody knows what is expected of him, even if it is only recording data and progressing this on a chart. People can only achieve results when they have performance measures outlined and agreed with their direct manager. There is a danger that people develop unrealistic expectations of others. The match between expectations of manager and managed can soon erupt when a review is in progress. Conflict can arise. This process must be managed. A tremendous responsibility is on the manager to manage the process of TQ with his or her people. This means he has to think of his people as his 'internal customers'. For his people to meet his expectations, he will have to develop 'requirements' which are communicated to them and tested so they fully understand. In other words, his people have to be involved in the TQ process. They have to be able to contribute and, at the same time, be guided by their manager. Decisions have to be made, targets set and milestones agreed. Some clear responsibilities and actions must be negotiated. At this stage it is important that these 'requirements' should not be too complex.

SETTING ACHIEVABLE REQUIREMENTS

It is easy for all to get too enthusiastic about TQ so that they set unrealistic goals for themselves and their departments. If this happens, and targets are not reached, morale falls and belief in TQ can decline. Change takes a tumble. Always set realistic goals and objectives at the implementation stage because most people see that they have two lines of responsibility. One is the work for which they are employed and paid, and the other is TQ.

CHOICE: DO I PERFORM MY WORK OR PROMOTE TQ?

At first there can be a conflict when people have to make decisions about what they get involved in. There is a tremendous pressure to do those things for which they are paid. The day-to-day work culture might be orientated towards 'firefighting', whereas TQ is preventative. So which work is completed – where is the majority of time allocated? In reality, people do those things and tasks for which they are employed and get involved in TQ action plans in some other time. At first in a TQ Drive people see 'work and TQ' as two separate entities. This creates internal conflict when they have to decide when they do their TQ work, which is the counter-culture of 'crisis management'.

The change from one culture to another is not easy and takes time, but gradually TQ and 'the work for which people are paid' become the same thing. There will be many conflicts along the way when operators and staff at all levels talk to their immediate supervisor and say:

"There seems to be a conflict here. I have to ship the product to the customer. We think there could be a problem with it. If we fail to ship we could lose future business. If we ship and the product fails, we could lose any further business. What should I do?"

This is a difficult problem and there is only one solution and that is to be honest. Explaining to a customer, either within or outside the organisation, the reasons for hold-ups or issues with possibly defective products is the foundation of honesty and trust which is central to TQ. If you lose a sale because of honesty, the company still has its integrity and there is always another opportunity with the client. However, if the product is shipped, inspected at Goods Inwards and rejected, the sale is lost because of poor quality. This is more serious, because poor Quality has been coupled with deception. The company can never regain its integrity, and the word may soon spread to other customers.

BAD NEWS TRAVELS FAST

When people experience good service, whether on a personal or organisational level, and are delighted with work that has been achieved, research suggests that these 'good feelings' are communicated on average to four or five people. If, however, we experience poor service from our internal and external suppliers, we tend to tell a few more people. Research indicates that on average we tell 24 people of our bad experience! Bad news travels fast. It isn't long before the stories about others are well and truly passing to everyone and the company's reputation is in the balance. This might not appear so serious within the company, but it is. Internal customers might not have a choice and still have to deal with you, but external customers can choose to vote with their feet.

INFORMED OF PROGRESS

Knowing what others have achieved in the drive for TQ is critical. This comes back to communication and the sharing of information. Testing for understanding is one of the most interesting parts of a review of progress. In many cases employees are aware of the progress which has been made within their area of work. They may be aware of the TQ responsibilities which their direct supervisor has undertaken. But do not assume that this is always the case. It is not. Test for the flow of information by asking simple questions. For instance:

"Please specify what you think your supervisor has done to promote TQ in your immediate work area."

You may find that a positive response to the question is low in some work areas and extremely high in others, but change the question to:

"Please specify what you think other supervisors in areas outside your own have done to promote TQ in their immediate work area."

The results are interesting.

QUALITY IMPROVEMENT TEAM

This group has the responsibility to implement TQ. It should be composed of most functional heads. But asking questions about the activities of the QIT can provoke some interesting replies. Questions include:

"Are you aware of the current activities of the Quality Improvement Team? Please state them."

"Are you aware of the specific actions taken and commitment given by your representatives on the QIT? If so please, specify progress."

"Has a member of the Quality Improvement Team talked with you about TQ and if so what did they discuss? "

These questions are not designed to catch people out. They are designed to obtain the information which tells us a little about commitment. These questions may not form the 'rigorous' questionnaire for research purposes, but the responses to the questions indicate the degree to which TQ is being taken seriously. Responses indicate where an injection of training or enthusiasm is required and can also highlight 'resistance to change'. This is assumed to be negative. Managers and supervisors alike may appear to be resisting change because they have not quite made the transition required (see Chapter 4) as a result of problems with learning or confidence. Often these fears are groundless, but can be addressed only when information on progress exists.

Information from a structured questionnaire administered properly can create the fine tuning to ensure that TQ is taking hold and becoming the dominant culture. Some companies fear that administration of such an instrument would kill morale if the results are widely dispersed. Companies should only fear a fall in morale if they are not committed to taking immediate corrective and preventative action. An attitude of putting right what was wrong is far more constructive than nailing people who did not do as we asked. This 'putting right' orientation is a sure symptom of things changing.

CORRECTIVE ACTION TEAMS

If small groups have been set up as part of the Implementation Phase such as Quality Circles, Corrective Action Teams (CATs), etc., it is wise to get a feel from the general work of such groups. If the questionnaire and interview technique are used, it can soon be established whether the groups are being taken seriously or not. For instance: *"If you are not already, would you like to become a member of a Corrective Action Team?"* If the response was no, then a supplementary question such as *Why?* will illicit the response which may reflect an attitude. Sometimes people have said, "I was not asked", "They are a waste of time", or "My manager has not encouraged me". Sufficient responses should give an indication of how these structures are viewed.

"Do you believe the progress of CATs has been effective?" with a supplementary question of *"Give us reasons for your response"*, provides us with a feel for the acceptance of CATs, the progress achieved and whether this has been well communicated.

Asking people for specific information is also a key element of review. To general questions it is quite easy for the respondent to give a stereotyped response. Specific questions can be more enlightening.

"Do you know of someone within your work area who is or has been involved in Corrective Action Teams?" and assessing the progress made and results achieved through supplementary interviewing helps obtain different bearings on the same issue.

Moving away from questioning about Quality Structures which have been developed, it is then possible to ask in a general capacity about overall involvement. The general response can then be honed down to specifics by a skilled interviewer.

"Are you in any capacity involved in promoting TQ?" A supplementary asks *"What role do you play?"* Responses which are general in nature and mean nothing more than a superficial 'psychological commitment' show there may be problems getting TQ to take hold.

QUALITY IMPROVEMENT PROPOSALS

It has been shown throughout that most Japanese companies are committed to total employee involvement. Ideas are forthcoming from all parts and all grades of employees in all functions. Toyota proudly boasts that it implements, rather than talks about, 5,000 proposals per day. If its competitors are producing less than 5,000 per day, even if it is 4,500, they are falling behind.

Many Quality Drives have specific initiatives to promote involvement through a process referred to as Error Prevention, Improvement Proposals, etc. (These were highlighted in the last chapter.) Questions relating to these processes can generate some interesting results and indicate where remedial action should be taken. It will show that certain areas in the company are producing 'improvement' while others are not. Statistics can be compiled and displayed. For instance, a Data Processing Unit and a Marketing Section in a company had given very few proposals for 'improvement' in relation to all the production areas and administrative and functions. Displaying the information prompted the joke that 'DP and Marketing had no problems'. It also created some interesting issues for discussion. Did not these two sections create problems for others – their customers?

Their response, after a fairly short period of time, was positive. They gradually came on board and started to become less 'isolationalist, elitist; more self-critical'. This was a significant shift in 'culture' in both instances.

Asking for a quantifiable measure of involvement can generate interesting statistics for display. *"How many Improvement Proposal Forms have you generated or been involved in submitting?"* Although some staff have not submitted ideas, they may have helped others. Some staff feel happier about working with others. This must be respected. People cannot be forced to become involved in a 'paperwork process'. However, we do expect them to become committed to the psychological process of wanting to put things right.

Asking further about the process whereby proposals were submitted is a method of establishing how much 'Leadership Behaviour' is evident in day-to-day management and supervision. *"If you have been involved in the generation of IPFs, would you like to comment upon the help received from your direct supervisor in order to complete the documentation?"* *"Do you know of others in your area who have submitted IPFs?"*

Additional questions can highlight the commitment to action taken in formalising the process of employee improvement. *"What action has been taken to encourage you in submitting IPFs? Please specify."*

COMMUNICATION

TQ rests upon effective training, leadership and communication. Assessing the effectiveness of the formalised structure of communication through briefing groups and through the 'process of informal communication' is of value.

"*Do you think finding out about progress of TQ is important? If not, why not? How do you find out about the progress of TQ?*" Here it is obvious that some optional choice is given, such as direct supervisor, briefing, newsletter, etc.

Examining the factors inhibiting the speedy transmission of progress is critical. "*Are you aware of progress of TQ? What in your opinion helps or hinders the communication of progress of TQ?*"

Further checking questions help to give some reliability to other questions. "*In your opinion, is the communication of progress of TQ adequate or not? Please explain.*"

TRAINING

With any Training and Development activity, there should be some formal appraisal of training workshops. Focus should be on what people have learned – not on whether they enjoyed a session. Often they are not the same experience. We do not have time here to discuss evaluation of training in its most sophisticated form, but we would expect a questionnaire at the end of the workshop requesting information on learning outcomes and processes. Most Personnel and Training Departments will have a framework for structuring a form of review, but time should be taken to ensuring that information required really has been elicited from the group. It may be appropriate to ask further questions. "*Do you require training to improve your contribution to TQ?*" "*If you do require training please specify the areas.*"

THE FUTURE

We may also wish to involve people in future progress and at this time if we can elicit a response, implement the idea quickly, recognise and value the contribution from the person, then we are half-way to promoting the required cultural change.

"*What suggestions do you have to promote TQ?*" This can be followed by a more specific question: "*How could we help you to promote TQ in your immediate work area?*"

IF YOU ARE NOT SERIOUS ABOUT FIXING THINGS, DO NOT ASK!

It also must be remembered that the design of questionnaires is important. What is relevant for one drive may not be so for another. More important is the administration of the questionnaire. An open flexible style, with interviewers trained in interviewing and research, is critical. It is probably more likely that an outsider will generate an honest response from interviewees/respondents. Some internal staff end up generating information that respondents think they want to hear!

The Questionnaire is an extremely powerful tool for reviewing progress – but if you are not prepared to take action quickly on your findings and conclusions, do not bother going through the exercise at all. At one company, a review of TQ was undertaken by a member of the Personnel Function at Head Office. Fifteen months later there was no feedback to the plant. The results had not been discussed. No action was taken. Excuses were in abundance, but the hopes and aspirations of some of the respondents who had been honest and wanted change were dashed by a failure to reply. As with all TQ practices, if you are not serious – do not do it!

IF AT FIRST YOU CANNOT CHANGE THE PEOPLE, CHANGE THE PEOPLE!

The results of the survey must be communicated to the Top Team, Quality Improvement Team, or whoever oversees the process, and fed back in a manner respecting the comments of those who took part in the exercise. The finger-pointing reflecting the 'you are not doing your job' attitude is counter-productive. Recognising that the reason for failure is equally because of poor direction, fear of trying something new rather than a negative bloody-minded attitude, is a good starting point. However, if resistance is evident and not in spirit with the principles of TQ, there is no option but to take necessary action. Removing the chief obstacles may appear harsh, but should not be avoided. Far too many senior company officers who are resistant to change are allowed to continue in their positions, slowly killing the company and the spirit, motivation and morale of their people. Remember the phrase: "If at first you cannot change the people, change the people".

SELECTION OF TRAINERS AND CONSULTANTS

As with all change strategies, the success of the programme can very much be dependent upon the personal skills of those chosen to implement these changes. Inasmuch as the choice of internal resources to act as a TQ Manager, this has been dealt with in Chapter 6, but the choice of external trainers and consultants is also particularly difficult. Obviously, the external people to consider will range from the independent consultant to the national and multi-national consulting agencies. There is no one right way to pursue TQ, so a range of people may be appropriate. You may need different people with different skills at different times. You may have to use a variety of agencies.

It is fairly obvious that a potential client will assess previous interventions, in which external consultants have been involved, but it is surprising how infrequently this is broached. Ideally, before a choice is made, it is important to visit some of the locations and talk with the consultant's other clients about success and failure. This is a true test of the calibre of the Consultancy.

Do not be drawn towards the larger consultancies just because they appear to have the reputation. What is important is the individual consultant you employ. Personal chemistry is probably more important than anything else – can you work with this person and will this person inspire others to challenge the way they do things? (The practice has now started to die of major consultancies using their best resources to obtain a contract and the poorest to implement the programme! But do ask who you are getting!)

SMALL OR LARGE : IT'S THE PERSON WHO'S RIGHT

Smaller consultancies may appear more responsive to change the way they do things and be less inclined to use a standard package, but they have limitations – their relative size can create problems. If they are good at what they do, they may have difficulty responding to a special need, ie. not enough days in the week. However, this can be compensated for by planning and appraising the possibility of problems before they arise.

What is the most important point is whether the consultant can establish rapport with the client and the client group. In other words, the managers of the organisation, its staff and employees. Social skills, influence and persuasion are extremely important, and employing someone without these attributes is asking for trouble.

CONSULTANTS SHOULD BE PEOPLE PEOPLE

It is obvious we would expect our external resource, man or woman, to have the knowledge of TQ and be a proponent of the behavioural sciences. The major point which this book is making is that TQ is behaviourally driven. The requirement to fully understand the people dimension is imperative with people trying to create cultural change. Understanding people is critical, but it is not just the understanding achieved through managing people, but rather through the formalised study of people in organisations. Understanding and having an appreciation of organisational theory and organisation behaviour is extremely important when trying to bring about significant change.

MANAGERS ARE NOT PEOPLE-ORIENTATED

Years ago when lecturing on postgraduate courses, I and my colleagues were amazed at the lack of 'people knowledge and skills' displayed by many senior managers who attended the course. It was evident that the 'technical competence' to do the job was what had contributed towards the manager's promotion. In some cases the lack of social skills and managerial vision and perception were missing to such an extent that we wondered how managers achieved any results through their people.

The poor inter-personal skills demonstrated made one wonder how they managed throughout the year. If a manager cannot or does not manage through influence and persuasion, then he manages through his authority. If his authority is the only way of getting others to do things, it is likely that the style employed is strongly directive and non-participative.

If this is the case, we in the UK have a major problem ahead of us. As a nation we are not committed to training our managers to the same degree as our European and American neighbours, yet we expect them to achieve the same results. We have to develop a national culture of training and development. This role is too important to leave to Government alone, but industry can lead the way.

TRAINING BUDGETS AND PORTABLE CABINS

A training manager told me that he spent 0.6% of the wage bill on training in the last financial year and pointed to his investment. It was standing outside in the yard, a 'portable cabin', summing up the problem of training in its entirety. We simply do not recognise the impact that training can make to performance. It is for this reason that when we appraise the skills of consultants we adopt the same criterion as for normal business and focus too much on the systems side and too little on the people dimension.

Employing a consultant who has the knowledge, the skills to influence, and be perceived as honest, is a major advantage to any organisation. Any consultant can manage through his position and authority, but the people with whom he or she comes into contact only accept this on a superficial level. A message which is to be believed has to be projected with passion and honesty. The way to influence people to turn their culture around is not by telling them that they have to do it, but by motivating, persuading and influencing them to want to change and take ownership of TQ.

Of course, there are other criteria which are important when selecting external consultants. Obviously, the choice will depend upon the experience of the consultant and how it was gained. There is a danger that the client will want such specific experience that he rejects all those without it – with the reason given as "We are different to every other company in our industry. We need someone who really understands us." This viewpoint is fine and often voiced but can create inherent dangers. Employing people who know the company and the culture so well can create problems with objectivity. Likewise, employing someone who will fail to challenge Management when necessary is not providing a good service to the client. There are times when a consultant must stand up and say things which a Management Team or senior officers would prefer not to hear. It is unpleasant, but necessary. A consultant should be someone who challenges the beliefs of others, who is prepared to be unpopular when the client would really prefer him to pursue the line of least resistance and low success. A good consultant or trainer should challenge the views and prejudices of others and should not be drawn by future potential business to say what is expected and acceptable!

ADOPTING AN INCREMENTAL APPROACH

To complete the section on implementing change and review, it is important to look at the process of managing change more fully, although this was covered in Chapters 4 and 5.

There must be a plan for implementation which should be owned by all. We would expect all senior staff to understand the critical times of the plan and understand the importance of meeting special milestones. All supervisory staff should understand the plan, so if they are asked by their people they can at least respond with a good overview. Supervisory staff, ignorant of the plan and progress, do not lend credibility to the drive.

There will be times when the 'Plan' slips two paces back or when the 'Plan' is no longer as realistic because of significant shifts in the organisation environment. There will be times when moves have to be made to counter a 'negative political climate' in a specific area of the company. These occasions are when Managers who are keen to progress changes have to take the responsibility for change on their shoulders.

Living in the real world, we are aware that even the best Plan can go awry. It is, therefore, the manager or supervisor who may have to temporarily run with TQ. This approach has been termed 'logical incrementalism'. Quinn, in his book *Strategies for Change*, indicates that when the formal planning progress breaks down is when some managers come into play and run with the ball. They may deal with politics, personal resistance, develop sub-systems previously neglected out of the formal process of planning, develop trust and psychological commitment. These actions are necessary and will only exist in environments where people are allowed to be free in their approach. Change and progress do not depend on the actions of the 'conformist' but the 'non-conforming', the person who challenges the way things are done. Encouraging this perspective, developing 'transformational managers' (see Chapter 5) whom you can rely on later if things go wrong, is critical to the organisation. Every organisation has these heroes. Most are discouraged and held in check. Encouraging the unreasonable for driving initiatives will reap benefits.

It is these managers who can anticipate change and move things forward in an incremental manner. They might not have achieved a great deal, but things are better than they were yesterday and perhaps that is the best way to sum up TQ! Implementation is based upon progress. Do not paint grand visions of the future if you have no way of achieving this vision. Just ensure that things get better in a tangible format every day. Publicise small wins and celebrate with your people. They are the resource you can rely on when things get tough.

SUMMARY

When reviewing progress it is important to deal with the big strategic issues to do with culture first, and then only secondly deal with the specific issues which relate to COQ, Customer Requirements and assessing how well these are embedded in the culture. Continuous review is really important so that we can, if required, amend and take remedial action.

Agreeing measures for both Hard and Soft S's is critical in generating data and provides feedback helping us to assess progress.

Bullet Points

- When reviewing progress, always focus upon the culture first. Assess how the culture has changed and how well the core values of the business are communicated to staff and customers.

- Evaluate how managers have focused upon changing their behaviour. Use 360 degree assessment on 'what it's like to receive behaviour' from them.

- Remember, change starts with self, so don't just work with the Hard S's, measure how people have managed themselves through the process of transition.

- Do not expect success overnight. However, this is not an excuse for doing nothing. Progress is dependent upon accurate feedback.

- Do not hide failure. If one area is not pulling its weight, take action. If its failure to take action is based upon personal doubt and competence, do not take punitive measures.

- If people are openly rejecting the TQ approach, you have no choice. If at first you cannot change the people, then change the people.

- Ensure that all criteria for review have been considered before assessing progress and designing Survey methods.

- Ensure that Cost of Quality measures are in place, understood, visible and have meaning. Research the service areas first.

- Do not rely only on physical evidence. Ask people if they know what measures relate to their areas!

- TQ can become the common language of a company and not only referred to just after attending TQ training workshops.

- The response from research on progress requires instant action. If you are not serious about creating change, do not ask for opinions!

- Bad news travels fast. We tend to be attracted to put right what is wrong and not to praise the good things. There will be blockages and hold-ups in TQ. Bad news travels fast. Ensure that the good news is publicised.

- Share success and information with others. Develop a newsletter and ensure that it is kept up to date. The first time that the newsletter fails to be printed or is two weeks late in distribution is the indication which the staff have been looking for to prove that TQ was just another 'fad'.

- Asking staff the likely successes of the Quality Improvement Team is a strong indicator of the QIT's commitment to communication.

- Publicise the success of Corrective Action Teams and Quality Proposals.

- Select external trainers and consultants with care. You can only promote TQ once. Ensure that they can work with rather than for you.

- Ensure the TQ solution matches your problem, not their package.

- Influence, persuasiveness and enthusiasm are outstanding characteristics critical for projecting TQ. Having consultants rely solely on their status and authority will not convince the most sceptical of shopfloor and administrative people.

- Ensure that TQ Drives are tailored to your needs and swift changes can be introduced where necessary.

- Ensure that all internal managers acting as trainers and facilitators are socially skilled. Change in behaviour comes about through dialogue, influence and discussion. Exhortation of slogans and authority can carry little real weight.

- Beware of the consultant with only one package to sell, the one he uses with all clients!

- Ensure that consultants are not just versed in systems but are also students of organisational behaviour. It is impossible to help co-ordinate and drive TQ throughout a company without a high level of understanding of people and their motivations and behaviours. This cannot be learned simply by watching. Experience is important, but must be supplemented by genuine understanding, research and study.

- Plans do go wrong on occasion, although they should not in a TQ drive. If they do, managers have to take responsibility to run with TQ for a short period of time. This means that the Managers have to be the champions of TQ. Have they been prepared for this role?

- Adopt an incremental approach to change. Learn from your mistakes.

- If things are better today than they were yesterday, all is going to plan. This is the vision.

This questionnaire was administered to more than 40 people in a 200-person plant. The results were the subject of a separate report. Cost of Quality Measures were the subject of an additional assessment. The conclusions of this report led to significant changes which created the enthusiasm and results required.

TQ QUESTIONNAIRE: ASSESSING PROGRESS

This structured questionnaire will be read to all interviewees and comments noted. In some cases the answers to 'closed ended questions' carry a supplementary question – this is for further analysis.

The questionnaire is broken down into a number of sections. The responses will be assessed as a percentage of the response from the total interviews. All additional comments will be appended.

COMMITMENT

1. When did you last speak with your supervisor about TQ?
    a. Within the past week   21%
    b. Last month   30%
    c. 3 months ago   38%
    d. Never   11%

2. Has your direct supervisor spoken to you about the role you can play in promoting TQ?
    a. Yes   50%
    b. No   50%
    Two responses were non-applicable.

3. Please specify what you think your supervisor has done to promote TQ.
    Responses included:
    TQ Newsletter (1)
    Nothing (9)
    Above-average encouragement (2)
    Progressed initiatives (1)
    Follows company policy (1)
    Regular support (1)
    Not a lot (2)
    Don't know (3)
    Made us aware (1)
    Assistance and help, created initiatives and helped fill in IPFs (3)
    Promoted changes in immediate work area (1)
    Started improving things (1)
    Suggestions accepted (1)
    The remaining 7 were not applicable.

QUALITY IMPROVEMENT TEAM

4. Are you aware of the current activities of the Quality Improvement Team?
   a. Yes   32%
   b. No   68%
   Three responses were non-applicable.

5. Has a member of the Quality Improvement Team talked with you about TQ?
   a. Yes   30%
   b. No   70%
   Four responses were non-applicable.

6. If (a) above, who was it and what did they discuss?
   People named include ......(a list of senior managers and supervisors). They provided information and encouragement to complete IPFs. Some respondents were not aware of the function and composition of the QIT (2).

CORRECTIVE ACTION TEAMS

7. Would you like to become a member of a Corrective Action Team?
   a. Yes   40%
   b. No   27%
   c. Already a CAT member   33%

8. If (b) above, why not?
   Don't feel that company is committed (1)
   Quite happy to contribute, but was never invited! (2)
   They don't give you time off (1)
   Not seen anything happen (1)
   Too many other pressures outside work (1)
   Composition of team is wrong – too many outsiders (1)
   CAT on XXXXXXX was a waste of time (1)
   III (1)
   It has to be done in your own time (1)

9. Do you believe the progress of CATs has been effective?
   a. Yes   59%
   b. No   41%

10. If (b) above, why not?
    Not involved (2)
    Proves more difficult to make things work (1)
    No feedback (3)
    Don't know (2)
    Making progress, slow in coming (1)
    Waste of time (1)
    Not seen results (1)

Believe some progress but don't have information (1)
No paperwork, no feedback (1)
Started rolling, now stopped (1)
Not progressed enough (1)

PARTICIPATION

11. Are you in any capacity involved in promoting TQ?
    a. Yes   52%
    b. No   35%
    c. Not sure   13%
    Three responses were non-applicable.

12. If (a) above, what role do you play?
    Most related to working as part of CAT and some said they had integrated the TQ philosophy into their normal work.

13. How many Improvement Proposal Forms have you generated or been involved in submitting? (41 respondents)
    7   completed zero IPFs
    10 completed one IPF
    8   completed two IPFs
    5   completed three IPFs
    5   completed four IPFs
    3   completed six IPFs
    3   completed ten-twelve IPFs

14. If you have been involved in the generation of IPFs, would you like to comment upon the help received from your direct supervisor in order to complete the IPF?

    Most agreed that the help they received was good and supervisors had been helpful. It appeared that supervisors adopted a reactive role rather than promoting quality initiatives. Many respondents suggested that they had to approach their supervisors – few supervisors adopted the proactive role.

15. Do you know of others in your area who have submitted IPFs?
    a. Yes   75%
    b. No   25%

16. What action has been taken to encourage you in submitting IPFs? Please specify.
    Most agreed that Manager X................ and Manager Y .... were the guiding influence and some suggested that the drive could have had greater support from the Management Team. A large number also commented upon the value of information in the newsletter and notice boards.

17. Do you know of someone within your work area who is or has been involved in Corrective Action Teams?
   a. Yes   74%
   b. No   26%

18. Do you think the work of CATs is of value?
   a. Yes   88%
   b. No   0%
   c. Don't know   12%

19. If response was (b) or (c) above, why? Please comment.
   Nothing has happened – things have stayed as they are! (1)
   No visible results (1)
   Don't know, no feedback, don't know what they do (2)

COMMUNICATION

20. Do you think finding out about progress of TQ is important?
   a. Yes   100%
   b. No   0%

21. If (b) above, why not?
   No comments.

22. How do you find out about the progress of TQ?
   (As a percentage of all employees interviewed)
   a. Direct Supervisor   20%
   b. Briefing sessions   23%
   c. Newsletter   67%
   d Other – please specify   32%
   e. Not aware of progress   8%
   In (d) above respondents referred to the following:
      Minutes of QIT
      Asking for feedback
      General unstructured comments from QIT members
      Accident
      Monthly reports
      Informal talks
      Boards

23. Are you aware of the IPFs which are submitted from your department and area?
   a. Yes   65%
   b. No   35%

24. Are you aware of progress of TQ?
   a. Yes   47%
   b. No   53%

25. In your opinion, is the communication of progress of TQ adequate or not?
    a. Adequate   19%
    b. Not adequate   71%

26. If (b) above, why not?
    No feedback on IPF's. . . low priority, too busy with other things (5)
    No feedback. . . should be compulsory (3)
    Info too general, not specific enough F/B, need to make it 1:1 (1)
    No communication since workshop (3)
    Could be better (4)
    Info from CATs not transferred to other areas (3)
    No enthusiasm (1)
    No return for investment, no COQ figures (1)
    Dicer and palletiser F/B too selective (1)
    Nothing apart from newsletters (1)
    Production demands are greater than quality (1)
    No feedback, bulletin is full of exhortations. . . not practical (1)

TRAINING
27. Do you require training to improve your contribution to TQ?
    a. Yes   50%
    b. No   50%

28. If (a) above, please specify
    Revision of TQ. . . refresher and update (12)
    Meetings management (1)
    Personal action planning. . . telling me what I can do (1)
    Equipment(job) related training (2)
    Everyone needs training. . . it sparks off ideas (1)

THE FUTURE
29. How in your opinion could we progress TQ?
    (Some respondents had multiple suggestions)
    More communication and impetus/boost (8)
    Briefing meetings. . . don't know what is happening (1)
    More job-related knowledge (2)
    Improve morale. . . interference from Amsterdam (1)
    Better feedback and communication (6)
    Promote TQ same as safety (1)
    Posters (3)
    Need milestones and report on progress (1)
    Not a great deal to do (1)
    Start again from the beginning (1)
    Complaints board displayed (1)
    Senior management take action (1)

Examples of how the system works. . . more successes (1)
Pace of activity (1)
Re-educate management – they still don't listen! (1)
Don't know how to do it! (1)
Build enthusiasm (1)
Employ people full-time to do TQ rather than adopt a haphazard approach (1)
Spending money is not the answer – everyone should do the job (1)
Change the attitude of staff. . . still 'them and us' (1)
More group work (1)
Develop specific TQ notice board (1)
Reduce management resistance (1)
Enforce meetings in working day (1)
We should get paid for TQ (1)

30. How could we help you to promote TQ in your immediate work area?
Similar responses to above.

CHAPTER 15

How Do We Create a World Class Total Quality Culture?

JUST DO IT!

There is a story told many times about Dr. Deming being harassed over breakfast by a journalist who wanted to know the real secrets of Quality Management. He asked Dr. Deming "What do we have to do in the West to compete and promote Total Quality?". Apparently Dr. Deming looked up from eating, stared the journalist coldly in the eye and told him to tell his readers, "Just do it, that's all. Just do it".

It is as simple as those few words. The companies who have promoted Total Quality have adopted the same philosophy. There is no instant fix which does not entail working with the core culture of the business. There is no secret that can be installed within a business that can move it from a 'fix it' to a highly 'performance-driven, customer-centred culture'. No one-day course has yet been developed which can turn a company on its head overnight and produce instant service excellence, Zero defect products, implement empowerment and self-managing groups or any other technique. Culture change is not a panacea, but is the closest you will get to one. The panacea is not a technique but a continuous process, a commitment to promote constant innovation and improvement and to succeed through people. We can, however, learn from others and implement changes. Some of the guiding principles follow.

We can learn from others in our cultures, but we should all go back to basics and learn from those who committed to the improvement process first. If you operate in manufacturing, this is essential. Those who have undertaken research or visited on study tours Japanese companies, and witnessed first hand their philosophy, are totally convinced that there is still a great deal to learn about implementation and continuous improvement. They are not just very successful in manufacturing – they also demonstrate the commitment in service and commerce. Nine out of the top ten banks in the world are now Japanese.

THE LESSON FROM JAPAN

Many had studied the art of Japanese management and recognised that Quality was a major factor which had provided these companies with their competitive edge. Many on such tours are surprised to find that the Japanese had neither more knowledge than us, nor applied techniques which were not available to us in the West. How then can they be so successful?

TQ IN THE WEST

TQ goes far beyond the philosophy and practices of Quality Control and Quality Assurance. It is a strategy which is concerned with changing the fundamental beliefs, values and culture of a company, harnessing the enthusiasm and participation of everyone, whether manufacturing- or service-orientated, towards an overall ideal of 'Right First Time'.

TQ has grown in recent years. Organisations in both the public and private sectors have recognised that quality of product and service is what can differentiate them from their competitors. It can be the most powerful barrier to entry into world markets, which organisations can pursue to guarantee a long-term future.

QUALITY STRATEGY

During my study tour, delegates were to visit and tour manufacturing locations and talk with Japanese senior management about their strategies of implementing Total Quality. The companies to be visited included Kawashima Textile (£313 million turnover); Sumitomo Electric, based in Itami, a major manufacturer of components to the automotive industry; Daiei, the largest chain of supermarkets throughout Japan (£7 billion turnover); Mitsubishi Motors; Kawasaki Steel (£7.2 billion turnover); Nippon Denso, a world leader in automotive electronics; Toyota, whose domestic production of cars was 30,000 per day; Shiseido Cosmetics; and Hitachi, which produces colour display tubes for TVs and LCDs and produces bubble memories and a host of other components.

Each of the visits was instructive and provided a number of lessons which we in the West could apply to the same effect. All presentations were made by the individuals who implemented TQ.

EIGHT LESSONS TO LEARN

1. Education and Training

The commitment to training and education of all managers and operatives is extremely high. The opinion from many of the managers talking with us was that "managers get the staff they deserve". In other words, the deeds and achievements of a work group are a direct reflection on the manager. A committed and effective work group meet regularly to discuss and initiate quality improvements. Groups who fail to do so are groups which lack motivation – probably because their manager has not spent sufficient time preparing them for preventing problems arising.

Emphasis is placed on quite sophisticated analysis. At one presentation at the HQ of Daiei supermarkets, four young women, members of a Quality Circle, shared with us their work on quality improvement. They used coefficient of correlation and regression analysis to examine statistical relationships and worked through a thorough approach to problem-solving including fishbone diagrams. Young women using sophisticated techniques surprised many on the tour. Theirs was a most thorough treatment. They fully understood statistics and their applicability to Quality improvement. What was even more surprising was that they were working in the service sector rather than manufacturing industry. There was a great deal of emphasis in other locations where Failure Mode Effect Analysis (FMEA) and Taguchi methods were common techniques used for anticipating and solving problems.

2. Fool-proofing

Fool-proofing, an approach to designing manufacturing technology in such a way as to produce zero defects, was much in evidence. Walking around Nippon Denso, an original equipment supplier to the automotive industry, one cannot help being surprised by the number of 'fool-proofing' devices in the machine shop.

Although robots were not so much in evidence, the layout and cleanliness of the work area was superlative. Housekeeping is very much an essential element of preventative action.

Operatives take a few minutes each day to assess their workstation and the equipment they will use. They run through a simple checklist and, if they find damaged or worn equipment, will notify the maintenance department immediately. There appeared to be an automatic drive to check and prevent problems arising.

We wonder how many stoppages on the shopfloor and waste in downtime could have been anticipated in some of our factories by workers and staff who are aware of problems, but insufficiently moved to take the requisite action.

3. Quality Circles

Unfortunately, too many managers in European industry think that Quality Circles are the beginning and end of TQ. In fact, research in the UK suggests that most Quality Circle initiatives have been less than successful because of lack of commitment from managerial grades – so why do they work in Japan?

We think the first factor is that Quality as an over-riding philosophy has been led from the top – not just in words but actions. Management have been keen to initiate quality improvements because they trust the experience of operatives and work groups. Quality

Circles are successful because the ideas they pursue are actioned, thus reinforcing the behaviour of all circle members.

The evidence which was presented to us regarding QC activity was staggering. Toyota maintain that on average they receive 180 ideas per employee each year, of which 97% are actioned. The Quality Circle acts as a vehicle to discuss these ideas and suggestions prior to being submitted to management for approval.

Circles seemed to meet outside their work time and were paid for their efforts. Methods of payment differed radically. Employees in one factory received a wage of a third their normal rate, because this was perceived as a training and not a job rate. Others received no payment but did receive incentives for the ideas implemented. Money did not seem to be a major motivator in itself. What seemed much more powerful was the opportunity to influence events and make work easier.

Perhaps the over-riding thoughts about QCs in Japan and the UK is that in Japan Circle members can significantly influence events. Actions are agreed by the management team and are put into immediate effect.

What we need to learn is that if we pursue the QC approach, as a tool of TQ, we must ensure that all operatives are thoroughly trained in SPC and other related techniques, that ideas which come from the circle are debated and actioned immediately and, if ideas are not feasible, this should be communicated immediately back to the Circle.

4. Communication

A major point highlighted by a Production Engineer was that for Quality to be the factor which linked all units and departments – then a pre-requisite for the TQ culture was an effective means of communication. It was evident that, in Japanese organisations, communication has a high profile. There were constant visual reminders of quality and in almost every company we visited we found organisational charts with photographs of managers attached. The operatives were aware of their supervisors and their responsibilities.

Quality Circles in themselves are an effective means of communication, but emphasis seems to be placed more on lateral communication than vertical. Not that the latter was not encouraged or applied, far from it. But managers seemed to realise that the key to effective communication is the emphasis placed on departmental communication.

For instance, the Japanese pride themselves on being generalists. This is not strictly true. They are specialists in their function, whether it be production engineering, research and development, management services or whatever. However, they are encouraged, through education and daily interaction, to mix with others. More importantly, they are taught to reject the specialist approach to problem-solving. They look at a problem wearing different hats and can tend to appreciate it from different perspectives. What is interesting is that this 'global perspective' reduces the misunderstandings which can be created between departments and functions. Conflict and negative stereotyping between organisational units does not arise.

Unfortunately, we in the West tend to assume that conflict is endemic within structures and take it as normal that the R&D boys fail to work with Manufacturing units, that Systems departments impose their will on other units and that Sales departments drive production. The Japanese seem to have developed a communication network and commitment to solve these problems. They do it simply by moving people, particularly at supervisory level, around through Job Rotation, and listening and responding to ideas from all quarters.

5. Automation

The Japanese have looked at robotics and automation and used them when necessary. 'When necessary' refers to processes where defects are difficult to control due to human error or where the nature of the work is boring and routine and where the quality standards can drop when the attention of operatives wanders.

This was evident not only in Toyota and Mitsubishi car plants, but also in Kawasaki Steel. On a visit lasting two hours, walking through rolling mills and past blast furnaces, we came into contact with only 12 people. The process was almost completely automated. Kawasaki Steel is using artificial intelligence to run its steel-making process to great effect. The majority of staff were housed inside moving gantry monitoring the process.

Obviously, automation requires a great financial investment, but this is a problem which the Japanese have resolved. Increases in productivity and quality cannot be made without a substantial investment in the future. They ensure that their future is well planned, examined and assessed, then debated again so that the choice to borrow and invest is the end of a natural sequence of events. The decision not to invest is anathema to them.

6. Measure and Display

The Japanese seem to have a passion for displaying their talents, not just in a creative but also an informative sense. In a Japanese company it is unlikely that you will pass a notice board which does not display current information. These are not the locations for historical data. You cannot travel very far without coming across a board which is proclaiming success in terms of productivity, reduction in defect rates, quality improvements and cost-reduction. In comparison, take a look at your departmental/company notice board!

The Japanese are sure to keep data on all movements within production. If a problem exists, they will have been monitoring performance using graphing techniques to illustrate problems.

When being shown around the training headquarters of Daiei, the supermarket leader, we noted posters which had been completed by operatives illustrating the drive towards quality. It was not the multi-colour, professional glossy, but the carefully designed message and hand-painted poster which adorned the walls. The Japanese put a great deal of effort into illustrating their progress and highlighting areas for concern. But would it catch on in the UK?

We are not talking about employees entering poster competitions. Measure and Display is a philosophy to encourage employees and managers at all levels to communicate in a visual manner. Part of this approach is to monitor progress and isolate disturbing trends. Let's face it, this is the purpose behind SPC. What we require is sufficient discipline to identify an activity which is giving us problems or be so radical as picking a process which has gone out of control.

Now that the process has been highlighted, we need to measure and display progress in order to understand the causes which create these problems. This illustrative approach is stimulating and creative. Writing and recording progress is the best way yet of keeping the attention of ourselves and others on the problem.

Consider the alternatives of the poor practice in many European plants: Posters on Safety and Quality which have occupied the same spot for the past three years and read but not remembered; charts which are not updated, company slogans and exhortations devised years ago but still suspended from ceiling lights today; notices three months out of date on boards, etc.

Keeping and displaying graphs, charting real progress, devising a tailored poster campaign with strategic emphasis never created quality by itself, but could not hinder the promotion of a sincere drive for quality. As long as a drive utilising a visual approach has more depth than the thickness of the printed paper, it will play its part in ensuring that quality is always in the mind of whoever is the recipient.

7. Quality is not just a Manufacturing Concept

Quality is very much rooted in the service as well as the manufacturing functions. Companies in the UK who practise TQ ensure that all aspects of service are 'Right First Time', including delivery, service contracts, invoicing, etc. This is very much in evidence in Japan, except that the 'Just In Time' principles exercised by most companies are directly related to JIT payments for services and goods provided, not 60- or 90-day payment terms.

Sumitomo Electric, suppliers of braking systems to major car manufacturers, cited an example which is common practice to the company, but was a surprise to many people on a study tour. If a manufacturer does find an error it is reported direct to the supplier. This does not happen often because the principles behind JIT suggest that a defective component causes a production line to stop. In this rare instance, the Operations manager, designer, production engineer, the foreman and the operative who made the component visit the customer immediately and sort out the problem so that the defect never arises again. This is a real team effort. This responsiveness is characteristic of the TQ approach throughout Japanese industry and illustrates the level of co-operation and harmony which is generated within and between departments. This team-building approach does much to halt the negative elements of allocating blame in favour of the philosophy of preventative action.

8. Long-Term Planning

Needless to say, the Japanese could not have created a meaningful TQ philosophy without a devotion to long-term strategic planning. How else would they have been so successful in the markets where they currently hold a competitive position? The Japanese had targeted the electronics, the car, motorcycle, television, video and audio markets many years ago and successfully entered and continue to invest in Europe.

THE PHILOSOPHY ON WHICH THESE LESSONS ARE LEARNT

Four basic factors can be outlined which all companies seemed to use to great effect to penetrate new markets and give them a competitive advantage. The major points fall within four areas.

COMMITTED TO HARD S's

Deming, Juran and others introduced the techniques and tools we now know as SPC (Statistical Process Control), QA (Quality Assurance) and TQC (Total Quality Control) into Japan many years ago. We are not ignorant of these practices, but we never seem to get around to applying the ideas in our own countries.

Some companies still have difficulties adapting to meet the requirements of BS 5750/ISO 9000, much less making the transition to TQ.

As far as Western practice is concerned, as I have said, many organisations have the systems but don't seem to apply them. Asking operatives to complete SPC charts is meaningful only if they are aware that some action is taken to resolve the problems they have encountered. If no action is taken, why bother? Quality Improvement Systems must have a function and be seen to lead to preventative action.

The Japanese have applied techniques, systems and procedures rigorously to ensure that quality is improved continuously. All operatives are fully conversant with these and the problem-solving tools which give rise to better quality.

The Japanese are also committed to the use of Production Engineers. They are not perceived as an indirect cost. The quote which seemed to tell so much about the priorities the West put on the role of preventative action in manufacturing processes in comparison to the Japanese is as follows:

The US has twice the population of Japan, sixteen times more lawyers, but only half the number of production engineers.

COMMITMENT TO SOFT S's: LEADERSHIP AND COMMITMENT

Managers are judged on the performance of others. They would lose face if they failed to consider options which would lead to defect reduction.

'Managers leading by example' seemed to be the underlying theme. One manufacturing manager from an automotive components supplier said he would "be personally failing his people if he did not instruct them in the techniques and practices of TQC".

Managers are directly rewarded for the efforts they make on cost-reduction, productive capability, defect rates and quality. The difference is that the Japanese do not compromise on Quality for a short-term fix or cost-reduction!

TRAINING AND PARTICIPATION

All operatives are trained in techniques geared for quality improvement. Training is a continuous affair and not a 'lick and promise' compromise. Operatives and staff are encouraged to put forward suggestions which are actioned. Most companies stated that they implemented 80% of ideas after investigation.

COMMITMENT TO CHANGE THROUGH PEOPLE

There are very few companies in Europe which do not state with pride that they are "people-driven". In reality, there are many cases where this is no more than exhortation and PR.

People are the organisation's most valuable resource. Although many manufacturing plants are highly automated, the improvements come from groups of workers who meet regularly to discuss improvement. The morale and motivation of workers is increased if their contribution towards 'zero defects' is recognised and praised.

Listening and analysing is something which we are not very good at practising. We tend to be action-orientated and rarely allow sufficient time to think through the next 'quick fix'. We need to be more patient and thoughtful in our approach to quality improvement.

MOVING TOWARDS THE PHILOSOPHY

We need to develop a commitment to a philosophy based upon building those things which led to achievement prior to entering into world class competition.

— Organisational Structure

Too many companies have too many levels of management. The more levels, the greater the communication difficulties and the slower the response time. We have to reject the 'multiple layers' and concentrate upon reducing these levels to three or four. More than this, we have to ensure that people talk to each other.

— Horizontal Management

We should devote time to increasing lateral communications between functions and departments. We fail to understand that work is achieved through integration, not vertical specialisation.

— Move From Product-led To Customer-led Strategies

Many of our organisations have developed a skill for leading the market with their product. When demand for the product declines, many feel that the product life cycle is nearing its maturity phase – so they develop a new range, disregarding the fact that the problem could be to do with Quality. We have to think of our customers more and develop products and services which meet their needs best. This is critical in the service sector. We forget the customer and his or her needs. We need to develop a Total Quality Service approach and recognise that this can come only from within the organisation. Advertising and Public Relations can do so much to project our product, but true TQ comes from meeting the requirements of our internal customers and suppliers. Getting 'close to our customers' comes from being self-critical and constantly looking for improvements.

— Valuing Our People

People is what this book is all about. If we manage our people with respect, if we value them and if we treat them with dignity, they can help us achieve the impossible. We have to develop Human Resource Strategies in Training and Development, Recruitment and Selection, Manpower Planning, Employee Relations, Career Development, Motivation, Team-Building and Job Design. We have to value people to win their commitment. We have to truly value them, not think of them merely as a tool or a factor of production.

— Cultural Change

We need to develop the culture where people can blossom and want to stay with the organisation, where there is a genuine opportunity to contribute and develop. Employees who are not developing are going backwards. We need to develop simple values and live by them.

— Quality of Working Life

Work is a central life interest for many people and in the time of the Demographic Timebomb we have to realise that people need to have a need to belong. We want people to be proud of their company and in non-company time talk glowingly about the reputation and commitment of the enterprise. Developing a sincere Quality of Working Life comes from the application of Human Resource Policies.

— Developing Partnerships

Learn to work with customers. Get involved in the design of new products and services. Work with suppliers to reduce errors and ensure that they are aware of your new developments. Work with competitors on joint projects. Look for innovation in the way business is organised, not just with competitors but also other industries.

— Leadership

Leadership is about emotion. There is little one can add. The people who lead the company have to understand the impact of their presence, actions and behaviour on others. Leading by example must be their guiding principle in everything they do.

— Change Management

We have to recognise that change is not constant but increasing at an accelerating rate. As well as valuing people, we need to love change. We must encourage others to want to change and improve everything they do.

TQ: A POLITICAL PHILOSOPHY

TQ is a means of achieving a strong competitive position, but it should be seen in wider socio-economic perspective. There is no reason why our school and educational system, our social services and National Manpower Planning, cannot benefit from this approach. Everything written in the book is easy to implement if you want to. It is simple, based upon fundamental principles of concern for others, a concern for planning and a motivation to succeed, achieve and improve performance. That is no more than any human being strives to achieve through his life.

THE FUTURE

The future holds many fears and opportunities for individuals, organisations and societies. We have the foresight and the opportunity to mould our future the way we think fit. We should take what we have and find ways to make things better. We need to reject the old view of finding ten ways to make a good idea fail in order to find one to make it work. We should encourage and motivate others to do the same.

The time for excuses has gone. We need to think over some fairly simple words and act upon them:

"Just do it, that's all. Just do it."

Bullet Points

- There are no special advantages that the Japanese and others have over us. It is their commitment to doing things right which is the guiding principle to their success. Nothing they use is not available in the West.

- Develop a TQ strategy and relate it to every function.

- Train people in all they need to know and beyond. People who are trained and feel they are valued can achieve anything.

- Commit to improving all aspects of people management.

- Systems and structures have a large part to play in Quality improvement. Do not neglect to give your people the best.

- Given the opportunity, people will tell you how things can be improved – but only if they feel they have dignity as a treasured resource.

- Effective communication will spread the word of TQ. Ineffective communication will fuel the fears of the doubters.

- Use automation when necessary, in work where there is a high defect rate or where the opportunity for self-expression is so low that the job itself creates opportunities for rework.

- Plan, measure and progress results side by side.

- Ensure that Quality initiatives start in service as well as manufacturing areas.

- Spend more time planning and preventing problems arising. Devote attention to long-term planning.

- Passion for Quality is not enough. Rigorous systems must complement the enthusiasm for TQ.

- Lead by example. Commit to real change.

- Spend as much as you can on training. It still will not be enough. Hire the best trainers. Train Line Managers to train.

- Value your people.

- Reduce the lines of management. Increase horizontal management and promote short-term job rotation practices.

- Move from product- to customer-led strategies.

- Change to a responsive people-orientated culture.

- Develop partnerships with others, your competitors and suppliers.

- Learn to love change.

- Live in the future not the past. You have to change now to cope with the environmental complexity of life in the 21st Century.

APPENDIX I
Video Training Packages

Transformations UK Ltd.
11 Alva St. Edinburgh EH2 4PH
Tel 0131-346-1276/226-4519 Fax 0131-346-1618

TQ & Culture Change Series

A Tool for Changing Behaviour: The Johari Window. 15 minutes. Philip Atkinson explains that any change requires managers to become more critical of their own behaviour and the impact that this has on those they manage. He describes the Johari Model of examining behaviour from the perspective of those things which are known to others and to oneself. A great video package for starting the process of personal change and one which focuses in-depth on the process.

£230.00 + Vat.

Building Lasting Customer Relationships. Critical for any organisation is the way we deal with and focus upon our customers. This 30-minute video concentrates upon the importance of encouraging customer complaints and examines the poor statistics associated with customer retention. The average service business will lose 80% of its customer base every 5 years. This video examines the importance of customer care with both the external and the internal customer.

£385.00 + Vat.

Change Management: Listening Skills. 15 minutes. Change is achieved only when others can be influenced by those who lead. The requirement for developing effective listening skills is outlined. The video illustrates the key problems associated with poor listening and suggests actions which managers can take to improve personal performance.

£230.00 + Vat.

Costing Quality. 30 minutes. Here Philip Atkinson explains the major components of the Cost of Quality and highlights literally hundreds of examples of Rework. The philosophy which underpins the investment in Prevention to eliminate Rework is well explained by highlighting the importance of working across functional boundaries and getting things right in the planning process.
£385.00 + Vat.

Creating Culture Change. A 45-minute video filmed in front of a live audience and focusing upon the mainstay of culture and what it means. Corporate Culture is explored and Leadership as a foundation for effective change is highlighted. Applicable in a variety of organisational contexts.

£250.00 + Vat.

Making Quality Happen. A 75-minute video filmed in front of a live audience of 350 managers. The key components of TQ are explored including Costing Quality, the Internal Customer, Right First Time and Preventative Action. The focus is on approaches to organisational change and the reasons for TQ failure.

£385.00 + Vat.

Problem Solving and Empowerment. 20 minutes. This features a facilitator within GE Capital running a Work-out session for staff from different functions. Brainstorming and problem solving are displayed within the group. A focused discussion on Empowerment provides an enthusiastic spur for organisations keen to pursue TQ.

£250.00 + Vat.

Simple Models for Personal Change. An extremely powerful video for use when running a programme focusing upon personal change. This would be ideal for examining behaviour in a team, leading and motivating, coaching and appraising others. Philip draws upon two models for personal change - the Conscious Competence model and the Johari Window. This 15-minute video is extremely powerful at getting people to adopt a more self-critical appraisal of the effect of their behaviour on others.

£230.00 + Vat.

TQ: Leading the Process. 35 minutes. This video focuses upon the importance of Leadership in shaping the corporate culture and draws upon several contemporary models of Leadership. Directors of GE Capital are interviewed and share their strong views on the importance of challenging and stretching staff.

£385.00 + Vat.

TQ: Steps to Implementation. This is the most recent video on the pitfalls of introducing TQ and Culture Change. During this 30-minute video Philip Atkinson outlines the key issues which relate to unsuccessful implementation of change. Philip highlights why 80% plus initiatives fail and focuses upon a tangible method of assessing culture and talking through corporate strategy, leadership, values and people management.

£285.00 + Vat.

APPENDIX 2

Recommended Reading

Busting Bureaucracy
Johnston, K B   ISBN 1-556-23878-9   1993   Business One Irwin

Competitive Strategy
Porter, Michael   ISBN 0-029-25360-8   1980   Free Press

Completeness
Crosby, Phil   ISBN 0-525-93475-8   1992   Dutton

Control Your Destiny or Someone Else Will
Tichy, Noel & Sherman,
Stratford   ISBN 0-385-24883-0   1993   Currency Doubleday

Credibility
Kouzes & Posner   ISBN 1-55542-550-X   1993   Jossey Bass

Empty Raincoat
Handy, Charles   ISBN 0-091-78022-5   1994   Hutchinson

Fifth Discipline
Senge, Peter   ISBN 0-712-69885-X   1990   Century Business

From Tin Soldiers to Russian Dolls
Van der Merwe, Sandra   ISBN 0-750-60974-5   1993   Butterworth Heinmann

Get Better or Get Beaten

Slater, Robert   ISBN 0-7863-0235-6   1994   Irwin

Knowledge for Action

Argyris, Chris   ISBN 1-555-42519-4   1993   Jossey Bass

Intelligent Enterprise

Quinn, James B   ISBN B0-029-25615-1   1992   Freepress

Leaders

Bennis and Nanus   ISBN 0-060-15246-X   1985   Harper & Rowe

Leadership:

Hughes, Ginnett

and Curphy   ISBN 0-256-10278-3   1993   Irwin

Liberation Management

Peters, Tom   ISBN 0-333-53340-2   1992   Macmillan

Managing Beyond the Quick Fix

Kilmann, Ralph H   ISBN 1-555-42132-6   1989   Jossey Boss

Mass Customisation

Pine, B J   ISBN 0-87584-372-7   1993   Harvard Business School Press

On Becoming a Leader

Bennis   ISBN 0-097-42889   1989   Hutchinson Business Books

Out of the Crisis

Deming, W Edwards   ISBN 0-521-30553-5   1986   Cambridge

Psychology of Customer Care

Lynch, James J   ISBN 0-333-55769-7   1992   Macmillan

Strategies for Change

Quinn, James B   ISBN 0-256-02543-6   1980   Irwin

Ten Steps to a Learning Organisation

Kline, Peter & Saunders   ISBN B0-915-55624-3   1993   Pfeiffer & Co.

The Customer Driven Company
Whiteley, Richard C ISBN 0-712-65235-3 1991 Business Books Ltd.

The David Solution
Stewart, Valerie ISBN 0-566-02843-3 1990 Gower

The Improvement Process
Harrington, H J ISBN 0-070-26754-5 1987 McGraw Hill

The Leadership Challenge
Kouzes & Posner ISBN 1-55542-061-3 1987 Jossey Bass

The Manager's Bookshelf
Pierce, John and
Newstrom, John ISBN 0-065-00707-7 1993 Harper Collins

The New GE
Slater, Robert ISBN 1-556-23670-0 1993 Business One Irwin

The Unwritten Rules of the Game
Scott-Morgan, P ISBN 0-070-57075-2 1994 McGraw Hill

Thriving on Chaos
Peters, Tom ISBN 0-333-45427-8 1987 Macmillan

Total Quality Learning
Lessem, Ron ISBN 0-631-16828-1 1991 Blackwell

Understanding Organisations
Handy, Charles ISBN 0-140-15603-8 1993 Penguin

Why TQM Fails and What to Do About It
Hitchcock, Darcy E ISBN 0-786-30140-6 1994 Assoc. of Qual. & Partic.

2001 Management
Davis, S M ISBN 0-671-67675-0 1989 Simon & Schuster

20:20 Vision
Davis and Davidson ISBN 0-671-77815-3 1991 Fireside Simon & Schuster

INDEX

Rushmere Wynne

are publishers of finance, investment and management books.
If you would like a copy of our current catalogue

Please write to:

Rushmere Wynne
4-5 Harmill
Grovebury Road
Leighton Buzzard
Bedfordshire
LU7 8FF

or Fax: 01525 852037
or Phone: 01525 853726